Literary Criticism and Cultural Theory

Edited by
William E. Cain
Professor of English
Wellesley College

A ROUTLEDGE SERIES

LITERARY CRITICISM AND CULTURAL THEORY
WILLIAM E. CAIN, *General Editor*

The Metanarrative of Suspicion in Late Twentieth Century America

Sandra Baringer

Routledge
New York & London

Published in 2004 by
Routledge
270 Madison Avenue
New York, NY 10016
www.routledge-ny.com

Published in Great Britain by
Routledge
2 Park Square
Milton Park, Abingdon
Oxon OX14 4RN

Routledge is an imprint of the Taylor & Francis Group.
Copyright © 2004 by Taylor & Francis Books, Inc.

Printed in the United States of America on acid-free paper.
Typesetting: BookType

Library of Congress Cataloging-in-Publication Data

Baringer, Sandra.
  The metanarrative of suspicion in late twentieth century America /
Sandra Baringer.
     p. cm. — (Literary criticism and cultural theory)
  Includes bibliographical references and index.
  ISBN 0-415-97076-8 (hb : alk. paper)
  1. American literature—20th century—History and criticism.
2. Suspicion in literature. 3. Literature and society—United States—
History—20th century. 4. Narration (Rhetoric) I. Title. II. Series.
  PS228.S85B37 2004
  810.9'3556—dc22
                                                    2004002085

Contents

Acknowledgments

I would like to thank the University of California, Riverside and the University of California Humanities Research Institute for financial support during crucial stages of the writing of this book. For reading the manuscript at various stages, thanks go to Katherine Kinney, Emory Elliott, Deborah Willis, John Carlos Rowe, and the members of my research group at UCHRI, Angela Davis, Gina Dent, Ruth Wilson Gilmore, David Theo Goldberg, Avery Gordon, and Nancy Scheper-Hughes, all of whom I also thank for the interdisciplinary perspectives afforded by our work together.

The Conspiracy Culture Conference at King Alfred's College, Winchester, England in 1998 was, I believe, very important for many scholars working in this area. Conference organizers Alasdair Spark and Peter Knight deserve special recognition for putting it together.

Kenneth Tilsen and Karen Northcott were kind enough to authorize access to the WKLD/OC archives at the Minnesota History Center of the Minnesota Historical Society in St. Paul, Minnesota.

An earlier version of the Silko chapter was published in *FemSpec* 2:2 (2001) as "The Terror of the Liminal: Silko's *Almanac* and Klein's Phantasy Paradigm." Editor Batya Weinbaum has graciously granted permission to reprint.

Chris Coyle tolerated the paper mess and provided verbal feedback which informs more of the book than he may realize.

I thank Joseph Childers for advising me to stop writing like a lawyer. That may not be exactly what he said, nor exactly what I have done, but it was useful advice in more ways than one.

And finally, I would like to acknowledge the courage and dedication of those who have participated in a support committee or other such group on behalf of someone they felt was wrongly accused. Some of them helped me directly or indirectly with this project; there are many others whom I have never met. Without them, our justice system would be in more trouble than it already is.

Introduction

Acceptance of the beast within as a given of millennial America achieved a sort of official status in popular discourse by the turn of the century. These narratives are beyond asking who killed JFK. Rather, they operate on the common ground of an assumption that our government conceals profound and terrible secrets from us. The only place left to go is to explore the ramifications of personal growth and values under such a regime, or in the case of the final episode of the *X-Files*, retreat to faith in an afterlife. Relatively humorous approaches were taken in *Men in Black* and *Conspiracy Theory* (1997), but subsequent films moved beyond this whistling-in-the-dark disavowal of anxiety to a more explicit engagement in the issue the following year in the *X-Files* feature-length film episode, *Dark City*, and *The Truman Show*, followed by *The Matrix* in 1999.

Several important critical works were written during this period as well: Mark Fenster's *Conspiracy Theories: Secrecy and Power in American Culture* (1999), Stephen Paul Miller's *The Seventies Now: Culture as Surveillance* (1999), Patrick O'Donnell's *Latent Destinies: Cultural Paranoia and Contemporary U.S. Narrative* (2000), and Timothy Melley's *Empire of Conspiracy: The Culture of Paranoia in Postwar America* (2000). Fenster argues that though these discourses may be interesting as a form of play, they have little potential for resistance. Mliler's book poses the Watergate scandal as the central organizing principle of cultural anxiety over surveillance and government corruption. O'Donnell's work, heavily informed by European post-Lacanians such as Zizek, Kristeva, Deleuze and Guattari, argues the existence of a postmodernist libidinal economy involving "the linkage between the desire for identificatory mobility and the seemingly contradictory drive for connection ... with national and historical destinies" (159).

Melley contributes the term "agency panic" to the discourse. His study addresses, among other things, notable postmodern fiction by Thomas Pynchon (*Gravity's Rainbow*), Don DeLillo (*Libra*), Margaret Atwood, William Burroughs, Kathy Acker, and William Gibson. Though Melley's analysis of film is limited to Ridley Scott's revisioning of Philip K. Dick in *Bladerunner* (1982), his argument about panic over exterior manipulations of memory, perception, and the fundamental question of personal identity is exemplified in a number of fin-de-siecle films: *Videodrome* (1983), *Brazil* (1985), *Total Recall* (1990), and *Strange Days* (1995), followed by the aforementioned *Dark City* (1998), *The Truman Show* (1998), and *The Matrix* (1999).

But the popular fascination with conspiracy theories is not merely ineffectual, nor is it directed primarily toward questions over the definition of self. It is a also a sinister symptom of real persecutory narratives that operate on real bodies, bodies increasingly marked by race and/or gender. If one looks at America through the cinematic lens, a moment may have existed in 1998 when the destabilization of reality was something that could be laughed about but generally speaking, these films exhibit a state of panic in the popular imagination.

Stuart Hall associates "moral panics" with crises in the legitimation of the state. The book by Hall and his associates *Policing the Crisis* (1978) addresses the production of moral panics over crime ("muggings" by blacks) as a response to, rather than a cause of deteriorating relations between blacks and police in post-World War II England. Considerable attention is given to questioning notions of "common sense" such as a general perception that crime is increasing when in fact crime rates remain fairly stable over long periods of time with minor fluctuations that are often pointed to as symptoms of a crisis. As in England, the social unrest in the United States in the sixties produced a crisis in the legitimation of the state and state control. The Nixonian "law and order" response to the crisis was partially, though not entirely successful in refocusing public attention from the misdeeds of the government to the supposed misdeeds of war protesters and activist organizations, branching out into a more general panic over social disintegration as represented by drug use, out-of-wedlock pregnancies, single parenthood, miscegenation, and feminist demands (bra-burning, for example, became an icon with significance far exceeding any rational relationship to any instances in which it actually occurred). The practices of the FBI under J. Edgar Hoover and the predilections of the press for sensationalist reporting worked together to fuel a continuing moral panic in the United States over social disintegration and crime that tripled the American prison population between 1970 and 1985.

In the popular imagination, prone as it is to relatively subconscious psychological machinations, this moral panic over social unrest and crime is projected back onto the government. It is a two-way street: the state's crisis in legitimation is projected onto portions of the population in such a way that the state can demonstrate its legitimacy by policing that particular group, and the public's moral panic over social unrest is projected back at the state. Government misdeeds occur, and social unrest occurs as well, but it is this process of projection and reflection that magnifies the scope of government misdeeds to the proportions represented by the full-blown paranoid fantasies of science fiction narratives where the government is so controlling the doors of perception that the subject is unable to discern who he is.

My approach to what I call the metanarrative of suspicion is grounded in Fredric Jameson's ranking of history over psychology, though my analysis of this metanarrative borrows heavily from psychoanalytic theory. Jameson argues that the "uninterrupted narrative" to which his concept of the political unconscious refers is the "repressed and buried reality" of the history of class struggle (20). Though he will allow that psychoanalysis may be "the only real new and original hermeneutic developed since the great patristic and medieval system of the four senses of scripture" (61), he nevertheless sees the nuclear family upon which psychoanalysis turns as a mere byproduct of capitalism (62). The nuclear family is not central to my analysis, though early experiences of infancy are. Class struggle in the history of the United States must be examined through an American history of enslavement and genocide of native peoples.

The concept of buried master narrative is key, but I call this narrative of suspicion a metanarrative because it is narrative about narrative: a narrative about what stories to believe. It is in some respects a paranoid narrative, or a narrative of paranoia, but I prefer the term "suspicion" because "paranoia" has come to connote a psychotic or "abnormal" state. On the contrary, the metanarrative of suspicion is one historically deployed in the service of power but enabled by the desire that all psychoanalytic methods seek to interpret. This desire, that which is often termed "pre-Oedipal," precedes the nuclear family and the Law of the Father; thus, it is that with which power must contend. There is nothing very abnormal about it.

This metanarrative of suspicion must be distinguished from the "hermeneutics of suspicion" described by Paul Ricoeur in his work *Freud and Philosophy: An Essay on Interpretation* (1970). His concern is with hermeneutics in its relation to epistemology, i.e. the philosophy of interpretation, and his thesis, broadly stated, is that the strategy of doubting as a precursor to postmodernism had its source in the work of Freud, Marx, and Nietzsche. The relationship of Ricoeur's thought to postmodernism in its more paranoid manifestations has been most succinctly explored in an essay by Linda Fisher. Fisher utilizes the term "hypersuspicion" to describe the concept of "suspicion radicalized into paranoia," and criticizes this tendency of postmodernism as a dead-end in which "postmodernism must eventually not just doubt, but preclude and deny, its own meaning" (113). Fisher is not the only scholar to mount such a critique of postmodernism, but her essay is notable for laying out the connections among Ricoeur's thought, psychological approaches to paranoia (Bywater, Shapiro), and postmodernism.

The hermeneutics of suspicion is an important term in the scholarship of postmodernism. But my approach is concerned more with the ideological functions of power than with postmodernism per se. The positive effect of postmodern attacks on master narratives cannot be the end of all master narratives, but rather a heightened awareness of master narratives. The metanarrative of suspicion is an important master narrative, at least in America.[1] Thus, though the hermeneutics of suspicion are certainly relevant to the metanarrative of suspicion, the metanarrative I attempt to describe is a more specific application of the strategies of master narratives, realism or otherwise, to the vulnerabilities of the human psyche to paranoid outlooks and responses associated with the pre-Oedipal state, particularly in connection with trauma. The ideological apparatus most overtly associated with power, namely the law and law enforcement, is in some respects more adept at "playing" this psychic vulnerability than at the more mundane and technical task of crime-solving.[2]

The metanarrative of suspicion tells us that people with power will lie to us. Why should this be so? One could argue that since they have the power, they have no need to lie. But to overgeneralize is, of course, to oversimplify. A lie, especially a big one, can be a means of retaining power.

For Freud, seeing is a sexual pleasure, perverse only when it becomes an end in itself, i.e. scopophilia. Film critics have pursued this concept to its logical conclusions: the seer, or voyeur, is exercising control over the seen object, the power lying both in the fetishizing nature of the gaze and in the circumstance of the voyeur seeing without the object's knowledge. This sets up the relationship of dominance and submission. When the object discovers that [s]he is being seen, the response may be fright or alarm. But once the seer is seen, the exhibitionist may attempt to reverse the power relationship by granting or withholding the object, or part-object, of the gaze.

The association of the gaze with the development of capitalism is most tellingly exemplified by Jeremy Bentham's panoptic eye as interpreted by Michel Foucault in *Discipline and Punish: The Birth of the Prison.* In the eighteenth century, most prisons were little more than temporary holding tanks for prisoners and often their families, the end being execution or transport to the colonies. As the need for extended incarceration and thus a more centralized and ongoing control over the prisoner grew, Bentham designed a new prison architecture so that the guards could see all the inmates from a central location. The significance of the panoptic eye that transcends the circumstances of prison architecture is that the prisoner adapts his behavior to the probablility, or possibility, of being seen. Thus the panoptic eye imposes self discipline whether the seer is watching or not.

This concept is second nature to any late twentieth century subject who has observed an unoccupied police car parked along a highway and consequently reduced speed. But it was somewhat novel in the nineteenth century, and it is no coincidence that the birth of the prison was followed by the birth of the detective novel. The "private eye" Sherlock Holmes novels accompanied a privatization of the "eye" of the police, contributing, by the end of the nineteenth century, to a "spy mania" (Seltzer 25, 39). The inimitable Henry James explored his own fascination with and repulsion from the "network of watchers" (39) in one of his earlier novels, *The Princess Casamassima.* Seeing without being seen is the measure of power in the novel, with multiple levels of watching and manipulation going on in the theatre (a metafictional critique) as well as on the street. Mark Seltzer describes James's project in this novel as "exposure and demystification of the realist mania for surveillance and his attempt to disown the policing it implies" (54).

If Henry James was ambivalent about the "intrusive voyeurism" (30) of the detective novel and its complicity in the empiricist and colonialist enterprises of sociology and anthropology in the latter nineteenth century, no such misgivings are apparent in the mainstream noir detective fiction that was to develop in the United States in later years. The guilty knowledge in novels such as Raymond Chandler's *The Big Sleep* is fully "othered" from the private eye to the invisible power structure—in this instance, the tar pits of the evil capitalists.[3] The detective in such novels routinely directs his guiltless and fetishizing gaze upon a distressed or diabolical damsel, and only in the end will the detective discover the true locus of the crime.

Why does this trope of surveillance and discovery, of the evil within, or without, as you will, have such resonance in American fiction? We want to believe, are willing to believe, that there are big lies all around us. We laugh at the *South Park* cop saying "move along, there's nothing to see here" because there is, of course, always something to see.[4]

The "paranoid style" described by historian Richard Hofstadter in his essay "The Paranoid Style in American Politics" is only beginning to be systematically examined in its literary manifestations. Hofstadter is careful to note that he does not see the paranoid style as a distinctively American phenomenon, but that he focuses on its American manifestations because he is an American historian. Hofstadter distinguishes between the "clinical paranoiac" and the "paranoid spokesman in politics" only in that the former sees conspiracies as directed against him individually and the latter sees conspiracies as directed against "a nation, a culture, a way of life" (4). He asserts that though

> a mentality disposed to see the world in the paranoid's way may always be present in some considerable minority of the population ... [m]ovements employing the paranoid style ... come in successive episodic waves ... the paranoid disposition is mobilized into action chiefly by social conflicts that involve ultimate schemes of values and that bring fundamental fears and hatreds, rather than negotiable interests, into political action. Catastrophe or the fear of catastrophe is most likely to elicit the syndrome of paranoid rhetoric (39).

Hofstadter notes that the catalysts in American history have tended to be "ethnic and religious conflicts" but that "elsewhere class conflicts have also mobilized such energies" (39). His historical survey covers the supposed Illuminati conspiracy to foment the French revolution followed by the invasion of the United States by Illuminati-inspired Jacobins, anti-Catholicism, anti-Masonry, anti-Mormonism, nativism, the populist American Protective Association of the 1890s, the Ku Klux Klan, and the Red scare of the 1950s, all to set up his discussion of the paranoid rhetoric of "new right" Goldwater Republicans extant at the time when he wrote the first version of the essay in 1963.

Another important political historian who has written on the subject is Michael Rogin, who takes up where Hofstadter leaves off to examine the role of political repression in encouraging "demonizing" modes of thought. In his 1987 book *Ronald Reagan, the Movie and Other Episodes in Political Demonology*, Rogin organizes paranoid episodes in American history somewhat differently than Hofstadter. Whereas Hofstadter surveys a number of movements throughout the nineteenth century and then jumps to the 1950s, Rogin sees the significant episodes as a pattern of three movements: first, the demonizing of Indians—"the first moment in American political demonology" (80); second, the demonizing of Marxists and labor organizers in the late nineteenth century—a series of Red scare episodes in the 1870s, 1886, and 1919 (63); third, the Red scare of the post-World War II cold war (68–80). Rogin's analysis is also consistent with Foucault's overall thesis about the growth of state power in the nineteenth century. Rogin finds the practice of paternalistic political suppression of Indians to be consistent with other arenas in which the paternal model was being deployed in the early nineteenth century: "slavery, the asylum, labor relations, and radical dissent" (51).[5]

The "episodic waves" of paranoid movements or cults appear most often where several of the factors discussed above are involved. "Social conflicts that involve ultimate schemes of values" (Hofstadter 39) may be ongoing, but are most likely to be intensified by circumstances such as the intensification of state repression and millenial/apocalyptic anxieties. Countersubversive repression by law enforcement is one side of a symbiotic relationship with subversive forces: repression may be a response to intensified social conflicts as well as a spur to more paranoid thought patterns among subversive groups. But political repression in the United States should be also viewed, at this point in time, as a developmental process that began with the Espionage and Sedition acts of 1917–18 followed by the birth of the FBI in the 1920s. The seemingly "episodic" nature of the McCarthy witchhunts and Watergate should be seen as part of a larger pattern. As for the millennial influence, other scholars have noted a century-end pattern. Elaine Showalter summarizes them as follows:

> The Salem witch trials took place in the 1690s; the mesmerism craze after the French Revolution, in the 1790s. In the 1890s, rebellions against imperialism and the class structure, controversies over prostitution and homosexuality, the rise of feminism, and the sexual plague of syphilis all joined with apocalyptic fantasies . . . (19).

This end-of-century anxiety understandably intensifies at the end of the twentieth century, due not only to the 2,000-year mark but to a number of apocalyptic prophecies by media evangelists, astrologers ("this is the dawning of the Age of Aquarius"), and assorted new age spiritualists and readers of Nostradamus.

Several scholars besides Showalter have published studies of the paranoid style in its various manifestations: Elisabeth Young-Bruehl's trans-disciplinary work

The Anatomy of Prejudices (1996); Daniel Pipes' historical approach in *Conspiracy: How the Paranoid Style Flourishes and Where It Comes From* (1997); the collaboration of a political scientist and a psychiatrit in Robert S. Robins and Jerrold M. Post's *Political Paranoia: The Psychopolitics of Hatred* (1997); Jodi Dean's undefinable *Aliens in America : Conspiracy Cultures from Outerspace to Cyberspace* (1998); Barry Glassner's *The Culture of Fear: Why Americans Are Afraid of the Wrong Things* (1999); Mike Davis's *Ecology of Fear: Los Angeles and the Imagination of Disaster* (1999).

Though sometimes Eurocentric in his reliance on a Marxian model of class struggle as teleological, Fredric Jameson's critical approach is a good starting place insofar as he acknowledges the importance of psychoanalysis as hermeneutic while at the same time foregrounding issues of class conflict. Rogin's work elsewhere in *Fathers and Children: Andrew Jackson and the Subjugation of the American Indian* (1975) has been perhaps the most fruitful attempt to examine the border clash on History's battleground between, in Jameson's words, "Necessity" and "desire" (102): that is, Rogin's conjoining of a materialist analysis of class struggle with the psychoanalytic study of desire in its manifestations within and beyond the nuclear family. In my view, Rogin's work succeeds because he departs from a more orthodox (in this country) Freudian approach to utilize the psychoanalytic theories of Melanie Klein.

The introduction to Eve Kosofsky Sedgwick's new collection of essays, entitled "Paranoid Reading and Reparative Reading; or, You're So Paranoid, You Probably Think This Introduction Is About You" (*Novel Gazing*, 1997) argues that the time has come to move on from New Historicist sleuthing-out of the hegemonic containment of all subversive narratives, that the hidden discourses of power are no longer much of a secret and thus a paranoid epistemology (i.e. the hermeneutic of suspicion) may have outlived much of its usefulness. She questions the "prestige of a single, overarching narrative: exposing and problematizing hidden violences in the geneology of the modern liberal subject," remarking that these liberal subjects are not so easy to find, anyway, where "a vast majority of the population claims to engage in direct intercourse with multiple invisible entities such as angels, Satan, and God" (18). Sedgwick adopts the Kleinian concept of reparation in her call for fewer paranoid readings of texts and more reparative readings of texts—pursuing pleasure and even hope, strategies by which "the reparatively positioned reader tries to organize the fragments and part-objects she encounters or creates" (24). But Sedgwick's approach sidesteps the elephant in the middle of the room: all those people talking to angels, Satan and God. What *about* them? Sedgwick is interested in more relaxing reading material than what will be discussed herein.

A psychoanalytic approach to a political problem runs the risk of universalizing that which can only be addressed fruitfully through a historical analysis. Nevertheless, I believe that Klein's model of the psychological state of infancy, in its very universality, can help inform why adult models of understanding can go wrong in particular historical moments. To discuss Klein it is necessary to discuss Freud, though Freud's work on paranoia was minimal, and his one case study was caught in a particular historical moment, in a particular historical family. Freud's essay "Psychoanalytic Notes Upon an Autobiographical Account of a Case of Paranoia (Dementia Paranoides)" is, as the title indicates, not based upon an analysis of one of Freud's own patients. Freud never met Dr. Schreber, the author of this singular account of decades of paranoid fantasies. Freud's basic conclusion was that Schreber, a noted judge of his time, was a repressed homosexual. But Schreber's father, the source of Schreber's "father complex [Freud 161], was not just any father, but a nationally prominent authority on authoritarian child rearing: "an orthopedist and educational reformer . . . known for his orthopedic devices to correct poor posture in children—devices that caused much more discomfort and pain than any worthwhile therapy. He is known to have used these devices on his son" (Oldham and Bone 6, Schatzman).

While the relationship of authoritarian child rearing and collective susceptibility to fascism have been explored in Theodor Adorno's *The Authoritarian Personality*, scholarship on the relationship of these two concepts to paranoia has been more fragmented: for the most part, psychology has gone one way and political science another. The application of principles of group psychology and the study of organizations to political movements has been rare, and Robins and Post's *Political Paranoia* is a significant work for that reason.

Robins and Post argue that "paranoia is a characteristic mentality of the late twentieth century," comparing the intellectual situation to the paranoia of late Tudor England, a "world . . . of absolute reason" (41). On this point, the overdetermined rationality of the paranoid worldview comes head to head with the notion of late twentieth century postmodernism that holds postmodern discourse to be polyvocal, fragmented, and indeterminate. In Lacan's view paranoia is a resistance to language, the paranoid never fully identifying with the Symbolic and "throwing back upon the world the disorder of which he's composed," so that paranoia results from "excessive reasoning rather than the collapse of reason" thus a condition of enlightenment (or Enlightenment)—the paranoid constructs something to manipulate the Symbolic. Paranoia is thus, according to this line of thinking, an intensification of normal processes rather than a departure from them, a practice of excessive and overdetermined reasoning engaged in even by Jameson and Lacan (Nicol). Sedgwick, however, has made an important point in insisting that this sort of discourse has its limits.

Contemporary clinical specialists in paranoia rely much more on the theoretical grounding of Kleinian object relations than on Freud: "The role of aggression as motive and the experience of helplessness in trauma were not adequately appreciated in (Freud's) formulations. We know now, for example, that many paranoid patients have histories of severe abuse as children" (Oldham and Bone ix). Nevertheless, Freud's commentary on Schreber has been useful in its discussion of narcissism, which contemporary psychiatrists interpret more as a matter of "self-esteem regulation" than as a stage in libidinal development, as Freud saw it (Bone and Oldham 7). Freud's case history of the Wolf Man has also proven useful insofar as Freud discusses therein the relationship of beating fantasies to paranoia: "the beginning of the realization of the common connection between paranoia and sadomasochism. The paranoid patient is concerned with attack and counterattack, with beating and being beaten. He or she is always ready to perceive provocation, insult, or injury" (Bone and Oldham 7–8). Clinicians use the Kleinian concept of "object relations" to describe the way the paranoid thinker relates to the world. "Objects" in this construct are other people, generally speaking (though this is a loose definition of a technical term). Before an infant develops the concept of a whole person, she sees others in terms of body parts—breasts, feces, etc.—and later "splits" these part objects into good and bad. The paranoid thinker has trouble seeing other people as anything other than completely good or completely bad, and thus it is said that such a person has a problem with "object constancy," that is, a stable relationship with another person that does not veer between love and hate (see generally Auchincloss and Weiss). Some psychiatrists have marked the distinction between paranoia and masochism as one of degree: "The paranoid operates at a more impaired level of object relatedness than the masochist. Masochism can be seen as the price paid for the maintenance of an object tie. The paranoid maintains the object tie only through aggressive acts and fantasy" (Bone and Oldham 11, summarizing Blum).

Early post-Freudian psychoanalysis used many terms in ways that can be confusing to contemporary readers schooled in the American Psychiatric Assocation's *Diagnostic and Statistical Manual of Psychiatric Disorders*. The most important of these terms for my purposes is Melanie Klein's phrase "paranoid-schizoid position," describing a "ubiquitous infantile stage of development" (Oldham and Bone 9). This term was her elaboration on Scottish psychoanalyst W.D. Fairbairn's description of a "schizoid position" in infancy, which he postulated as preceding Klein's "depressive position." What Fairbairn meant by "schizoid" was essentially the same as what Kleinians mean by "splitting"; the concept of splitting relies upon the premise that the infant, first of all, perceives others (initially the mother or primary caregiver) not as a whole being but as a collection of "objects" such as the breast—obviously a significant object in that it is the provider of nourishment. The infant deals with hunger or other more painful and anxiety-producing experiences by a perceived ego disintegration—"the anxiety of being split up in bits" (Hinshelwood 159)—which in turn becomes fear of persecution by a fearful object—Klein's famous "bad breast." This paradigm is not inconsistent with Lacan's notion that the ego only comes into being through its perception of others in the "mirror stage."[6] At any rate, Fairbairn's schizoid position of ego disintegration in the infant is followed by Klein's "depressive position," the term she used to describe the depression the infant experiences through guilt at having hostile feelings toward the caregiver, that is, the "bad breast." Once entering the depressive position, the infant can begin to negotiate relationships with objects that are based on love and respect—"object constancy"—rather than alternative hostility and idealization.

Klein amended Fairbairn's term "schizoid position" to "paranoid-schizoid position" to better reflect the existence of the persecutory fears undergone by the infant in this stage (Hinschelwood 158).   All of this happens, in Kleinian thought, in the first three months of life, since Klein placed the onset of the depressive position at age four to six months. The terms "schizoid" and "depressive" are used as descriptors of developmental stages rather than pathological conditions, as they are used in contemporary American diagnostic practice. And obviously, all of this radically predates any Oedipal stage, whatever view one may have of that paradigm. The material relationship of the developing ego with the Other is a relationship with a maternal rather than a paternal figure. However, the common use of the terms "good breast" and "bad breast" should be taken metaphorically rather than literally. The source of nurture may be a bottle as well as a breast, and may be any caregiver, not necessarily the mother. The point is that the infant psyche is almost totally focused upon oral nourishment.

Klein's model of the infant psyche was unpalatable to many, if not most, Freudians. Both Klein and Anna Freud moved to England from the continent in the years preceding the outbreak of World War II, and they continued to feud there for years, though the Kleinian model of child psychology was to eventually become much more prominent in England than it ever has in the United States. Despite her disagreements with Anna Freud over analytic techniques with children, Klein constantly made attempts to align her theories with Sigmund Freud's and almost never overtly challenged them. This explains her preoccupation with Freud's "death drive" as the cause of splitting in the paranoid-schizoid position. The term is somewhat problematic in that it is needlessly controversial: one need not acknowledge the innate existence of a "death drive" to acknowledge the existence of aggressive instincts in an infant.

Julia Kristeva's work on the chora and the abject is informed by Kleinian concepts, particularly in *The Powers of Horror* (1982); Kristeva specifically discusses Kleinian theory in *Black Sun: Depression and Melancholia* (1987). The concept of the abject will be most fully explored in the chapter on Silko. Another more recent book that deals with late twentieth century conspiracy theories, however, completely ignores not only Klein and Kristeva but the entire range of scholarship on paranoia. Elaine Showalter's *Hystories: Hysterical Epidemics and Modern Culture* (1997) attempts to reintroduce the nineteenth century and Freudian diagnosis of hysteria into an analysis of social phenomena that could just as accurately be described as paranoid. Though Showalter disagrees with French medical historian Etienne Trillat's 1986 announcement that "hysteria is dead; that's certain" (Showalter 2), she does note that in actuality hysteria has simply been reclassified as "anxiety neuroses, obsessional disorders, manic depression, or borderline personality disorders . . . somatization disorder, conversion disorder, or disssociative identity disorder" (17). Showalter's book provides a fascinating and clearly written history of hysteria, but some of the contemporary examples she focuses on in the third section of the book—chronic fatigue syndrome, Gulf War syndrome, recovered memory, multiple personality syndrome, satanic ritual abuse, and alien abduction—could benefit from consideration of the relevance of paranoid thought patterns, object relations theory, and the application of these models to large group scenarios.

The six chapters that follow explore different types of texts engaged in various sorts of conspiratorial or paranoid narratives. Though fiction in its 'traditional' form may receive more attention that any other single type of text, law enforcement narratives, social work (as opposed to sociological) narratives, autobiographical narratives, visual media, and the internet also enter into the analysis.

The first chapter, "Crucifying the White Man: Douglass Durham and the Master Narrative of the Seventies Savage," involves study of the strategy of the FBI in dealing with political activist and extremist groups. The FBI has a well known history of the paranoid style in its own operations, and a text I will examine as exemplary of its strategies and the results they produce is the testimony of Douglass Durham before a US Senate subcommittee in April 1976. Durham was an undercover FBI informer who infiltrated the American Indian Movement. He presented to the subcommittee an alarming scenario of planned revolution to be orchestrated at multiple sites across the country in connection with the bicentennial celebration. None of the events materialized, though probably many FBI operatives would still claim this was due to its preventive action in seizing Marlon Brando's mobile home full of dynamite.

Durham is a storyteller. A popular joke among defense lawyers goes, "When are informants lying? Only when their lips are moving." But to call his exaggerations and misrepresentations "lies" would be an oversimplification. Durham's story changed over time, and it bore a complex relationship to what AIM wanted to hear as well as to what the FBI wanted to hear. To a large extent, Durham may have believed most of his own story, even as it underwent transformations, but what he believed is less important than how his story reflected larger social anxieties about communism (attack from outside the boundaries) and the revenge of the defeated savage (the beast within).

As Catherine McNicol Stock points out in her study of "rural radicals," the left/right paradigm is of limited usefulness in addressing rural protest movements (5). The American Indian Movement, though it started among urban Indians, came to advocate increasingly on rural issues, representing in its most controversial episode at Wounded Knee the interests of traditional Lakota attempting to maintain a rural subsistence lifestyle. The FBI's strategy against AIM bears an important relationship to the later rise of the rural radical right and the FBI's more recent ineptitude in laying siege to those who feel they are being persecuted, justifiably or not. Narratives of savagery and communist infiltration can escape the confines of a master narrative and turn on their source.

The psychology of paranoia and the abject always has an important role in the analysis of any social phenomenon that involves scapegoating, and so these concepts are also important in the study of racism. Continuing upon the road mapped out by Hofstadter, my second chapter, "Lynching the White Woman: William Pierce's 'Day of the Rope'," examines the discourse of American white supremacism by way of a study of two novels written under the pseudonym Andrew Macdonald by National Alliance leader William Pierce. *The Turner Diaries* (1978) is a contemporary (seventies) counterpart to Nasnaga's *Indians' Summer* (1975) from a white racist perspective, wherein white survivalists prevail over an oppressive (gun-controlling) multicultural government and proceed to exterminate the entire nonwhite population of the earth. This novel rehashes and expands upon the pre-postmodern conspiracy theory of the Jewish banking cartel that controls the world. This chapter also covers MacDonald's *Hunter* (1989), a novel that develops in more detail the theoretical underpinnings of *The Turner Diaries*.

The contemporary radical right values the concept of heritage, and constructs that heritage in ways evident not only in the term "militia movement" but also in its overtones of self-identification as Scottish or Scotch-Irish. The elements of religious zeal, self-education, an authoritarian model of family coupled with family fragmentation, and a pugnacious model of male bonding echo the culture of the Jacksonian frontier. Whether this reflects an actual social history or a reconstructed appropriation of a romanticized model of ethnicity is irrelevant to the end result in terms of the racism and other forms of Other-ing that are embedded in this narrative of identity. The radical right arose from circumstances of economic oppression and has become a compelling contemporary example of what can happen when an analysis of class exploitation is subsumed by a narrative of ethnicity.

Conspiracy theories are the special progeny of police and prosecutors, whose narratives predate the novel. This premise underlies my attention to law enforcement narratives of suspicion. The third chapter, "Women's Work: Child Sexual Abuse Prosecution in the 1980s," addresses a text exemplary of the *bete noir* of local law enforcement organizations in the eighties: the child sexual abuse prosecutions against day care workers. Aside from the fact that innocent people have spend years in prison as a result of these prosecutions, this phenomenon is significant as one manifestation of the rise of a new ideological apparatus: the psychology/social work industry. The recovered memory and satanic ritual abuse phenomena and the recent revelations of child abuse within the Catholic Church are all a part of the same dynamic operating here, but it is those who are the most socially vulnerable who are imprisoned.

Deborah Willis asserts that "witchhunting at the village level . . . may largely have been a form of women's work" (14). Though she speaks of early modern England, the same generalization seems to apply to at least some contemporary law enforcement functions at the village level: those involving children. Both abuse and neglect proceedings involving removal of a child from the parental home and criminal prosecution of child abusers most often hinge upon the testimony of psychologists and social workers. These professions, at least insofar as they involve children, are overwhelmingly women's professions. The level of education of such expert witnesses is most often a masters degree in social work or counseling. It can be argued that their expertise in psychoanalytical theory is roughly equivalent to a police academy (or even law school) graduate FBI operative's expertise in political theory: they may have some knowledge of it, but it is not the focus of their training. The methodology that has been used in prosecutions such as the McMartin case in Los Angeles and the Little Rascals case in Edenton, North Carolina partakes of the isolated and insular nature of law enforcement investigations endemic to our legal system. Thus bizarre texts of persecution are constructed by mental health professionals, literally out of the mouths of babes, that resemble nothing so much as a Hieronymus Bosch painting. The challenge herein is to attempt to assimilate cultural child rearing patterns, individual and collective/historical traumatic events, and the influence of state and ideological apparatuses into a theory that accounts for the contemporary social phenomena of conspiracy theories and the texts that have arisen from them.

In the field of American fiction, Thomas Pynchon is foremost in exploration of the politics of paranoia—one could say that it is his life's work. For that reason and because of my focus on post-sixties texts, the fourth chapter, "'Frailty, Thy Name Is Woman!': Motherhood and Treason in Pynchon's *Vineland*," recapitulates from the perspective of the late eighties the emergence and subsequent oppression and fragmentation of the New Left in the late sixties and early seventies. Of particular interest herein is the Nietzchean philosophy gone awry of the arch villain Brock Vond and Pynchon's articulation of the undercover informant strategy used by the FBI to undermine and destroy political activist groups.

The fifth chapter, "Yellow Woman and the Destroyers: The Terror of the Liminal in Silko's *Almanac of the Dead*," discusses a novel published one year after *Vineland*. This novel constructs a conspiracy of degenerate Old World racist aristocracy engaged in drug dealing, arms dealing, and human organ dealing, with the ultimate objective of abandoning the planet to the teeming masses, escaping to an orbiting biosphere when the earth becomes ultimately inhospitable. Concomitantly, a mass movement of indigenous Americans march north from Chiapas to the U.S., initiating the prophesied displacement and/or removal of "all things European" from the North American continent.

The sixth chapter is "Beyond the Foucauldian Complex: Inscriptions and Reinscriptions of the Power Paradigm by American Prison Writers." This chapter describes the culture of sexual and racial domination in American prisons through selected writings by late twentieth century prisoners. As the ultimate contemporary site of persecution, American prisons are the home of a contemporary literature of persecution. This literature is a focal point of many of the key elements of the metanarrative of suspicion, and the dramatic increase in the American prison population in the past two decades is symptomatic of the centrality of these discursive practices to contemporary American culture. The concentration and development of the more severe forms of such discursive practices in the prison environment spill over into the general culture in such a way that the metanarrative feeds on itself and proliferates.

A persecution complex is very deeply historically embedded in the national consciousness, and it continues to replicate itself in ways that are somewhat exacerbated by both our earlier historical heritage and by twentieth century developments in our law enforcement system.

One element that encourages the proliferation of paranoid thought patterns is isolation and insulation from other modes of analysis. This can be seen among some activist groups, and can probably be best documented from contemporary studies of white supremacist groups who have established their strongholds in geographically isolated areas such as northern Idaho and West Virginia. But isolation and insulation also describes the operative mode of modern law enforcement in the United States. Anglo-American legal theory generally promotes the idea that our common law (Anglo)-based system of investigation and prosecution is more 'enlightened' and less 'medieval' than the continental inquisitorial system: judges do not have broad prosecutorial powers in the Anglo-American system as they do in France, for example. The evolution and history of the FBI in this country bears examination as the prototype of the insular, separate-power model of law enforcement and investigation. As such, significant questions arise as to the feasibility of entrusting such an organization with the power that it has come to bear.

The FBI has incurred the wrath of the extreme right more for enforcement actions such as those against David Koresh and Randy Weaver than for its paranoid thought patterns. But there is a connection between the paranoid thought engendered by insular styles of operation, the deliberate sowing of suspicion and, most recently, the lack of respect for human life that has been apparent in the Waco and Weaver actions. The recent actions against right wing extremists are continuations of the same patterns exhibited against Black Panther and AIM groups in previous decades. This is not to say that the effect is the same, or to imply that the extreme right and the extreme left should be subject to the same ideological analysis. The situation with David Koresh demonstrated the need for law enforcement to utilize more reliable psychological expertise in dealing with paranoid mentalities. On the other hand, the enormous and elaborate attention that law enforcement has invested in studying leftist African American and Native American organizations has not significantly improved its ability to investigate crime in minority communities. Toni Cade Bambara's novelistic account of the investigation of disappearance of black children in Atlanta in *Those Bones Are Not My Child*, for example, illustrates not only suspicion by the police of the black community, but the particular vulnerability of parents to being the primary suspects when a child has disappeared.

Many postmodern theorists have been overly celebratory of the subversion of "master narrative" by Bakhtinian notions of multiple voiced discourse, destablization of the "terrorism" of the Real, etc. A descent into a world of the cacaphonous voices of Babel cavorting in carnivalesque fashion may be cathartic, but to maintain oneself perpetually in such a liminal state (Kristeva's *chora*) is to choose a life of individual or collective psychosis.[7] Silko's novel *Almanac of the Dead* takes the reader to such a world, and the concept of catharsis, and particularly carthartic humor, is important to interpreting the novel. *The Turner Diaries*, on the other hand, is a text that exhibits a manifestation of the paranoid-schizoid position that is even more frightening in its "realist" presentation than the hyperbolic sadomasochism in Silko's novel. These texts exhibit horror in different ways, and "visiting" them is useful insofar as it aids in demystification of some of the darker corners of the human psyche.

The mythical analog to the paranoid-schizoid position of the human infant is the liminal world of the trickster. Tricksters are always testing themselves against an Other, defining their boundaries. The infant likewise must grow and assert its independence from the mother, and the struggle for autonomy and "object constancy" continues through life. On a social or cultural scale, subjects must maintain "object constancy" with master narratives. Like the trickster, a subject must constantly negotiate boundaries between herself and the discourses that construct her world. The relationship between subject and discourse should not be one of universal suspicion, but rather of selective trust, the goal of reparative practices. No one master narrative should be allowed to exercise dominion, but to counter a master narrative with a metanarrative of suspicion of all narratives or a position that all narratives are equally "real" offers a universe in which meaning degenerates into chaos. Where meaning degenerates into chaos, paranoid constructs can arise, assert themselves, and cause real consequences. These consequences mark the bodies of the dead, the abused, and the imprisoned.

With respect to the investigation of the disappearance of black children in Atlanta, Bambara says "even the radicals, white and Black alike, did little more than react to the authorities' agenda, as if there were no alternative way to organize or to think" (651). Constructing alternative ways to think is even more difficult than constructing alternative ways to organize. Reexamining notions of "common sense" is an essential first step toward reconstructing and refocusing narratives of suspicion. Just because scapegoating and demonization may be universal tendencies does not mean that we do not have the intelligence to rise above them. The substitution of the spectres of "bad people . . . for bad policies" (Glassner 6) is intellectually and politically lazy: a practice unworthy of our leadership and ourselves. It is particularly imperative to avoid scapegoating and demonization when faced with real threats and acts of aggression that are specifically intended to terrorize. We must learn, as a collective body of people who control the most powerful military force in the world, how *not* to collectively respond to aggression with the thought processes of infants.

Chapter One

Crucifying the White Man

Douglass Durham's Reinvention
of the American Indian Movement

It is unlikely that the April 2003 arrest of homeless Denver man and accompanying issuance of a fugitive warrant for a Canadian will put to rest the controversy over the murder of Anna Mae Aquash. Though a total of ten assorted FBI, BIA and local sheriff personnel immediately gathered at the creekbed where the body was found on February 1976, their interest in anything except getting the body into the ground fast initially seemed to dissipate until they decided to exhume the body within a week after burial for a second autopsy. The BIA pathologist who conducted the initial investigation had concluded that she died from exposure and inebriation, failing to notice the bullet hole in the back of her head. He cut her hands off her corpse and sent them to Washington, D.C. for identification. After the second autopsy the FBI returned the hands in a wide-mouthed jar to attorney Bruce Ellison (Brand 13–20, Matthiessen 255–62). That was the end of any substantial law enforcement investigation into her death at the time.

Even though persistent questions about Aquash's death eventually resulted in the recent indictments, the only new evidence is likely to consist of conflicting stories from various suspects. It has long been known that the two people indicted were among those Aquash was last seen with when she left the Denver area in 1975 headed for Pine Ridge. But the prevailing view among American Indian activists was probably best articulated by a friend of the arrested man at the time of his arraignment when she stated, "There's never going to be anybody looking into what the feds did—how they had their hand in all of this." (Abbott, "Second Man Sought").[1] Since Douglass Durham had been outed by AIM as an FBI informant almost a year prior to when her body was found, it is unlikely that he was directly involved in the events that lead to her execution, but that probability marks the beginning, not the end, of the story. Jordan S. Dill, whose web page on Durham calls for a Congressional inquiry into Aquash's death, argues that Durham's military and CIA connections should be, in the long term, more significant to Indians than his relatively brief FBI association: "Indian people should be especially interested in Army Intelligence, because—Army v. Indians, traditional, ya know. They are still in the field."[2]

In the 1939 John Ford movie *Drums Along the Mohawk*, the patriot frontier militiamen are surrounded by Mohawks fighting for the British; they must send a messenger to a nearby fort for reinforcement. The first messenger is returned by the redskins, his arms and legs tied in a crucifixion posture across the top of a haywagon which the savages then set on fire before the horrified gaze of the besieged townspeople. This image is replicated in Durham's narrative, three years after the supposed incident, of the mock crucifixion of a white man on Easter Sunday by the American Indian Movement during its occupation of Wounded Knee in 1973. Durham's crucifixion story resurrects the frontier narrative of the savage beast in the wilderness lying in wait for the white man. But it is Durham himself who took on a new life during those three years between Wounded Knee and his final debriefing before a right-wing senatorial subcommittee in 1976.

Douglass Durham's otherwise dubious career is notable due to the high position of trust and power to which he rose in AIM: chief of security and 'second-in-command' in the sense that he had become Dennis Banks's closest advisor. While Durham played a large part in making AIM one of the most paranoid of activist organizations at a time when at least some degree of suspicion was necessary for such groups to survive, his statements about AIM were to become paranoid narratives in themselves, shaped along the course of his speaking tour for the anti-communist John Birch Society during the year following his exposure.[3] A newly discovered hearing transcript of Durham testifying in an obscure federal venue in May 1975 helps elucidate how, when, and why Durham's story changed.

Durham has been portrayed by scholars sympathetic to AIM as a wife-beating, misogynistic pimp whose real career is with the CIA. However much of this characterization may be true, it tends to imply that his motivations toward AIM were malevolent. But it can be argued that his attitudes about AIM were complex and changed over time. The psychology of the long-term undercover operative is necessarily 'abnormal.' Living in a close, almost familial grouping with people when one's mission is to betray them is not a situation conducive to functional human relationships, as former FBI undercover agent Cril Payne explained with remarkable lucidity in his account of his investigation of the New Left in the Pacific Northwest. Durham never wrote a book about his experiences, though apparently he had intended to;[4] one must interpret his state of mind through his testimonial narratives. These narratives are important in themselves as significant pieces of the metanarrative of suspicion in which activist politics have been embedded since the McCarthy era (with roots much earlier). Moreover, an understanding of the individual psychological operations that may be performed upon information about a collective 'significant other'—particularly a racialized 'Other'—can enhance our understanding of the dynamics of scapegoating and collective paranoia.

Durham was born September 26, 1937 in Omaha, Nebraska. The son of a telephone company employee, he lived in several places before graduating from Roosevelt High School in Des Moines, Iowa in 1955 (Lamberto). According to the interview with Lamberto in April 1975, he spent several years in an Indian elementary school in Hayward, Wisconsin, though by the time of his Congressional testimony a year later this had shrunk to several months (United States Senate 16). After several years in the Marines which included some time stationed in Cuba (according to Durham), he was employed by the Des Moines Police Department from 1961 to 1964. His career began to unravel when his pregnant wife died in 1964 from cerebral edema, a condition that would almost undoubtedly have occurred from a blow to the head. The police department conducted an investigation and though it found no evidence of foul play, Durham was discharged from the police department in October 1964 on the basis of a psychiatric report declaring him "unfit for office involving public trust" (Giese 3).[5]

Documentation of Durham's pre-AIM history is problematic. Virtually all of the information on Durham's background recounted in AIM histories—Johanna Brand's *The Life and Death of Anna Mae Aquash* (1978), Ward Churchill and Jim Vander Wall's *Agents of Repression: The FBI's Secret Wars Against the Black Panther Party and the American Indian Movement* (1988, 1990), Peter Matthiessen's *In the Spirit of Crazy Horse* (1983, 1991), and Rex Weyler's *Blood of the Land: The Government and Corporate War Against the American Indian Movement* (1984)—rely primarily on two sources: a lengthy article by Paula Giese and Durham's self-reporting. Giese, a reporter for the northern Minnesota alternative newspaper *North Country Anvil* in the mid-seventies, had worked as a legal investigator for the Wounded Knee Legal Defense/Offense Committee (WKLD/OC) during the 1974 Minneapolis trial of Dennis Banks and Russell Means for activities related to the Wounded Knee occupation of 1973. Interestingly enough, biographical information about Giese in the list of contributors for the *North Country Anvil* in a late 1975 issue does not mention her WKLD/OC background, though the articles she was contributing concerned AIM issues and a large amount of unattributed copy in *Akwesasne Notes* during this period appears to have been written by Giese. Rather, she is identified as "a former wire service reporter and University of Minnesota humanities professor" (16:70). Giese's primary article on Durham, "Secret Agent Douglass Durham and the Death of Jancita Eagle Deer," appeared in 1976 in the *North Country Anvil* (a condensed version appeared in *Covert Action* in 1985). Her article was based in part on Durham's own commentary, tape recorded when Dennis Banks, Vernon Bellecourt, and lead WKLD/OC counsel Kenneth Tilsen confronted him at a meeting in a Des Moines hotel room on March 7, 1975. Also present at the hotel meeting as a mediator was John P. Adams of the United Methodist Church and National Council of Churches, who wrote the most comprehensive account of Durham's story in an article in *Christian Century* (reprinted in *Akwesasne Notes*). Kenneth Tilsen, who viewed Durham's story as "all bullshit," threw away the tape and gave the transcript to a now-unidentifiable journalism student (Northcott).[6]

Giese died in 1997. Her 1976 article tells a sordid tale of gun-running for the CIA in preparation for the 1961 Bay of Pigs invasion, "'running' a string of 'girls'" from a 24-hour café on Des Moines' North Sixth Avenue called the Why Not?, later running an "automated call-girl service" enhanced by his skills as a photographer, and "fronting for Mafia interests" (2–3). Much, if not all of this information seems to have come from the March 1975 press conference and subsequent published interviews with Durham. Unfortunately, Giese does not cite her sources and some of her facts are unverified. For example, she claims that a police investigation into the death of Durham's first wife was triggered by his marriage three weeks later to "one of the Why Not? girls" (2). Durham's wife Donna Exline died on July 5, 1964, and Polk County courthouse records of Durham's divorce from his third wife (in 1977) give the date of his third marriage as July 24, 1965 (though Durham characterized this marriage as his second to reporter Lamberto).[7] Giese remarked in her 1976 article that "Wife No. 2 seems simply to have disappeared" (11), though it is unclear to whom she refers; Durham was married to the same woman from 1965 through 1977, and his son from his first marriage still lived with his third wife at the time of the 1977 divorce. A greater problem occurs with the report that Durham was "convicted of larceny in an odd Mafia-political case in 1971" (Giese 3). This statement was made in connection with a colorful narrative of "mov(ing) rapidly up in the Midwest hierarchy of organized crime . . . operat(ing) several restaurants, fronting for Mafia interests . . . 'I was considered (by local law enforcement officials) to be head of the largest criminal organization in the state of Iowa,' he boasted to AIM attorneys in tape-recorded, witnessed interviews conducted March 9–12 [1975] in Chicago" (Giese 3).[8] Giese's error as to where the interviews took place—they were held in Des Moines, Iowa and Des Plaines, Illinois (Lamberto)—is minor and understandable since the press conference on March 13 was held in Chicago, but the more serious problem is that no conviction appears in either federal or state court records for the area. Durham was charged on June 23, 1970 with the crime of "false pretense." According to the information (charging document) in Des Moines Municipal Court (#70–12893), he "did wilfully and feloniously and by false pretense obtain money to the value of more than $20.00 from Tom Greesaman with the intent to defraud." He was released on $1,000 bond and the case was bound over to the Polk County grand jury, which reviewed the case on December 2, 1970 and did not issue an indictment. The charge was "ignored" along with a companion case, meaning that the case was dismissed.[9] Apparently Durham invented the conviction as part of his story to Ron Petite and Harvey Major of the Des Moines AIM chapter; according to Dennis Banks, when Petite and Major recommended Durham to Banks "they told us that he was a former pig, busted for burglary and dismissed from the police force" (Matthiessen 120).

Giese spent a lot of time with Durham in the summer and fall of 1974 when they were investigating the rape charge of Jancita Eagle Deer against William Janklow. This endeavor was tangential to the defense team's presentation of evidence of prosecutorial misconduct in the Dennis Banks/Russell Means trial. It is not entirely clear why Giese and Durham continued with the Eagle Deer matter after the defense team declined to present Eagle Deer's testimony in connection with their motion to dismiss; WKLD/OC felt the matter's relevance to the Wounded Knee issues was at best attenuated. The investigation did result in getting Janklow disbarred from the Rosebud tribal court following Dennis Banks's petition and Eagle Deer's testimony in October 1974, but it is widely believed that public perception of the charge as a smear campaign contributed to Janklow's election as South Dakota's attorney general in November 1974 (Matthiessen 108–109). Karen Northcott, a WKLD/OC legal investigator who is still a legal investigator in Minneapolis, stated that Giese "may have had a personal relationship" with Durham during this time, and that Giese's article in the *North Country Anvil* over a year later was her own project and not produced under color of any association with WKLD/OC. Northcott characterizes Giese's narrative as exemplary of AIM at its most paranoid. Though Northcott's remark about Giese and Durham may be speculative, it is fairly well established that Giese was working with Durham at a time when other AIM and WKLD/OC women apparently had as little use for Durham as he did for them. For one thing, some of them had noticed that he dyed his hair black. They saw him as "Dennis's boy": an arrogant sycophant who appointed himself as gatekeeper to Banks; Northcott told Matthiessen, "He never talked to the Defense Committee staff except to give orders . . . we were just too lowly. Doug Durham was full of himself . . . " (111).

It is possible that Giese and Durham had in common personal conflicts about their own ancestry. Durham claimed while with AIM that he was one-quarter Chippewa; immediately after his exposure he revised this to a "smattering" of Indian blood on his father's side and several years at a Chippewa Indian elementary school (Adams 490); two months later, testifying at a motion hearing in Lincoln, Nebraska, he denied all Indian ancestry. Giese was characterized by Matthiessen as white, but the website Giese created in 1995 states that her Indian ancestry is Canadian; another website displaying a logo designed by Giese identifies her as Anishinabe, i.e. Chippewa or Ojibwe.[10]

At any rate, Durham became involved with Jancita Eagle Deer soon after tracking her down in Iowa. Giese's article reports extensive personal knowledge of Durham's abusive relationship with Eagle Deer, and the main thrust of the article is to implicate Durham in Eagle Deer's death.[11] Durham has also been accused both by AIM leaders and by several responsible journalists and scholars of complicity in the deaths of Harvey Major (Des Moines AIM leader) and Anna Mae Aquash, the most influential woman among the national AIM leadership.[12] Jordan S. Dill's internet accusations are viewed by some as paranoid fantasy (most notably the South Dakota-based newspaper *Indian Country Today*), but his statement that Durham had lived in a born-again Christian commune in Dallas, Texas is supported by divorce records in Polk County, Iowa at least insofar as the fact that Durham was living in Dallas in 1977 and was still living there in 1982. Even Dill distances himself from the rumor that the commune is actually Satanist (the web page says that Durham "lives in some sort of born-again Christian communal house, that was said to be a cover for Satanists [I don't have anything definite on this]"), but the general scenario described is not inconsistent with the sort of assignment a career federal informant might be involved with in the nineties. Right-wing 'Christian' communes are at the nexus of contemporary conspiracy radar, both receiving and transmitting.

Though it is primarily Durham's fictional embellishments and distortions which are the subject of this discussion, there are at least some facts about his association with AIM that are not in dispute. His contact with AIM began when he was asked by a Des Moines alternative newspaper *Pax Today* to accompany him to the Wounded Knee occupation as a photographer, where his FBI connections helped in getting through the roadblock.[13] He was only inside Wounded Knee for a few hours, a factor which becomes significant in analyzing his later testimony. Upon his return to Des Moines he was asked by the FBI to attempt to make some contact with the Iowa AIM chapter, a project aided by his published Wounded Knee pictures. Des Moines AIM members were impressed with his photography and writing skills; Aaron Two Elk said "Durham's background sort of gave us a special insight about the way the police worked . . . and he was a pretty good writer, was able to raise money and all sorts of stuff, so we looked at him as a real asset in those early days" (Churchill 213).[14] But by then, Two Elk said, Durham was already 'bad-jacketing' another AIM member, i.e., spreading the rumor that he was an informant (213). By and by, Durham gained the confidence of AIM leader Dennis Banks and rose to a national leadership position as head of security for AIM. As the FBI moved toward prosecution of Banks in connection with the disturbance at the courthouse in Custer, South Dakota, Durham accompanied Banks to the Northwest Territories in Canada where Banks remained a fugitive but eventually returned to face prosecution in Minneapolis. Durham's identity was discovered by AIM in November 1974, after the nine-month trial against Banks and Means had ended in dismissal for prosecutorial misconduct.[15] According to Banks, only Ken Tilsen, Banks, Clyde Bellecourt, and Russell Means knew about it and decided to watch him for a few months "to see where he might lead us" (Matthiessen 120). But meanwhile, Durham managed to put on a bizarre sideshow at a hearing in Ventura County, California, where he testified at a sanity hearing on behalf of AIM defendant Paul "Skyhorse" Durant, masquerading as a psychologist from the University of Iowa who "knew all about the Indian mind."[16]

Tilsen, Banks, and Vernon Bellecourt confronted Durham in Des Moines on March 7, 1975. After the taped interviews were completed, AIM sponsored a press conference in Chicago on March 12 at which Durham presented the first version of his story to the public. According to the *New York Times* report, Durham said he was "relieved" at his identity finally being discovered because

> he had come to respect Mr. Banks and to believe that A.I.M. was a 'legal, social organization that wasn't doing anything wrong.' . . .

He said that "after serving in the Marine Corps, he joined the Des Moines police force, working in a burglar-infested neighborhood, but left the force after his wife died . . . He later worked in and then managed a series of restaurants, some of which became hangouts for burglars, Mr. Durham said.

At the same time, he added, he was learning to fly a plane and to scuba dive, and was developing skills as a photographer, studying locks and burglar tools and reading about psychology . . .

Mr. Durham's swarthy skin, dark eyes and high cheekbones give him an Indian look . . . (Kifner)

John P. Adams, present during the three-day interviews, similarly quotes Durham as saying that "Dennis Banks is a rational and responsible man. He is a viable, logical and peaceful leader of a necessary social protest movement . . . I turned 180 degrees . . . I saw AIM as a social protest organization that is not illegal, does not do anything wrong, and in fact . . . is morally right. The only thing I saw wrong about the American Indian Movement was that it was being infiltrated" (493–94). It may be argued that Durham's admiring characterization of Banks and AIM during the interviews and at the initial press conference was self-serving and disingenuous, that he was still in the presence of AIM leadership and had been locked up with them, so to speak, for days undergoing interrogation. But he stuck with this story for at least a couple of months.

On May 31, 1975 Durham testified in Lincoln, Nebraska before Judge Warren K. Urbom at a motion regarding two of the nonleadership Wounded Knee cases.[17] He was called as a defense witness, although there is no indication that he came forward voluntarily. On June 19 the judge ruled against the defense motion based on his opinion that the connection of Durham's infiltration of WKLD/OC to these particular cases was, at best, attenuated. But at the hearing, several defense lawyers had their shot at Durham in an attempt to find out whatever they could about his involvement with WKLD/OC activities. Beyond the cases at hand, they hoped to produce evidence of FBI misconduct to introduce at an upcoming Wounded Knee hearing in Cedar Rapids (94).

The testimony opened with this exchange:

DEFENSE ATTORNEY ELLIOTT TAIKEFF: Mr. Durham, are those prescription glasses you are wearing?[18]
DURHAM: No, they are not.
TAIKEFF: Will you please take them off so that I can see your face?
DURHAM: Sure. (10)

Among the many published pictures of Durham, none show him wearing glasses, though he did wear contact lenses while undercover with AIM to darken the color of his eyes.

Aside from confounding his usual appearance, Durham's first interjection of information into the narrative beyond what was being specifically requested of him was his statement, in response to a general question about infiltrating any political organizations in Des Moines, that "I am politically naïve and I never did really get that involved" (14). Later on in the hearing, Durham is asked if the WKLD/OC volunteers "came there because they were politically motivated" (the attorney is attempting to establish that the FBI's motivation was investigation of a political group rather than investigation of criminal activity):

> DURHAM: No. I think this was a greater motivation than that.
> TAIKEFF: Well does this greater motivation include what would commonly be understood by the words "a political motivation?"
> DURHAM: Well there had been discussions about that. AIM was not a political organization.
> TAIKEFF: But I am asking about the people who came to work on the committee.
> DURHAM: I can't speak for the individual motivation, whether it was political or not. I know there was a lot of spiritual motivation from some of the things they had to live with all of their life, and if that was the result of politics on the Pine Ridge Reservation, I am sure there has got to be some political reason for them being there in that respect. Some of these people have been beaten down in Pine Ridge, and they had good motivation. Whether it can be called political or not—I am not sure of the label. (49–50)

There are several interesting aspects to this exchange. First, Durham's preferred adjective to describe AIM has shifted from "social" or "social protest" to "spiritual." This is perhaps the most accurate description that he ever gave of AIM. "Social protest" is a term of the white sixties counterculture. Its meaning as applied to Native concerns is distorted by the culturally embedded inflections of its origin. "Spiritual" is a term Indian followers of traditional beliefs use to describe their religion ("religion" is a disfavored term due to its implications of dogma and hierarchy—another instance of the limitation of the English language). AIM has been perpetually misunderstood as a political, even Marxist organization (particularly in the context of anticommunist paranoia) whereas most people with any extensive contact with AIM leaders understand that the movement is grounded in traditional Native spirituality: a spirituality which is performative and in which connections to land and to ancestors play primary roles. Thus the occupation of Wounded Knee was as much a religious ritual as a political demonstration.

The attorney asking the questions completely ignores the significance of Durham's term "spiritual motivation" and follows Durham's answer with a leading question designed to give Durham a definition of a "political" organization to see if he agrees with it; Taikeff asks if "their purpose in coming there was to bring about certain changes in the lives of American Indian people" and "to generally improve their prospects and their general living conditions." Durham answers "yes" to both questions. So the attorney is treating Durham as a hostile witness reluctant to say that AIM is a political organization by employing a cross-examination technique to force Durham to say "yes." Durham was clearly attempting to avoid saying that AIM was a political organization, presumably to protect the FBI and himself from the ramifications of unlawful surveillance of a political organization, or even discourage further political surveillance of AIM. Senator Frank Church's Senate Select Committee on Intelligence had been investigating domestic spying and counterintelligence programs of the FBI and CIA for several months at this point, since January 1975. But surely the FBI is placed in just as bad a light infiltrating a spiritual organization as a political organization.

Moving on from the "political organization" issue, the attorney asks about the "people who worked on the legal committee" (48). Durham, however, redirects the specifics of his answer to the situation of Lakota Indians living on the Pine Ridge reservation. Though Lakotas certainly had a strong presence on the legal committee, the committee also included a wide range of lawyers, law students, and other volunteers, Indian and non-Indian. This response hints at the probable presence of Lakotas in the courtroom audience, and at any rate it was their interests which were fundamentally at stake. Durham is speaking to and on behalf of them more than he is speaking to the attorney. Durham comes across as the one who is looking at the "big picture" while the attorney is chasing after minutae; Durham speaks to living conditions at Pine Ridge while the attorney is more concerned with the living conditions of white legal volunteers.

Durham is consistent throughout the hearing in maintaining that AIM is a nonviolent organization. He volunteers the information that "never once was a demonstration ever planned to be violent" (99). He says that he advised defendants, and in particular Dennis Banks to plead not guilty because "it was my belief" that they were not guilty of criminal acts in connection with Wounded Knee and the Custer, South Dakota courthouse riot (103). He says "I don't know what criminal conspiracy is. I have never seen one yet, I don't know what one is, to be honest with you" (59).

Durham is not entirely cooperative with either the defense attorneys or the prosecutors in this hearing. The defense attorneys are attempting to establish that the FBI had no business infiltrating AIM and that Durham's presence at defense strategy sessions was so invasive of attorney-client privilege that convictions should be thrown out. The U.S. Attorney then attempts to show on cross-examination that not only were illegal acts being performed by AIM members, whether or not at the behest of the leadership, but that contacts were being made with Communist countries as part of a plan for Banks to go into exile if necessary—a plan that could be interpreted as a conspiracy to obstruct justice. Assistant U.S. Attorney Keith Uhl is also trying very hard to establish that AIM was planning violent acts. But under cross examination by Uhl, Durham affirms again that "demonstrations planned by the American Indian Movement were planned not to be violent" (Uhl's words, 153). He reaffirms that this was true of "all that I knew of." Uhl is not satisfied with this answer because he has knowledge of a report made by Durham to the FBI regarding actions planned for the 1976 bicentennial year. Durham initially denies recollection of such a report, but eventually says "I recall a one-page thing on the possible violence in '76 . . . I reported excerpts, among other things, from a speech, statements made by some of the leaders that there would not be a peaceful two hundredth birthday for the United States if Indians weren't given better treatment, or something to that effect. They planned to 'get on' [sic] in some areas" (154–155). Later, asked about a list of possible assassination targets, Durham says "I recall being quizzed by the FBI about this blacklist for assassination . . . I could only speculate what individuals could be on the list" (167).

As noted, Durham's remarks seem to be directed toward an Indian audience rather than to either set of attorneys. It is likely that there were at least a few AIM members and supporters in the courtroom at this hearing; it would have been unusual if there were not. Thus, he focuses on Pine Ridge natives when being asked about the defense committee, he speaks at least once in rural/Indian vernacular,[19] and he interjects gratuitously sympathetic remarks concerning people whom he has been assigned to investigate: the repeated statements of "my belief" that Banks was not guilty (102) and an earlier description of demonstrators at Greenwood Park in Des Moines protesting, "and rightfully so," the accidental death of a motorcyclist due to an unmarked barrier (13).

As with his confessional-type story to AIM leaders, their attorney, and Methodist mediator John P. Adams, Durham's testimony in federal court is given from a defensive posture. He is surrounded by people hostile to him; no one, not even the federal prosecutors with whom he is barely acquainted, is his friend or advocate. Serious consequences can ensue if he says the wrong thing. But Durham is an intelligent and competent professional witness; he does not say the wrong thing. He says nothing that would invoke any further anger and contempt than he has already earned from AIM and its supporters, but at the same time he says nothing that the AIM lawyers are able to successfully use in getting any further convictions or prosecutions derailed.

Durham's testimony at this hearing is most significant when set in contrast to his lectures on tour with the John Birch Society and his testimony the following year before Senator Eastland's Internal Security Subcommittee because it establishes that he was still willing to profess some degree of sympathy for, and even solidarity with, AIM in a public forum. As hostile and coercive as the environment of a federal courtroom might have been in this case, it was more controlled and protective of his interests than being holed up in a hotel room with four men and a tape recorder. He could have said all sorts of damaging things about AIM and walked away—he chose not to.

By this time, however, especially in light of feature articles about him and other newspaper coverage in Iowa and Nebraska before and after the court hearing,[20] he was rendered somewhat useless for undercover work in the Midwest. The John Birch lecture tour gave him some needed income, but in playing to an entirely different audience, his narrative about AIM underwent significant revision.

The John Birch Society was founded in 1958 by Robert Welch, named after an army captain and Baptist missionary killed by Chinese communists shortly after World War II. Its mission was to expose communists everywhere; even Dwight D. Eisenhower was a Communist agent according to Welch's publications and despite such wild claims, the group grew to a membership of eighty thousand by 1967 (Bennett 317–19). A large portion of this membership consisted of Midwestern farmers and so when AIM became an activist presence fairly close to home, someone who had been "inside AIM" would be a popular speaker. It is clear from Durham's court testimony in Nebraska that the FBI had been interested in ferreting out any contacts between AIM leaders and Communists. Thus the ground had already been laid for elaboration and embellishment of this theme.

The only significant change in Durham's story from the March interviews and press conference to the May 31 hearing had been that he no longer claimed to be Indian.[21] But by October 1975, the John Birch Society was announcing his lectures with a flyer headed, "**A.I.M. is a military operation.**" Featuring a picture of Durham with shorter hair and a trim beard (a departure from his previous, Indian-style long hair and clean shave) the poster continues: "It is a foreign army using guerrilla warfare to destroy America. A.I.M. terrorists have stashed dynamite on the Rosebud Reservation, and in Wisconsin, New Mexico, Kansas, Nebraska, and Iowa! **Hear Doug Durham, Former A.I.M Leader, tell what he learned while 'Inside A.I.M'.**" The back side of the flyer continues with the following statements in quotation marks intended to indicate quotes from Durham:

> **The American Indian is** now under attack by the revolutionaries of A.I.M.—criminal renegades armed with Soviet AK-47 assault rifles and backed by federal funds.
>
> **A.I.M. has tried to create** the impression of popular support but most Indians reject it because of its totalitarian philosophy and criminal activities.
>
> **A.I.M. plans to carry its terrorism** to Indian reservations and towns nationwide—where it will continue its **Looting** and **Butchery** and **Arson** and **Kidnapping**.
>
> The A.I.M. Leaders Are Gangsters.[22]

If this sort of rhetoric seems reminiscent of late nineties paranoid discourses of the nineties white militia movement, it is because some of the specific narratives of foreign communist troops poised on the borders in Canada and Mexico have their source in John Birch Society publications. But here, the "foreign army" is already within and among us: looting, butchering, fire-setting, baby-stealing "renegades" with a "totalitarian philosophy." The juxtaposition of "renegades" with "totalitarian" is oxymoronic: renegades by definition are rebels against authority. Furthermore, the vast array of published material on AIM invariably demonstrates that its leadership and membership structures are so loose as to confound white middle class notions of any sort of legally recognizable cohesive group, let alone one with a top-down totalitarian philosophy. The alarmism over the Marxist connection seems particular quaint in retrospect in light of the serious schisms that were to develop between AIM and its American leftist supporters, as articulated in Ward Churchill's anthology *Marxism and Native Americans* (1982).

What accounts for this rapid about-face in Durham's narrative? Any narrative is the product of an interaction between a narrator and an audience, but the audience has even more influence on the narration of a professional informant. Moreover, significant events had transpired between May and October beyond Durham's need for a steady income. The John Birch tour was started after the deaths of two FBI agents on the Pine Ridge reservation June 26, 1975 when FBI agents approached a remote cabin near Oglala where a group of AIM families was camped out, allegedly in search of a young man who had stolen a pair of cowboy boots. The event, which has been covered in several books and TV documentaries,[23] eventually led to a life sentence for Leonard Peltier and acquittals on grounds of self-defense for Darrelle Dean Butler and Bob Robideau. Peltier was convicted in a separate trial from the other two defendants and most scholars agree, though the prosecutors vehemently deny, that the conviction was unjust.[24]

Meanwhile, compounding the ongoing Church Committee investigation, the Rockefeller Commission (created by President Ford around the same time, in January 1975, in response to December 22, 1974 disclosures by the *New York Times* of CIA involvement in domestic surveillance) delivered its report in early June 1975, finding that the CIA "over the years committed acts in violation of the 1947 National Security Act or domestic laws" ("Justice Agency" 21).[25] This event contributed to general public concern over government spying, and three days before the Oglala firefight, the Church Committee had sent a letter to U.S. Attorney General Edward S. Levi announcing its intent to conduct interviews of Douglass Durham. According to an FBI memo, this request wasn't received by the FBI Legal Division until June 27, the day after the Oglala firefight, and on that same day Church Committee staff member Patrick Shea "requested we hold in abeyance any action on the request in view of the killing of the Agents at Pine Ridge Reservation, South Dakota." The Church Committee's investigation of Durham was never resumed (Churchill 251).

The FBI was promoting a general atmosphere of hysteria about AIM's intentions following the deaths of agents Williams and Coler on June 26. Though a bomb shattered some windows at the Mt. Rushmore visitor's center at 4 a.m. on June 27 (Matthiessen 202), most of the violence was clearly being perpetrated by agents of law enforcement. By July 22, U.S. Commission on Civil Rights chairman Aurthur J. Flemming was complaining to the U.S. Attorney General about the FBI's "full-scale military type invasion" of Pine Ridge that had intensified after the June 26 incident (Matthiessen 250). A few weeks earlier on June 8, Russell Means had been shot in the back by a BIA agent and then charged with assaulting the officer who shot him (he was acquitted [146, 611]). On July 1, his brother Ted Means announced a July 4 march to Mt. Rushmore in honor of Joe Stuntz, the Indian who had been killed in the Oglala firefight (202). In response, while continuing to ransack Indian households all over the area, the FBI circulated a memo on July 2 predicting that an AIM suicide squad was going to attempt to blow up Mt. Rushmore on July 4. Though nothing remotely like this happened (a tobacco ceremony was held there [Churchill 250, 439]), a group of Indians "tired of being buzzed by an FBI Huey" did shoot down a helicopter north of Pine Ridge village, with no injuries reported (Churchill 250, Matthiessen 203).

Meanwhile, American patriots were starting to plan for the bicentennial celebration of the following year. The FBI was not being paranoid in understanding that South Dakota Indians, and particularly AIM, hated Mt. Rushmore, but no evidence seems to exist to support a report of a suicide squad. The monument and the bicentennial are the sort of trigger symbols, like the American flag, a threat to which can provoke a variety of irrational responses. Thus paranoid anticipation both within the FBI and in the farm country surrounding the Black Hills and Lakota region, fueled by the ongoing war on the Pine Ridge reservation, was hardly to be unexpected.

On October 14, Durham spoke at a Bircher lecture in Rapid City, South Dakota of AIM's supposed intentions to disrupt bicentennial celebrations the following year. "In preparation for the scheduled deceleration," he said, "AIM has established training camps around the country in which political indoctrination, marskmanship, and guerrrilla warfare are taught." Later that day, a bomb went off in the BIA Law and Order Building in Pine Ridge (home of tribal chairman Dick Wilson's GOONS—Guardians of the Oglala Nation). Wilson blamed AIM; AIM leader Clyde Bellecourt blamed the John Birch Society. A week later, Durham stated in a lecture at Mitchell that AIM would engage in "indiscriminate killings of whites" (Matthessen 240–41).[26]

One would think that amidst all these terrorist preparations, Durham might be traveling and speaking under heavy security; he certainly had more to fear from AIM than anyone. But on the contrary, AIM members who attended one of his lectures in Valentine, Nebraska

> couldn't take no more, so we went up there on the platform. A friend of mine told Durham to step to one side, and he kept an eye on him while I told those people the real truth about life on Pine Ridge. We're not Communists, I said . . . and gradually the hoots and yells died down, and they were turning to each other, discussing what I was saying. So Durham knew that he was losing 'em, and he comes my way while I'm still talking,

and I'm still talking when I let him have it; next thing you know, he's picking himself off the floor with a bloody mouth (Bill Means, quoted in Mattheissen 241).

Bill Means apparently suffered no ill consequences from this encounter; he says "afterward, them white people come up to me, not really knowing what to say, you know, but just trying to make me feel better some way, and themselves, too" (241).

Akwesasne Notes had reprinted John P. Adams's fairly evenhanded and sympathetic *Christian Century* article based on the March interview tapes of Durham in the early summer 1975 issue. Paula Giese's much more critical and provocative report focusing on the death of Durham's former lover Jancita Eagle Deer was printed in the *North Country Anvil* in the March-April 1976, around the same time she implicated him in the circumstances surrounding the "AIM Camp 13" murder in Ventura County, California in the early spring 1976 issue of *Akwesasne Notes*. The latter article included an assertion that Durham had been talking about Giese in his John Birch speeches, "calling her a 'big time Commie,' giving out her home address in hopes of stirring up a cut-rate assassination" ("Your Information" 7). The following issue (Early Summer 1976) of *Akwesasne Notes* described an unsigned letter the newspaper had received from Houston, Texas. The editors interpreted the letter as

> a carefully constructed professional effort to get Paula Giese assassinated
> . . .
>
>   The author of the letter claimed to be a disenchanted FBI agent who had left his position . . . To establish his credibility, he wrote a detailed description of the interior of the AIM office, including the location of the peanut butter.
>
>   Then, he promised he would give *Akwesasne Notes* a detailed complete list of all the infomers, spies, and provacateurs . . . To get this, all *Notes* had to do was to publish his letter.
>
>   The writer then came out with the accusation that Paula Giese was an FBI agent, getting paid thousands of dollars a month. The totally untrue and impossible fable continued to say that Giese had been responsible for the capture of Dennis Banks, the shooting of Russell Means, and other dirty deeds, and that is was a shame that such brave Indian heroes had to suffer—Paula Geise should die, the writer said ("*Akwesasne Notes* Target").

If the stakes were less serious, one might interpret this media exchange between Giese and Durham (if it was Durham) as almost amusing. Giese's articles on Durham, though generally accurate, were spiteful, speculative, and perhaps paranoid, to the point that WKLD/OC distanced itself from them (Northcott). Durham's slander of Giese in his speeches seems childish, and the anonymous letter sounds paranoid. But the letter was actually a failed attempt to play on the assumed paranoia of the *Akwesasne Notes* staff which, given the generally paranoid environment that existed at the time, is to be commended for its good judgment in disbelieving the accusations. AIM people were dying right and left. Harvey Major of the Des Moines AIM chapter was dead, as was Anna Mae Aquash, whose body had been discovered in February 1976.

It was in the midst of such an atmosphere that Durham testified before Senator James Eastland's Senate Subcommittee on Internal Security on April 6, 1976 to investigate "Revolutionary Activities within the United States: The American Indian Movement." Matthiessen calls Eastland a "professional flag waver" (318); a right-wing anti-communist, Eastland is also on record as an advocate of "the untainted racial heritage, culture and institutions of the Anglo-Saxon race."[27] Churchill and Vander Wall discuss the hearing under the subchapter heading "The Douglass Durham Show" (272–281), an apt description because no other witnesses were called. The hearing transcript indicates that Eastland was the only senatorial member of the subcommittee present.

Unfortunately, however, Churchill and Vander Wall's otherwise excellent book on FBI repression of AIM and the Black Panthers erroneously places Durham's Congressional hearing testimony in April of 1975 rather than 1976 (272), leading to their characterization of this testimony as a "prelude" to the John Birch tour (280) rather than what was, the final product of many practice runs before Bircher audiences and an obviously productive relationship between Durham and whoever was producing the advertising flyers. The quotes on the flyers key in on the hot-button phrases that would 'work' the audience, and Durham learned how to elaborate the script. One can only speculate on whatever relationship may have existed between the FBI and the John Birch Society that may have assisted Durham in landing this job, but one does not have to allege a conspiratorial relationship to note that by circumstance alone, the JBS acted as shill for the FBI in coaching Durham in developing his narrative of terroristic communist savages in our midst. Likewise, Senator Eastland offered a forum for an FBI narrative that was still, even after the death of J. Edgar Hoover in 1972, focused on the premise of the communist menace. The hearing operated on the margins of official sanction—fellow subcommittee member Birch Bayh later denounced it (Brand 108–09), but it served the purpose of the FBI in disempowering AIM; it helped dry up funding sources, keep spiritual leader Leonard Crow Dog in prison, and extradite Leonard Peltier from Canada (Churchill 279, 445).

Durham's Congressional testimony is perhaps of more historical significance for containing the first public manifestation of the "kill a cop a day" bicentennial conspiracy theory that was to emerge a few months later in the form of the notorious "Dog Soldier teletypes" (to be discussed later). But the most fantastic feature of Durham's narrative was his description of the Easter Sunday crucifixion of a white man said to have been performed during the Wounded Knee occupation three years earlier. Durham himself was only at Wounded Knee for a half day at most, to take pictures, and took pictures of nothing remotely similar.

Though Durham claimed this man was hung up and beaten for six hours within full view of federal marshals, there have been no independent reports of such an incident either before or since Durham told his tale to Senator Eastland; those who were at Wounded Knee invariably confirm nothing like this ever occurred (Churchill 274).

Even the lawyer conducting the questioning at the Congressional hearing must have been dubious about this amazing story: Durham volunteered it in his opening statement (5–6) and chief counsel Richard L. Schultz ignored it in his subsequent questioning. One can only speculate that Senator Eastland took this sort of behavior among Indians as par for the course; he remained virtually silent throughout the hearing. Bruce Johansen and Robert Maestas discuss the crucifixion story in the chapter of their book aptly entitled ""The Making of a Savage: The FBI's Creative Writer's School," describing it as "a new play on an old theme: the savages taking out their heathenism on all that is Christian" (52). The story also has interesting psychological implications involving its "white man" that are deserving of analysis, but first it is necessary to examine the broader objectives of the hearing.

An overview of the questioning conducted by the chief counsel warrants the conclusion that three main objectives were being pursued: to establish that AIM planning a series of violent acts over the bicentennial summer (the 'dog soldier' prototype), to establish that AIM was fully ensconced within an international network of communist organizations, and to establish that AIM had engaged in fiscal malfeasance with federal grants and food stamps. These objectives were consistent with the last three of what Durham had stated as five FBI objectives for his undercover assignment a year earlier at the Nebraska hearing: alleged criminal activities, caches of arms, and foreign involvement (the first two objectives were the movement of leaders of the American Indian Movement and the status of individuals in executive offices of the American Indian Movement [34]). But Durham's hand always seemed to be in the middle of such activities, where there was any credence to them at all. He was not merely an informant, but a slanderer and provocateur. For example, Durham himself had released an unauthorized memo on AIM letterhead February 6, 1974, cited in a February 9 FBI memo from Minneapolis to Washington about AIM's "plans for the immediate future" involving "systematic violence" (Churchill 223, 434); this was apparently the memo brought out on cross-examination at the Nebraska hearing (153–55). According to women close to the situation (Candy Hamilton and Nilak Butler), Durham's ongoing advocacy of "guerrilla warfare" led to Anna Mae Aquash's insistence that he was "out of line" and his subsequent ill-will toward and attempted bad-jacketing of her (223, 434). According to Churchill and Vander Wall, Durham himself introduced and promoted Marighella's *Mini-Manual of the Urban Guerilla* to AIM members (274). As for foreign involvement, they point out that "virtually every concrete interaction between 'AIM' and any of the 'suspect' foreign entities posited came, not through *bona fide* AIM members, but through

Durham (a known FBI infiltrator), George Roberts (a suspected CIA infiltrator), or both. The entire spurious issue is thus indelibly marked with the stamp of COINTELPRO-type orchestration" (278).

A tedious portion of the Congressional hearing is devoted to the submission of cancelled checks, telephone bills, and other such office receipts from the Des Moines AIM chapter. Here again, after pages of testimony about the misappropriation of funds from a Office of Economic Opportunity grant to pay the travel of Dennis Banks and Ron Petite to Canada after the Custer indictments, it turns out that the funds were actually deposited in a different account and thus the checks had been signed by Durham himself (37–44, 127–29).

During his year on the John Birch lecture circuit, Durham seems to have developed a fuller understanding of the meaning of "criminal conspiracy" than he claimed to have had at the Lincoln hearing—at least, he came to the Eastland committee prepared to define terrorism: "This move toward terrorism and threats of violent acts seemed to be an increasing phase in AIM. The terrorist, of course, is essentially a criminal who is just seeking his influence and power with criminal methods to terror, intimidation, and violence. He certainly is not a soldier but there is a tendency to refer to them as soldiers or the 'Dog Soldiers' in AIM" (8). Durham supported his claims that violent acts were intended for the summer bicentennial celebration with quotes from public speeches by Russell Means and Clyde Bellecourt pertaining to "blowing out the white man's birthday candle" and intimations about "the unhappiest birthday party you've ever had in your life" (68, 76). Durham's more specific statements regarding the bicentennial conspiracy, those regarding "any patriotic symbol" as "an immediate target for attack," are unattributed: "I was told . . . I was told" (68). When pressed for the source of such statements, he claimed that John Trudell "discussed with me directly snipings, and indiscriminate shootings of non-Indians," a carefully worded statement that is not inconsistent with the assertions of others that it was Durham who was always initiating such "discussions."[28] He refers to one of his exhibits as quoting Leonard Crow Dog "advocating the massacre of our government" (77) when the actual quote reads "We are not going to massacre the white man, we are going to massacre his attitude and his government" (185). But the most attenuated piece of evidence he provides in support of the bicentennial terrorism theory—and also the one that most clearly ties Durham's testimony to the Dog Soldier teletypes—is his citation of a UPI wire service report of a speech given by William Kunstler to Corky Gonzales's Mexican American Crusade for Justice in Denver two years previously on May 18, 1974 (also the source of Means's "birthday party" rhetoric). Kunstler said, "I promise you revolution by 1976. It is better to die in the streets than to go down without a whimper" (151, a hearing exhibit)—a statement Durham misquoted in his testimony as "It is better to die in the streets than live on our knees" (67). This statement is consistent with Durham's assertion that, among a cavalcade of entities including the People's Republic of China, the PLO, the IRA, and the Symbionese Liberation Army, it was the National Lawyers Guild who exercised the "largest amount of influence" on AIM (53), as Kunstler was a member of the National Lawyers Guild. Kunstler's statement can hardly be attributed to AIM just because AIM invited him to give a speech. But according to Durham, Carter Camp, an AIM member but hardly one of its shining stars, repeated this statement a year later on June 5, 1975: "I promise you revolution in'76. It will be America's unhappiest birthday, and America guarantees it." (68).

In closing, Durham delivered his final shot at Paula Giese, calling her a "non-Indian" who "personally told me that she and attorney Ken Tilsen were Trotskyites" (78).

As evidence of a conspiracy to disrupt the bicentennial, the case made above would fall apart under cross-examination or even a rebuttal argument. But a Congressional hearing, especially one modeled after HUAC procedures, need not provide such checks and balances. Eastland was the only Senator present at the hearing (1) and Committee member Birch Bayh explicitly refused to participate, condemning the report issued in September 1976 as "totally unacceptable . . . hav[ing] no other purpose than to discredit a number of individuals, including . . . the American Indian Movement" (Brand 108–09). Nevertheless, the testimony was made available to prosecuting attorneys with attendant damaging effects in the Peltier extradition case in Canada in June 1976 and a sentence reduction hearing for Leonard Crow Dog (Churchill 445) and supplemented the media event created by the FBI with the release of the so-called Dog Soldier teletypes on June 21, 1976.

According to this FBI press release, Rudolfo 'Corky' Gonzales and his Denver-based Chicano group had a rocket launcher and were plotting with AIM and SDS (Students for a Democratic Society, a New Left anti-war group from the late sixties that was inactive by the mid-seventies) in "setting up terrorist groups" to "kill a cop a day" by "lur[ing] law enforcement officers into ambush"—an enterprise to which AIM was expected to contribute "2,000 warriors . . . trained in the Northwest Territory." According to Churchill and Vander Wall this memo had actually been prepared in May 1975 and withheld for an "opportune moment" (281, 445); one may recall that Durham's testimony about the Corky Gonzales group pertained to an event in May 1974 according to the UPI report transcribed and attached to the Eastland hearing as Exhibit 30A (151). The following day, June 22, 1976, the FBI released the second "teletype" based on information received from "a source, with whom insufficient contact has been made but who is in a position to furnish reliable information" going into great detail with names (including the son of liberal South Dakota Senator James Abourezk) and locations of supposed weapons caches.[29] Abourezk denounced the teletypes as a "smear campaign" (Mattheissen 283) and they were to become generally discredited by the fact that no such violent actions or weapons caches ever materialized. The trial of Dino Butler and Bob Robideau for the deaths of the two FBI agents in June 1975 had commenced on June 9, 1976, and if the FBI was attempting to whip up a bicentennial hysteria in order to obtain a conviction, it failed; they were acquitted on grounds of self defense.

Despite the pyrrhic AIM victory represented by the Butler/Robideau acquittal, Durham's overall career in regard to AIM was a resounding success in the sense that insiders tended to attribute the group's demoralization to his efforts. An anonymous source said

> I can't think of any one person who did more damage to AIM than Doug Durham . . . Durham just absolutely destroyed trust inside the organization . . . Nobody could be sure how far it went . . . and people were getting killed right and left . . .
>
> You could say that a lot of the spirit went out of the movement around what Durham did . . . But Dennis [Banks] was never the same after he got taken in. And a whole lot of that early feeling, the *openness* of AIM disappeared. It got to be small groups who already knew each other real well (Churchill 232–33).

Durham's lies are clever, professionally attached to the truth like a well-done hair weave. For instance, a trip to Arizona to investigate two separate shooting incidents becomes "a potential uprising down there, which I effectively quelled" (62, 145–49): simple word choice invokes the entire mythology of the Hollywood western. Durham has learned to play on the way in which Americans have internalized the Hollywood language of "renegades," "uprisings," and such to the point where they confuse fact with fiction. If he had been sent by, say, a white militia group to investigate two shooting incidents, would he characterize the trip as "quelling" an "uprising?" And if he did, would he be believed?

Elsewhere, he elaborates on the visit to Judge Nichol's home mentioned briefly mentioned at the Lincoln hearing, where prosecutor Uhl had appeared to be familiar with the story that the judge's wife had been issued an honorary AIM membership card, drawing it out on cross examination and then dropping the subject (161). At the Eastland hearing almost a year later, Durham constructed a much more detailed version of this meeting involving artifacts, coffee, cookies, and a discussion of a change of venue motion that would have been improper outside of the presence of an attorney from the other side (54). Then, when asked if he had ever previously testified under oath and been cross-examined about this "rather extraordinary story," he said that "it was brought out by the U.S. Attorney in Lincoln . . . It was a 7½-hour hearing . . . The defense attorneys did not object or cross-examine me, relating to this particular item" (55). Thus he slipped in a defamatory charge against Judge Nichol, accusing him of ex parte communication regarding a pending case and going on to imply that the matter had already been fully explored, when in fact the version presented at Lincoln had contained no mention of such an ex parte communication at the Nichol home.

Another example of Durham's fact-bending ability involves welfare-bashing. He asserted without apparent foundation at the Eastland hearing that "approximately half [of the people occupying Wounded Knee] had been employees of social welfare programs financed primarily by government grants (5). Since the federal government was and is the major employer on the Pine Ridge reservation, this information is not as shocking as Durham appears to make it. He plays on the welfare stereotype when discussing the Des Moines AIM chapter as well; some of the OEO grant had allegedly been "passed around among some of the members of the American Indian Movement to buy beer, cigarettes, gas for their cars, bullets, and what have you" (42). Apparently AIM members had no need for food; when offering to introduce into evidence Dennis Banks's food stamp card, Durham claims some of the food stamps were stolen, sold for cash at an 80% discount, and the money used to buy weapons, but then admits that although he "did not directly observe the sale of Dennis' food stamps, I observed the sale of food stamps of like nature of people in a bar in Minneapolis" (64).

Though a psychiatric report on Durham made at the request of the Des Moines Police Department in 1964 apparently diagnosed Durham as a "violent schizoid" (this pertaining to an investigation of the death of his pregnant wife [Giese 5]), there seems to be a general consensus that he was intelligent, articulate, and coldly rational. Oglala elder Vivian Locust described him as "more like some kind of machine, a robot." She said, "he didn't act like no human being. And I'm not sure what to say he *did* act like. No conscience. No guilt. No remorse. No human emotion *at all.* I'd say he acted like a snake, but that's not fair to snakes. Snakes aren't that cold" (Churchill 233). The saga of Doug Durham perhaps demonstrates that one can be cold, unemotional, and functional and still be extremely disturbed.

Durham's interaction with AIM is oddly reminiscent of a case study described in a psychiatric anthology on paranoia, that of a doctor who slowly poisoned his patients with misprescribed medications. This patient described to psychiatrist Harold P. Blum an obsession over his food being poisoned arising out of an incident during reserve military service after medical school wherein he received a phone call threatening his life. His wife's pregnancy brought on a crisis related to a problematic history with his mother, and in addition to misprescribing drugs for his patients he started engaging in compulsive sexual behavior with aides and nurses. Eventually his therapist convinced him to "relinquish medicine in favor of research" and the patient managed to redirect his fears of being poisoned and poisoning of patients into the "socially and scientifically acceptable poisoning of guineapigs" ("Paranoid Betrayal and Jealousy" 109). When he first became involved with AIM in 1973, Durham was already heavily invested in an undercover career that, to say the least, involved a high degree of anxiety. Over time, he perpetrated upon AIM a slow poisoning of its collective psychological health even as he "ministered" to the needs of both AIM and the FBI in his "official" capacity. While Durham saw himself as "conducting a kind of sensitivity program about AIM for the bureau [FBI]" (Adams 494), at the same time he was engaged in substantial fundraising and public relations work for AIM. Adams points out that

Durham became the "primary liaison" of the Des Moines chapter with the Open Bible Church and later, in a successful bid for $85,000 to post bail for Dennis Banks from the United Methodist Church, "offered a strong moral argument, complete with scriptural quotations" (490–91). Though many are now of the opinion that Adams's account is unduly sympathetic and even gullible, Adams did have significant and productive contact with Durham over a long period of time; he says "Durham was frequently in contact with church representatives on behalf of Dennis Banks and other AIM leaders. Sometimes the only AIM representative in a church meeting, he spoke convincingly of AIM's objectives, plans, and needs" (494).

Of course, Durham was essentially just doing his job as an undercover FBI operative in spreading paranoia and discord while gathering information. Paranoia is as central to Durham's discourse about AIM—he testified to Eastland that "AIM and many other similar movements are very paranoic. Their suspicions of each other and Government go in some cases beyond even the absurd" (8)—as it was to become in the movement's discourse about itself. It seems unlikely that Durham could have perpetrated so much paranoia, discord and violence upon the group without internalizing some of this hostility and aggression himself; an object relations model sheds light on Durham's statements to people such as Giese that he was dying of leukemia (Giese 8).[30] Though it is impossible to sort out all the fabrications from the truth with such an individual, it is certainly possible that he actually thought he had cancer.[31] Durham himself had explained to reporter Nick Lamberto, "In this business you have to be paranoid"; it would be unrealistic to expect such a successful operative to be anything other than a "charismatic nut" (Giese 12).

It is more than likely that he would have been—and presumably still is— unable to sort out the lies from the truth in his own mind. Perhaps his 180-degree turnaround from the admirer of Dennis Banks and his "social protest organization" to the denouncer of paranoid terrorists was sincere in the sense that with the social reinforcement he received on the John Birch lecture circuit, he actually started to believe his own lies and distortions and those being fed to him by the FBI. Totally lost from the road of the American individualist, whether law-man or out-law, hero or anti-hero, his subjectivity was entirely determined by his audience or context. Part of such a psychological reorientation would be the further development of a persecution complex, one to which Giese's published assaults would have contributed. This is one way to look at the bizarre emergence of the Easter Sunday crucifixion story at the Congressional hearing. In this battle of cross-fictions, all sides emanating from Durham's professionally fevered psychological command center as "Director of Security," it is Durham himself, in his reconstructed role as bearer of the white man's burden, who must imagine himself being crucified on the plains of Wounded Knee. Thus he projects his own persecution complex onto the nation with this resonant image of an anonymous white man being beaten by AIM.

A man is being beaten, indeed. Freud's essay "A Child Is Being Beaten" concerns his interpretation of the beating fantasies of his women patients. He traces a progression from the first scenario, "My father is beating a child," to the second, "My father is beating me," to the third, "a child is being beaten." The third stage marks the erasure of the patient/victim from the scene of violation and removes her from an active, albeit masochistic role to the passive, sadistic role of spectator. One need not totally subscribe to the incestuous desire and gender variations with which Freud invests this basic scenario to understand it as a potentially powerful coping mechanism for someone who perceives him or herself as the victim of abuse. Difficult as it may be to view Durham as victim as well as perpetrator, it is important to fully examine who was abusing whom. As psychiatrist Morton Schatzman has remarked on Freud's foundational case study in paranoia, Dr. Schreber was unable to recognize that it was his father who had abused him in the past and not God who was abusing him in the present.[32]

Russell Means asserts that Durham was like "a woman, *worse* than a woman; we used to give him pocket money, send him out for coffee! When he told people he was dying of leukemia, we just laughed at him. Banks needed a flunky, but even Banks used to chew him out in public . . . we just *used* him, that's all, blew him up way out of proportion to publicize FBI infiltration" (Matthiessen 124). This statement provides telling insight into Means's personality; allegations about sexism among the AIM leadership have been public knowledge for years, but rarely does someone so publicly indict himself. Furthermore, Means seems to protest too much (at the other extreme, it has been asserted that Durham embezzled more than $100,000 in donations [Brand 99]—a lot of pocket money). Nevertheless, feminization or emasculation is a powerful strategy in a sexist culture and Durham's primary culture, the culture of undercover law enforcement, is no exception. In the culture of the snitch, one attorney told documentary filmmaker Ofra Bikel, informants are "like prostitutes" and information is "the coin of the realm" (*Snitch*). Durham had been a snitch for several years before being assigned to AIM. In the rigid hierarchy of law enforcement, the free-lance professional informant lacks the respect accorded an agent who goes undercover. At times Durham tried to portray his departure from the Des Moines police department as voluntary, so that he could operate more freely as an undercover agent, but that is not how it generally works. Free-lance informants range from those forced out of regular law enforcement, as Durham was, to wannabes who can't quite make the grade in the first place, to criminals facing serious time who turn informant to stay out of prison. Some of the other known AIM informants, Jil and Gi Shafer and Virginia DeLuce ("Blue Dove") were something of an anomaly as they seemed to be in it for a combination of glamour and political motivation, but most informants overall—Louis Moves Camp and Myrtle Poor Bear, for instance—fall in the latter category, those vulnerable to arrest and conviction. Such people are often subjected to an incredible onslaught of threats and coercion, forced to betray even members of their own family and thus becoming even more marginalized from functional relationships than they already are, as Bikel's documentary about informants illustrates. They are not treated as peers by regular law enforcement agents. In the terms of the sexist subculture they inhabit, they are feminized. In the same way that infiltration of an organization can be perceived as a form of rape or violation, the total control which law enforcement agents sometimes wield over the personal life of an informant can also be perceived as a type of rape. An understanding of this dynamic sheds light on Durham's apparent abusive relationships with women, particularly someone as young and vulnerable as Jancita Eagle Deer was—someone he could totally dominate.

It can probably never be fully known the extent of the power the law enforcement superstructure held over Durham; certainly it would seem, given what is known, that he developed enough skills between 1964 and 1973 that he could have left "the life" if he wanted to. If he liked it and took the AIM project as a challenge, as he said, then it was because he got something out of this sort of deception and manipulation psychologically. It did give him an opportunity to meet a lot of women on the edge. But there may have been a racially-based as well as a gender-based dynamic involved. There is no compelling reason to accept at face value Durham's facile retraction of his claim to Indian ancestry. In the latest version, given at the Congressional hearing, he stated he was "Scottish-Irish, English, and German" (3) the three European ethnic groups who have been in the United States the longest and whose descendants are thus the least likely to be of "pure" European ancestry. It certainly served his purpose to become white as he moved to the right, but there is no particular reason to believe his latter self-characterization any more than any of the previous versions he gave about this or any other aspect of his life. There is a deep and hidden culture of denial in the Midwest (and probably elsewhere) among assimilated light-skinned persons of mixed ancestry of the generation of Durham's parents and grandparents, and he may not have been sure himself what he was.

Schatzman notes, regarding the Schreber case, that Schreber as a child was raised in a way that impaired ego boundaries; Schreber's father, who was a famous authority on child-rearing in 19th century Germany, raised his children to be "permeated by the feeling of the *impossibility*" of keeping anything from their parents (128). Someone so heavily immersed in the panoptic eye may learn to defend his ego boundaries by becoming a pathological liar, or at least function better when given a justification to lie, as for instance, by becoming an undercover informant (or continuing to be one after the need no longer exists). The situation becomes even more attractive to a certain personality type when a part of the job description is to engender paranoia in others—to ensure that they see "an FBI agent behind every mail box" (qtd. in Davis 10).[33] Schatzman calls a person who engenders paranoid states a "paranoidogenic" person: "He is, I believe, someone who persecutes or is persecuted by . . . possibilities of his own being that he regards as bad and that he tries to destroy 'in' others" (115–16). Following is Schatzman's "recipe" for this process:

Regard part of oneself, *That*, as bad (or made, obscene, impure, dirty, dangerous, etc.).

Fear That will destroy oneself if oneself does not destroy That.

Destroy That in oneself by denying That is part of oneself.

Deny the denial, that anything is denied, and the denial of the denial.

Discover That in other people.

Fear That in them will destroy them, others, or oneself if That is not destroyed.

Adopt means to destroy That in them, even if this entails destroying the people in whom one has discovered That. (116)

Replacing "That" with the word "Indian" in the above paradigm produces an interesting, though perhaps oversimplified, hypothesis about Durham's long-term motivations wherein he retaliates against real Indians for his own (unnameable and in some venues unspeakable) Indian identity. One could also replace "That" with "FBI Informer" in attempting to understand the zeal with which Durham pursued the bad-jacketing strategy from within AIM at a time when he was, if he is to be believed, a "convert" (Adams 493) to the movement.[34]

Some might ask what real different it makes if someone in an organization is "undercover" if in fact they are performing acts in furtherance of the organization's objectives. This question is perhaps even more compelling to those who have unwittingly collaborated with an informant and have thus, in a sense, been intellectually and emotionally 'violated' by that person. If Durham's obsessive bad-jacketing of others was a result of his own paranoia (or, even if not), and if the deleterious effects of this were outweighed by the money he raised, his public relations contacts, his piloting abilities and other technical skills, what does it matter what motivations lay in his innermost 'self'? And conversely, if someone of good and honorable heart is nevertheless truculent and divisive in demeanor and effect, does it ultimately matter whether or not that person is an undercover informant? It does matter, because to hold otherwise is to concede to the master narrative of suspicion: the narrative that implements the state's objective that everyone believe the panoptic eye peers from behind every mailbox. The deep penetration of this discourse of suspicion into the American Indian Movement should serve as an exemplar of what can still happen in other groups and what is already happening in certain respects in American society at large.

Durham said to John Adams, "no citizen in the United States escapes the possibility of being a subject of surveillance. If movement groups are infiltrated because they have the potential for committing crimes, then it is only a small step to the full invasion of any citizen's privacy, for every individual has the potential for committing a crime" (Adams 495). Adams, in pursuing this discussion with

Durham, was making the point that in infiltrating AIM the FBI also infiltrated the church organizations AIM dealt with and that government interests would have no compunction about going even further in this direction. If everyone's acts are so constructed by social imperatives that everyone may potentially commit a crime, then everyone is a proper subject of surveillance with "potential" becoming the threshold criterion of probability.[35] An actuarial calculation replaces the concept of trust that is as essential to the healthy functioning of large groups as it is to small groups. The shrinking zone of privacy in the United States and on its borders, even pre-9/11, approximates this standard. No longer is probable cause required for surveillance, nor reasonable suspicion, but "mere" suspicion based on "profiles" of persons and their habits: driving, reading, or otherwise.

Those who see no particular problem in being always under surveillance because they do not think they ever do anything wrong should consider another problem with the master narrative of suspicion. Its purpose is the construction and reconstruction of sub-narratives (thus its larger status as a metanarrative), and such narratives can have real destructive consequences. These narratives may be as small in scope as "Who killed Anna Mae?" or as large as "Where is the enemy amassing its troops?" When Durham's undercover status was exposed, reactions among AIM leadership ranged from shock to denial and redirection of suspicion against each other. He had penetrated to the heart of the troops and when the dust settled, some of the things that remained visible were the bodies of dead women.[35] As a result of this first narrative of suspicion created by Durham, Anna Mae's ghost still haunts any number of people who were on the Pine Ridge reservation in December, 1975.

As for the larger narrative, the real destructive consequences of the FBI's rein-vention of AIM as an army of communist-duped Dog Soldiers impinge on the narrator as well as those narrated against. In Durham's evolved and expanded 1976 narrative of the American Indian Movement, the communist enemy had infiltrated to the heart of the country and its Dog Soldiers were ready to strike and wreak havoc on the bicentennial celebration. This was a provocative variation on the master narrative of the communist Other, but the more provocative a narra-tive of suspicion becomes, the more likely it is to escape control of the master. This is particularly true when the master is willing to employ marginal and barely controllable individuals like Douglass Durham and groups like the John Birch Society to further its ends. The master cannot control all circumstances, and circumstances can also conspire.

Three circumstances conspired to send the course of this master narrative veering off in a new and disturbing direction. The first was the dissipation of AIM and the other raced "enemies within" (the Black Panthers, the Brown Berets, etc.) as a threat; this much the FBI would count as a success and within its control. The second was the growth throughout the late seventies and early eighties of a survivalist movement frightened of a nuclear holocaust. The third was the breakup of the Soviet Union. These latter two circumstances contributed to the growth of an insular culture in a defensive posture which had suddenly lost a suitable Other upon which to project its fear and hostility. It would have to reinvent one, and it did. The FBI's politicization of law enforcement throughout the century has enabled and even promoted the sort of scapegoating discourses that we call the paranoid style in American politics. When a populace steeped in discourses of racism and persecution loses the spectre of a foreign Other against which to direct its fears, it is easy for some of the more marginalized and threatened to turn against older imagined enemies. Accordingly, the survivalist movement evolved into proliferating 'cells' of white supremacists for whom the government itself, and particularly the FBI, replaced groups such as AIM as the enemy.

Despite the excesses of the survivalist narratives, it behooves us to remember that the United States Army is "still in the field." The current trajectory of fear against the "new" foreign Other promises to engender ever more fantastic, though perhaps not so new, narratives by undercover informants about the crucifiers of white men.

Chapter Two

Lynching the White Woman
William Pierce's 'Day of the Rope'

Though contemporary scholars disagree as to the degree that conspiracist thinking still poses a serious threat, for most of them, demonization of women or "bad mothers" has historically played only a minor role in manifestations of collective or political paranoia. Daniel Pipes, an expert in Middle Eastern history whose major contribution to the subject is the word "conspiracism," narrates the history of Western conspiracist movements from the Knights Templar through the Freemasons and the Illuminati without mentioning the European witchhunts. Oddly, considering his focus on anti-Semitism, he also has little to say about the Spanish Inquisition. Robins and Post's *Political Paranoia: The Psychopolitics of Hatred* devotes seven pages to the Salem witch trials. Of these "body count" analyses,[1] one may argue that the persecution of women gets minimized or trivialized, but the body count approach does compel the observation that paranoia is very closely associated with power, and positions of power or perceived power historically have been occupied, for the most part, by men.

William Pierce's second neo-Nazi novel *Hunter* (1989) opens with the cold-blooded murder of a "bushy-haired mulatto" man and a white woman; the protagonist has embarked on an individually conceived program of killings of mixed couples in an attempt to engender an epidemic of copycat killings among (to his way of thinking) the silent majority of white males repulsed at such contamination of their racial purity. Minimal emotional affect is associated with the killing of blacks in Pierce's work; his protagonists feel a twinge of regret at killing women of their own race only if the women are attractive. In this case, however, the woman is "dumpy, pasty-faced" and he feels an "icy calm" as "their skulls literally explode into showers of bone fragments, brain tissue, and blood" (2). Neither the man nor the woman would seem to be threats to even the paranoid mind, but they are: all black men are rapists in Pierce's novels, and those who willingly consort with them are race traitors. The threat is contamination of the white bloodline. On the "Day of the Rope" near the end of *The Turner Diaries* (1978), "many thousands" of such white women are executed, but so are thousands of men. The women wear "I defiled my race" placards while the men, "the politicians, the lawyers, the businessmen, the TV newscaster, the newspaper reporters and editors, the judges, the teachers, the school officials, the 'civic leaders,' the bureaucrats, the preachers, and all the others who . . . helped promote or implements the System's racial program," wear placards saying "I betrayed my race" (162–63).

The Turner Diaries (1978) could be described as a war manual for racist electricians. It should be read along with Mel Tappan's *Survival Guns* (1976), "an encyclopedic tour of the world of survival and combat firearms" (Clayton x) and Bruce D. Clayton's *Life After Doomsday: A Survivalist Guide to Nuclear War and Other Major Disasters* (1980). Clayton says that he became interested in the antinuclear movement while earning a Ph.D. in ecology and then became alienated by their fatalistic attitude about chances of survival (ix). The major focus of his expertise seems to be in analyzing radioactive fallout patterns, but the book covers all aspects of living without an infrastructure. It lacks the political overtones of later survivalist literature as the survivalist culture became less heterogenous and moved to the right during the Reagan years. Reagan, one may recall, also felt that a nuclear war was survivable. Clayton even includes a section on preserving the literary canon with insecticide, plastic, and foil. But rather than recommend a list of books to save, he recommends that everyone select a reference book, "a textbook related to your profession," and a third book of individual choice (142).[2]

The rise, or rather reinvigoration, of the American militia movement in the nineties is a heterogeneous phenomenon resistant to definition. To a larger extent than has been acknowledged, it has roots in fears of nuclear holocaust and the associated survivalist movement dating back to the seventies. Not all "survivalists" are militia members nor are they all racists. Nor can all individuals involved in these groups be accurately characterized as the "far right": Michael Kelly coined the term "fusion paranoia" in his 1995 *New Yorker* essay to describe the crossover appeal of survivalist, conspiratorial thinking to leftists left behind by the Reagan era. Though skinheads and white supremacists do populate urban areas, the conspiracist thinking of the militia movement is primarily situated in rural areas and connected to a rural subsistence lifestyle. American Indian Movement leader Russell Means has publicly expressed sympathy and even solidarity with the Freemen of Montana, and though other American Indian Movement figures now distance themselves from Means's political posturing, few people (aside from Paula Gunn Allen[3]) recall the "Black Hills International Survival Gathering" of 1980 which brought together environmentalist ranchers and mineworkers, the American Indian Movement, the Rainbow people,[4] and leaders of the anti-nuke movement. It was not until later in the eighties that the term "survivalist" came to connote the radical right. By that time most of the urban "back-to-the-land" types had wearied of the tedium, isolation, and minimal cash flow of rural life and the survivalist core that was left tended to be more "rural" in its heritage.[5]

Catherine McNicol Stock argues in *Rural Radicals* that the militia movement and related manifestations of the far right are a continuation of the rural radical politics of Shay's Rebellion, the Whiskey Rebellion, and late nineteeenth century

Populism. She explores the culture of vigilantism associated with rural activism and its relationship to demonization of others by race and class. The historical figure who most fully embodies these principles is Andrew Jackson, who pushed the Indians west to make room for Manifest Destiny, linked workers and farmers together as equals in the nation's productive life, and fought against monopolies (Stock 53). Actually, Jackson was a lawyer, and more of a land speculator than a farmer (Rogin, *Fathers and Children* 81–85), but he lived on the frontier. Jackson's most famous vigilante act was his refusal in 1832, as President, to enforce the Supreme Court decision that would have allowed the Cherokee to retain their lands in Georgia (214), thus setting in motion the forced removal of the Cherokees to Oklahoma known as the Trail of Tears. It is the embedding of a discourse of racism within a culture of vigilantism that links America's past to a present in which the demonizing gaze of the American with status anxiety has veered from Indians, to blacks, to Communists, and to Jews.[6]

Even if the contemporary radical right is not entirely racist in its demographics, it is the racist conspiracy theories associated with the contemporary militia movement and its associates that present cause for concern. Ken Toole of the Montana Human Rights Network presents the problem by way of the "funnel" paradigm (Stern 107). People with a variety of problems or issues—farm debt, IRS problems, loss of lucrative BLM grazing leases, unemployment, religious fundamentalism, hunters and gun hobbyists—come into contact with the racist theories of the Aryan Brotherhood, Christian Identity movement, and other white supremacist groups. Much in the same way that all persons who report contact with extraterrestrial beings come to describe the same aliens and the same experiences, these people get funneled into a way of thinking that accounts for their problems. As political scientist Robert S. Robins and social psychiatrist Jerrold M. Post put it, a conspiracy theory offers "a mental form of one-stop shopping" (295). And like a funnel cloud, once within the paradigm, the psychological affect becomes more intense, uncontrollable, and dangerous.

The leading works responding directly to the April 1995 Oklahoma City bombing were Morris Dees' *Gathering Storm: America's Militia Threat* (1996) and Kenneth Stern's *A Force Upon the Plain* (1996). Both authors are lawyers; Dees is associated with the Southern Poverty Law Center which maintains an extensive website on the radical right, and Stern is a former defense attorney for American Indian Movement leader Dennis Banks. Stern, who has worked for the American Jewish Committee for over a decade, asserts that three events triggered the rise of the militia movements in the nineties: the Waco action, the Randy Weaver action, and the Brady bill. The Oklahoma City bombing symbolized the rise of the militias and focused media attention on them, but Timothy McVeigh was not directly connected with the militias. Rather, McVeigh's action was symptomatic of the heterogeneity and independent proliferation of these forces.[7] And though the three events cited by Stern infused new energy into the forces of the radical right, the discourse was already in place. The movement has its "intellectuals" and its key texts, and its players have been engaged in active utilization of the internet since the mid-eighties (228).

One of these intellectual leaders is William Pierce, author of *The Turner Diaries* (1978) and *Hunter* (1989) under the pseudonym Andrew Macdonald. According to the Southern Poverty Law Center, one of the primary watchdogs of the radical right, this "soft-spoken, bespectacled" leader of the National Alliance was born in Atlanta and holds a doctorate in physics from the University of Colorado. He was an assistant professor of physics at Oregon State University from 1962 to 1965 and left for employment as a senior research scientist at the Advanced Materials Research and Development Laboratory of United Aircraft's Pratt and Whitney Division in Connecticut. A member of the John Birch Society during the early sixties, in 1966 he

> abandoned his job and the Birchers for full-time neo-Nazi activism, apprenticing under America's then most-notorious neo-Nazi, George Lincoln Rockwell, founder of the American Nazi Party. Pierce soon became one of Rockwell's most trusted lieutenants. After Rockwell's assassination in 1967, Pierce quickly rose to the top of the organization. By the early 1970s, he was leading a neo-Nazi splinter group—the National Youth Alliance—that became today's National Alliance. In 1985, Pierce moved National Alliance headquarters from the Washington, D.C., suburb of Arlington, Viriginia, to a 265-acre site in rural Pocahontas County, West Virginia. He said he wanted to escape constant reminders that the white race was in decline and that the country had been taken over by "non-whites, race-mixers, homosexuals and feminists" (1).[8]

A psychiatrist or, in fact, most people reading Dr. Pierce's work would probably characterize him first as racist and only secondarily as paranoid. This is consistent with Oldham and Skodol's findings regarding the screening of patients for psychoanalysis: that even when paranoid people do seek psychiatric treatment, they are less likely to be accepted for psychoanalysis than persons with other personality disorders, and those who are accepted for psychoanalysis tend to have relatively less severe forms of paranoia (Oldham and Skodol 163). Psychologists understand paranoia as a condition that is relative or situational. Thus a political dissident in Stalin's Soviet Union, "should he win asylum in the West . . . might well find himself diagnosed as suffering from a paranoid illness" if he were to continue behaving the same way in the West that he did in the Soviet Union. On the other hand, "the thoroughgoing paranoid is not able to don his suspiciousness as a protective garment, discarding it when it is no longer necessary" (Robins and Post 30). The situational nature of the disorder contributes to the problem of which Freud's Dr. Schreber was a prime example: not only can the paranoid personality be extremely intelligent, but ability to function professionally can proceed relatively unimpaired. Schreber maintained a career as a judge for years. But paranoia, though a closed system of thought that is immune to evidence or influence from the outside, can operate back and forth between a leader and a group of followers in a symbiotic relationship in which each feeds off the other's paranoid tendencies, thus creating what one might justifiably call a culture of pathology—a culture that collectively holds beliefs that seem irrational if not insane to outsiders.[9]

Pierce's role in the racist subculture demonstrates what Robins and Post call "role suction"—"when a foundation of discontent is present . . . the group can induce a leader to behave in a paranoid or caretaking manner" (102).[10] Pierce himself is from an older generation than most contemporary militia movement members and followers; it seems most likely that his beliefs are based fundamentally in a racist and segregationist Southern background. He gravitated to conspiracist neo-Nazi thought in the mid-sixties, at a time when his racism must have placed him in an increasingly marginalized position in the academic environment of Oregon State University. Since Rockwell's death, Pierce has been the leading 'scholar' of neo-Nazi thought in the United States, but it is only recently that his books seem to have achieved widespread circulation. Perhaps Pierce behaved and thought no differently in the eighties and nineties than he did in the sixties and seventies. But the funnel of discontent has clearly 'suctioned' him into a leadership role for many malcontents. His mid-eighties move to rural West Virginia resonates with the ideals of the Jacksonian frontier; as the Scotch-Irish settlers from whence Andrew Jackson came migrated to the southern frontier to escape religious persecution, Pierce came to what is left of the southern frontier to escape his imaginary persecutors—"non-whites, race-mixers, homosexuals and feminists."

The copyright page of the second edition of Pierce's second novel *Hunter*, published in 1989, claims that 61,000 copies were in circulation as of 1998. According to David Bennett's historical overview of far right groups, Rockwell's American Nazi Party never had more than a few hundred members. Meanwhile, the anti-Communist Minutemen of the sixties had 5–6,000 members, and the neo-Ku Klux Klan groups of the sixties had a maximum of 60,000 followers at most by the end of the sixties (325–26). By 1977, the FBI estimated that membership in the Ku Klux Klan and "Klan-style front groups" had declined to a maximum of 22,000 (347). Then came the resurgence of the far right in the eighties, with a new tone. The Order, though small in number, was modeled on the secret brotherhood of that name in *The Turner Diaries*, a novel perhaps best known for having been found in McVeigh's trunk at the time of his arrest. According to Bennett, the Order had "split from Aryan Nations because the parent group provided too much talk and not enough action" (349–50).[11] After the Order assassinated Denver radio talk show host Alan Berg in 1984, it was publicly silenced by the prosecution of twenty-three members in Seattle in 1985 (349). Since then, the new neo-Nazi organizations have continued to grow. There are many; among the more notable are the Aryan Nations,[12] its religious arm, the Church of Jesus Christ Christian, and in the nation's overstocked prisons, the

Aryan Brotherhood. No doubt aided by the incarceration of the leadership of the Order, the Aryan Brotherhood offers purpose and community to white drug dealers, drug users, and petty criminals.

This "new white culture" speaks of Pierce in almost reverent tones. Avid users of the internet, they publish their praise in Amazon.com's "Customer Comments" as well as on their own well-developed networks. From Middlesbrough, England, a reader remarks that *The Turner Diaries* "shows the brilliance of Dr. Pierce and how the white race could and should be the supreme race in the future." A reader from Novi, Michigan says that "Dr. Pierce shows a clear, insightful understanding of the racial problems facing us today." Another reader from Tampa says "Many events described in this book are not that unrealistic," and a reader from Murfreesboro, Tennessee offers a list of related race reading, including an anthology of racist essays from Hume, Kant, and Hegel. Perhaps a more direct confirmation of the book's "truth" comes from by way of a comment about journalist James Ridgeway's book *Blood in the Face: The Ku Klux Klan, Aryan Nations, Nazi Skinheads, and the Rise of a New White Culture.* A "neo-Nazi skinhead" reader from St. Louis who finds Ridgeway's writing "deceptive" advises, "If you really must know how Klansmen, Identity Christians and skinheads think, get a book straight from the source (like *The Turner Diaries*)."

Pierce wrote *Hunter* after the downfall of the Order. Much of the novel consists of tendentious Socratic dialog in which the characters discuss various textual sources and strains of thought within white supremacist dogma. Since *Hunter* has not achieved the notoriety of *The Turner Diaries*, its sales are not heavily inflated by the curiosity of concerned academics and liberals. Thus Amazon's "customer comments" on this novel are virtually unanimous in their praise. From "the United States": "Finally a book that expresses the ideas of every THINKING white person." From Foley, Alabama: "I can hardly go shopping without thinking of the opening of the book. Without a doubt the author knows the true enemies of our people and uses this book to show what can be done." From "New Hampshire, USA": "It is a fantastic book about the struggle for the realization of truth and the fight against tyranny . . . just as significant as Orwell's *1984*." From Chicago: "It has clarified my vision of the world and politics." From Saginaw, Michigan: "a masterfull [sic] work that is a MUST READ for any interested American Patriot!" From Aurora, Illinois: "It may be fiction, but be prepared to learn many facts . . . Riveting and exciting, you will find it hard to put down once you've begun!"

Such responses, particularly the last one, compel reflection on prevailing aesthetic standards, not only of New Criticism, but of the popular fiction market. It is hard to imagine how anyone could find the tediously didactic intellectual "history" that comprises so much of *Hunter* "riveting and exciting." It seems, rather, "pompous . . . dogmatic and full of borrowed authority"—one psychologist's description of a "rigid" obsessive-compulsive style which becomes paranoid delusion in its extreme forms (Shapiro 51–52). One can only conclude that this audience craves not only scenes of graphic and cold-blooded murder, but an exegesis of race and conspiracy theory that they feel has been denied them elsewhere: thus the appeal of the forbidden fruit. The paradigm of the international Jewish conspiracy satisfies their hunger for a one-stop explanation for everything that is wrong with the world. Though they are not illiterate nor, in many cases, even uneducated, they are simply unreceptive to other explanations. As group psychologists have long explained, "especially under circumstances of group trauma, a group may be receptive only to a leader with paranoid tendencies and may psychologically recruit such a leader" (Robins and Post 85). Starting perhaps with nothing more than an ill-focused anger at society and some degree of racism, the group, like the paranoid person, can become "dominated by one concept . . . subordinating every other value to it and willing to commit any act to fulfill it. The complete dominance of this idea means that paranoid fanatics live within a closed ideational system, a sealed castle of invincible ignorance immune to competing considerations" (175). Such is the nature of the paradigm of the international Jewish conspiracy.

Pierce is far from unaware of the paranoid nature of his discourse. But he deals with it by way of a reversal strategy, deflecting anticipated objections back at the other side. Thus in *The Turner Diaries* it is liberals who are bigots: Earl Turner's girlfriend Katherine "had none of the bigotry, none of the guilt and self-hatred that it takes to make a . . . liberal" (29). Turner refers to the "conspiracy theory" of conservatives, the "world's worst conspiracy-mongers—and also the world's greatest cowards" (63). *Hunter* pursues this "you're the paranoid" strategy even further, discussing the "paranoia" of leftists and Israelis (118, 186). Protagonist Oscar's girlfriend says of a Jewish graduate student who obnoxiously pursued her in college, "he *was* weird; he thought the explanation for everything that happened was a conspiracy on the part of some special-interest group, and that things were never what they seemed to be" (128). Oscar's mentor Harry Keller explains that Jews are "taught that the world is out to get them" (194). But Keller explains that though the Jews got their race consciousness from self-generated persecution and that even the misguided Christian Identity people, Mormons, and other "true believers" have developed some degree of race consciousness from persecution by the Jews, the true race consciousness of the superior race does not come from such base circumstance: "Our consciousness, instead of being based on a feeling of personal danger . . . depends on our capacity for abstraction" (195). This capacity for abstraction, incidentally, exists only in white males, who must explain it to their womenfolk. Women have intuition but are "impervious to reason" (98); Adelaide's "mental world was smaller, her horizon closer . . . her focus was on the trees, not the forest" (51).

At times, Pierce is adept in *Hunter* at accommodating obvious flaws in his evidence. He acknowledges that the *Protocols of the Elders of Zion* was "too neat to be genuine" (115) and that the people who write the anti-Semitic tracts are "careless with the facts" (92). Consequently, he has the Socratic Harry Keller quoting the Bible and the Talmud for most of his theories about the twentieth century

Jewish conspiracy. Oscar raises questions and objections, and Harry answers them. But though they read the Bible as compelling evidence about contemporary Jewish intent, Pierce's characters in *Hunter* are not Christians.[13] They sneer not only at standard Christian beliefs but the Christian Identity movement,[14] whose adherents they are actively recruiting, as well: "Do you think that people who believe Jesus walked on water and rose from the dead can't accept a nutty version of history? Not all of those people are uneducated hicks ... there are somewhere around a hundred million White folks in this country who already believe things no more bizarre than the Identity doctrine" (156).

The driving imperative in both *The Turner Diaries* and *Hunter* is that the world must be ruled by the white race. Pierce "teaches" this imperative to the reader in stages, utilizing opening strategies that focus on more immediate visceral fears: in *The Turner Diaries,* the fear that government search parties will come and take everyone's guns, and in *Hunter,* the fear of black-white miscegenation (specifically, black men with white women). The straw man device of a complete ban on all firearms (the Cohen Act) is only one of many such alarming premises in *The Turner Diaries*—others include marauding black men who gang-rape white women anywhere and everywhere, the deputization of black men from "the welfare rolls" to seize guns and make sure everyone's papers are in order (68),[15] a white liberal mob trashing a bookstore and beating up the clerk (78), black mobs killing a white cat (79) and cannibalizing white children (151), and Kappy the Kike, a white slave trader who buys teenage girls from hippie communes (84).[16] The patriotic buttons being pushed in *The Turner Diaries* are the second amendment right to bear arms and the first amendment freedom of movement and assembly. *Hunter,* in this regard, personifies attacks on freedom in the figure of Congressman Horowitz, whose Horowitz Act (apparently a massive piece of legislation cited in various contexts throughout the novel) imposed draconian affirmative action reporting requirements (5), let Haitians into the country and kept white South Africans out (18), and set up a national board of censorship on "hate literature" (205). But despite these homages to the Bill of Rights, by the midpoint of each of these novels the narrative is hinting at the need for more discipline and control. A pseudo-Nietzschean subtext is first introduced in *The Turner Diaries* with a description of the American people as a "herd of cattle" whose capacity for idealism has been destroyed by the Jewish conspiracy so that they can only respond to fear and hunger (101). Turner's diary implies that there will be no more TV after the revolution (63) for Americans who "can shamelessly continue their crass pursuit of pleasure under the most provocative conditions imaginable" (135). After the revolution, most of which occurs in 1993, the people are "hungry for authority and discipline" (199).

The Turner Diaries ends in a true Holocaust with a body count of sixty million (the Holocaust of World War II was, of course, fabricated by Jews). The entire Asian continent east of the Ural Mountains is virtually sterilized with nuclear explosions, becoming the Great Eastern Waste roamed by "bands of mutants"

whose final extermination may require another century (210). Pierce has asserted
that the first novel was a dystopian warning and not a call to action. *Hunter* has
a more subtle agenda: "our race is the principal agent, the power of higher organization, the process which is the active principle of God" (195). Harry blushes
when he mentions God because this idealistic concept is the hidden, rather than
the public face of Nazism. However, the Nazi God is not Christian; Christian
fundamentalists are cattle seeking "a share of the pie in the sky" (196). They need
both race consciousness and, again, discipline. *Hunter* is much more explicit on
the issue of discipline, establishing first the Hobbesian principle that democracy
can never work because "Nature abhors a vacuum" and some group will always
"impose its own agenda on society" (96). But the narrative sets up a conflict
between two models of white supremacist totalitarianism: the stealth model operating within the FBI and the underground model operating as the decentralized
National League. William Ryan, the FBI operative who eventually gets his own
SS-style agency, the Committee for Public Security, is ready and willing to supply
the "order and discipline that "this country needs" (135), referring to the citi-
zenry, "the Ph.D.s and the corporation executives as well as the cab drivers and the
housewives," as "a bunch of fucking animals" who "don't think; they only feel
and react according to a batch of conditioned reflexes" (139). The protagonist
Oscar Yeager works with both Ryan and the National League throughout most of
the novel, but eventually kills Ryan, not because he is such a fascist, but because
he is willing to keep working with the Jews for a decade or two after calling off all
elections while consolidating his power. Yeager says,

> Well, I'm certainly no advocate of democracy . . . I just can't go for any
> scenario which involves maintaining the present racial situation and the
> present Jewish media control. You may achieve stability. You may have a
> stronger, more smoothly running government. But the government isn't
> an end in itself. It's the race that's important. It's the race's mission of
> improving itself, of bringing forth a higher type of human being, that's
> important. (243, 245)

Like the Nazis of the Hitler era, Pierce is engaged in cynical manipulation of his
readership. This is not to say that he does not believe in his own philosophy, but
that few of the readers he is recruiting would qualify for the enlightened elite entitled to pursue "the active principle of God." His strategy is tailored to the
American herd, manipulating them with talk of first and second amendment free-
doms much as the National League's TV evangelist manipulates mainstream
Christian fundamentalists with an electronic halo, "channeling" Jesus's voice to tell
them of the beast in their midst (250). Only some of those with the drive to slog
through all the dogma of the final half of *Hunter* will understand that Pierce is
proposing a totalitarian government.

Pierce's choice of a pseudonym, Andrew Macdonald, likewise strikes a chord with his American patriot audience. The Scottish motif merits analysis because its sources and manifestations in late twentieth century popular culture are fairly complex. In the face of the growing recognition of multiculturalism, many white Americans have started to develop an increasing interest in their own cultural roots. This can be seen in a variety of practices ranging from genealogy networks on the internet to whiteness studies in English departments. Interest in pagan and tribal aspects of cultural history has been especially popular in Germany. Though Nazis identify with German paganism as part of their race pride, much of this interest (in Germany) is more benign, manifesting itself in New Age spirituality and a fascination with Karl May novels and American Indian art, literature, and religious practices. Americans with such interests, however, tend to identify paganism more with Celtic culture, in part because of anti-German sentiment in the U.S. dating back to World War I and exacerbated by the rise of Nazism. The remnants of Celtic culture are most manifest in Scotland and Ireland. Though a claim to Irish heritage is perhaps the most popular construction of Northern Euro-whiteness in recent years, as evidenced by the popularity of St. Patrick's Day, there is a growing interest in Scottish cultural artifacts as well. Bagpipes are one example. Bagpipe players serenade students at the Riverside campus of the University of California, Japanese bagpipe players march in St. Patrick's Day parades (an example of the conflation or confusion of Irish and Scottish cultures as neo-Celtic), and bagpipe players in kilts appear at a white supremacist gathering filmed in the documentary *Blood in the Face*. According to Militia of Montana (MOM) leader Ken Trochman, bagpipes were one of the things that first attracted him to Aryan Nations meetings: "I went to the Aryan Nations compound four or five times. Once it was for a bagpipe festival. I love bagpipes" (Stern 70).[17]

Scottish stereotypes in mainstream popular media have followed an interesting course. One of the most recognizable is Scotty in the original sixties *Star Trek* series, a masterful engineer who could hold his liquor and had a more ethnic accent than either Uhura or Sulu. A more hyperbolic development of the eccentric Scot appears as Willie, the school custodian in *The Simpsons*. Willie speaks in a brogue that is often barely comprehensible, lives alone in a shack on the school grounds, behaves unpredictably, and has extraordinary physical powers; while performing heroic feats he often appears feral or werewolf-like. In one episode he is deported to Scotland during an anti-immigrant hysteria. In the cartoon sitcom *South Park*, the poor kid, Kenny, has two unemployed parents, both alcoholic. The mother beats the father, who wears a hat that says "Scotch" in large letters across the front. Since Scotch whiskey is hardly the beverage of the poor, this must be interpreted as an ethnic marker. Like Willie, Kenny's father is an ethnic stereotype that fulfills a need (or more accurately, desire) for such stereotypes in an era in which negative stereotyping of racial minorities is no longer acceptable. These characters are a more subtle version of the Polish joke, which survived in popular culture for several decades after the Polish immigrant population generally assimilated into the middle class.

The media also provides positive Scottish characters, though there are mildly problematic aspects to them as well. *Braveheart* was an extremely popular movie starring Road-Warrior-Mel Gibson as William Wallace, the Scottish national hero who defeated the English at the battle of Stirling in the late thirteenth century. In educating viewers about the colonialist history of English incursions into Scotland that are rarely covered in standard American textbooks, this epic narrative has provided a sense of ethnic pride to Americans of Scottish descent who cannot particularly relate to the heritage of the Pilgrims or the Puritans. But it is doubtful that Wallace, when he was publicly executed in London in 1304, cried "freedom!" as he did in the film. "Scotland forever!" would have more clearly expressed the political issue at hand: Wallace fought for national sovereignty and ethnic autonomy, but not against the concept of monarchy. "Freedom!" is an American battle cry. This skewing of history does not necessarily render *Braveheart* "bad" for viewers, but the version of ethnicity presented in the television series *Highlander* is more insidious. The television series is a spinoff of a movie by the same name and companion to the popular teenage game Magic: the Gathering, which sustains the same subculture that played Dungeons and Dragons in the eighties. The "Highlanders" are a group of men with occult powers who are fated to pursue and kill each other throughout the centuries until only one of them survives. Only decapitation kills them. Not all of these *über*-men are Scottish, nor are all of them even white, though the hero has the unmistakeably Scottish name Duncan. The series attracts viewers interested in Celtic mythology and viewers drawn to Scottish heroes. The series is by no means reprehensible in aesthetic quality or in the sociopolitical issues addressed in some of the episodes, but it is fundamentally the story of a superior race of male warriors.

Historically, Scottish and Scotch-Irish immigrants were among the first to arrive in North America from Europe. Scottish immigrants in the seventeenth century included some who had been banished by Cromwell in the 1650s and generally, those who left due to religious intolerance (Dobson 39, 40, 63). Many Scots emigrated to Ulster in northern Ireland during the seventeenth century for the same reason.[18] These Ulster Scots were to become "one of the most important ethnic groups to settle in eighteenth-century America—the Scotch-Irish" (16). Thomas Pynchon satirizes the Ulster Scots in his novel *Mason and Dixon* as Pennsylvania frontiersmen whose irascibility bordered on the pathological. Though hyperbolic, Pynchon's characterization is not historically unfounded. One of the Ulster Scots' most famous offspring was Andrew Jackson. Michael Rogin describes Jackson's family background in *Fathers and Children*: his parents and two older brothers came from Ireland and "joined the Scotch-Irish migration south from Pennsylvania to the outlying southern frontier" where Andrew was born in 1767. His father died before he was born, his older brothers both died of illness during the Revolutionary War, and while Andrew was still recovering from smallpox, his mother left him to care for two sick cousins and died of cholera shortly thereafter, leaving him an orphan at 14. Having to share his mother with his cousins was not a new circumstance; his mother had run his invalid aunt's household since his infancy (39). As an adult, Jackson was chronically ill, particularly with digestive problems. His famous violent temper, along with his gambling away of his patrimony, eventually resulted in total estrangement from the extended (though in this case, fatherless) family or clan that was such an important element of Scotch-Irish and frontier culture (41).

Rogin discusses Kleinian concepts about "oral bliss" and "primitive rage" in relation to separation from the mother and resulting hostilities expressed in terms of devouring and being devoured. In terms of problems with what Kleinians call "object constancy," the splitting process overwhelms a more integrated adult picture of human relations, and others—or the Other—is alternatively idealized or demonized. Central to Rogin's concerns are the way that these hostilities played out in the Jacksonian era's splitting of the Indian of cultural discourse into the noble savage and the "starved wolf" and concomitant orally tinged hostility toward the Indian—for example, Thomas Hart Benton's assertion that one tribe after another would be "swallowed up" in the westward expansion (119–22).

Though Rogin does not clearly connect Jackson's family upbringing to this discussion, treating it in a different section of the book, the connection of Jackson's personal life to the larger cultural picture informs his entire argument. Jackson "grew up in a society characterized by fighting, boasting, and short tempers" (Rogin 43). A clearer picture of this can perhaps be seen in the Davy Crockett legends which, though prototypes of the Southwestern tall tale, are based in fact. Crockett likewise came from a frontier Scotch-Irish family. According to one of Crockett's tales, he ran away from home after his father took after him with an "old hickory" ("Old Hickory" was Andrew Jackson's nickname) for getting into a fight with another boy at the country school. Carroll Smith-Rosenberg's fascinating discussion of the Davy Crockett legends describes them as a structuring of the liminality of adolescence (though, like Jackson, Crockett did not have an adolescence according to modern-day expectations)—Crockett is beastlike, scalping Indians and sharing "injun gravy" with his dog (98)—occupying a border state between human and savage cannibal, between civilization and wilderness, between adult responsibility and a Peter-Pan-like perpetual childhood. More specifically, Smith-Rosenberg argues that Crockett marks "the liminality of the socially and economically marginal" and "the social and economic inferior . . . unwashed, uneducated, ungrammatical" (101).

Smith-Rosenberg's description of a Crockett/Jacksonian marginality can apply just as well to the skinheads and other young recruits of the militia movements of the eighties and nineties:

> the sons of artisans, suspended between the hope of emerging as successful entrepreneurs and the fear of sinking into the industrialized and unskilled work force, farmers' sons seeking to chisel out new bourgeois professions, clerks caught between the hope of rising into partnerships and the fear of ending their days as bureaucratic ciphers (101)

Many skinheads are the angry young sons of farmers and the working class beset by corporatization and globalization; their fathers may have worn Davy Crockett coonskin caps as children in the fifties. The skinhead persona is, as Smith-Rosenberg describes Crockett, "loose, liminal, and wild" (95).

Rogin's analysis of frontier Scotch-Irish families bears remarkable resemblance to some of the things that have been said about the susceptibility of the German people to Hitler. However, one has to wonder in both cases which is worse: to grow up without a father, or to grow up with a father who beats one with a hickory stick. The authoritarian family model of susceptibility to fascism was explored in Adorno and Horkheimer's one thousand page empirical study *The Authoritarian Personality* (1950), building on the prewar theories of Erich Fromm and Wilhelm Reich. Schatzman's *Soul Murder* argues this case from the history of Dr. Schreber's abusive upbringing of his famously paranoid son. More recently, cognitive scientist George Lakoff has mapped the dichotomy of the authoritarian versus the nurturing family onto the nation, arguing that conservatives expect the government to rule in authoritarian and punitive ways while liberals conceive the role of government as providing a safe haven to those in need. In the context of Lakoff's paradigm, Andrew Jackson's demonization of Indians makes sense as part of a larger picture of an intensifying reliance on a model of the authoritarian family applied on a political/national scale. The more authoritarian the model, the more hostility is generated; thus more splitting of objects into idealized and demonic roles is likely to occur. On the other hand, deprivation of parental care—loss of an object—can cause the same kinds of problems. Disruptions of maternal nurturing, i.e., feeding problems, in infancy is a classic feature of the Kleinian model of paranoia, seen in numerous case histories (Blum, Oldham and Bone). Robins and Post argue that the experience of many German youth raised without the fathers lost in World War I led to "an idealization of the absent father, a searching for a strong, powerful, nurturing figure" (299). Blum's discussion of the relationship between paranoia and sadomasochism (both, in his illustrative case history, arising from a father not fully available to his son) is consistent with the historical association of paranoid fears with the desire for, or susceptibility to, an authoritarian ruler.

This is not to say that the white supremacist fans of William Pierce necessarily have the capacity or inclination to elevate Pierce to the role of a totalitarian leader. The militia movement is probably too heterogenous for the neo-Nazi element within it to take control, and Pierce does not seem to have the desire to become a public figure. But this strain of thought in American culture is too dangerous to be ignored. Though its body count may be small so far, it is not insignificant, and it would be reckless to assume that the sentiment that produced the Oklahoma City bombing has subsided. This is particularly true in light of the growing prison population in the United States. Prison is nothing if not humiliating, and the fear of humiliation is central to paranoid pathology. As subjects becomes sensitive to humiliation, they become "unable to be indifferent to the implications of anything in the world around them. Sadomasochistic cycles of attack and counterattack ensue. The paranoid then maintains object ties based substantially on hatred" (Bone and Oldham 13).

So, then, problematic family backgrounds can contribute to a paranoid style of thinking, as can societal stressors—the humiliation of imprisonment or unemployment, the trauma of war, etc. But "such beliefs also require and are shaped by specific traditions (for example, designated demonized groups) and specific narratives (such as tales of orgies parodying the Catholic faith)" (Robins and Post 43). It becomes apparent in comparing Jacksonian southern frontier culture to contemporary American white supremacist culture that the demonized groups have shifted from Indians and Catholics to blacks and Jews. But the tradition is a continuous one. The religious zealotry and fierce individualism of the Ulster immigrants became a part of the narrative of American history and patriotism not only because they were a major immigrant group of the eighteenth century but because their culture produced the nineteenth century heroes Andrew Jackson and Davy Crockett.

In some sense, the Scotch-Irish immigrants to the southern frontier were entitled (if one is willing to accept the premise of entitlement) to a persecution complex; they were a twice-displaced people. Even if emigration to Ireland and later to the colonies was voluntary, it was pressured by religious intolerance and economic distress. On the other hand, if when they first left Scotland many of them were "individualists, religious fanatics with an anti-Papal bent, and determinists" (Jackson 8) these tendencies could only contribute to, as we say nowadays, problems in social adjustment. The persecutory fears that constructed the evil 'part-objects' as Indian and as the Mother Bank in the Jacksonian era (Rogin) are related to the paranoid style that has been documented in later developments from anti-Catholic and anti-Mason hysterias through the populist demonization of banks in the late nineteenth century and on to William Pierce, the Jewish banking conspiracy of the Nazis, and Pat Robertson.[19] Likewise, the mythology of the Jacksonian era underlies a large part of the myth of frontier individualism that has been so well documented by Slotkin and others in studies of later literature, from the late nineteenth century through Hemingway and the Hollywood western.

Like the economically beset, fatherless children of Germany in the twenties, followers of the contemporary radical right seek a leader who can provide them with an explanation for their unfocused distress and an enemy upon which to project their hostility. As with the Germans, anti-Semitism is initially secondary to these needs, but when a coherent paranoid narrative is provided they are susceptible to it. This dynamic explains the appeal of Pierce's novels to some of those being sucked into the funnel of racist hatred. It may be difficult to see these young white men as traumatized in light of the race, class, and gender privilege they still maintain compared to other demographic groups with much bigger economic and social problems, but they are not comparing their situation to other such groups. They compare their situation to what it seems to have been in a fuzzily romanticized past and what seems to them to be their right; the right to bear arms, kill their meat and their enemies, and provide for their families. Robins and Post assert that "paranoid mass movements arise only in disintegrating societies" (97). One need not be a William Bennett to recognize that the society of the patriarchal provider has disintegrated. It has gone the way of the wilderness swept clean of Indian savages where a man could sit on his front porch and not be able to see the smoke from his nearest neighbor's chimney.[20] Unfortunately, the nostalgia for this sort of autonomy (fear of loss of autonomy is one of the seven central elements of the mind of the paranoid [Robins and Post 7]) contributes to isolating practices–moving to remote rural areas, associating only with others of like mind–that further exacerbate susceptibility to crackpot theories that a broader range of exposure to information and intellectual thought might counteract.

Catherine McNicol Stock opens *Rural Radicals* with a cartoon in which voices from a farmhouse are plotting to use their farm subsidy checks to build a bigger bomb. She remarks on the importance of the contradiction of hatred of the federal government and dependence on it in rural politics (9). Though Stock's focus is on farming, a similar contradiction exists in the angry disputes over the threat to ridiculously underpriced grazing leases on federal land in the west (discussed by Stern). Threats to farm subsidies and grazing leases offer a classic invitation to paranoid thought under the Kleinian paradigm: the federal government is both good mother when it provides and bad mother when it withholds; thus a paranoid-schizoid response projects all sorts of angry hostility onto the nurturer. The "sugar tit" as figure of speech for federal funding is common in a wide variety of professions, not just farming. But paranoid thought processes can project and displace hostility onto other figures as well: thus the economically disenfranchised can project complex economic problems onto the figures of racial minorities moving into positions which were previously within the realm of white privilege. Radical right thought comes closer to the truth when it turns its demonizing gaze on multinational corporations, but unfortunately racializes the problem here as well by attributing their power to an international Jewish conspiracy. The power of large corporations dates back to the late New Deal when "government programs validated the ambitions of big farms, big industries, and big labor unions. Small producers were still important, of course, but not for what they produced as much as for what they—like all Americans . . . —consumed" (Stock 151). Here again is the problem with the left/right paradigm: twentieth century liberalism has contributed to the development of the multinational paradigm of late capitalism.[21]

Be that as it may, Pierce is as little concerned with the problems of capitalism as he is with democracy or individual liberties. Though the philosophy behind *The Turner Diaries* manifests itself in the nuclear war of racial extermination in the latter half of the novel, *Hunter*'s racism is overt in the opening scene of race-motivated street crime. *Hunter* works at developing unexamined racism into a white Aryan identity. Oscar Yeager's mentor Harry Keller has to point out to Oscar that both their surnames are German; Oscar "blushed" at this assertion because "He thought of his name as English—and it was.[22] But it also was German, he knew.

The only difference was that the English spelled it with a 'y' and the Germans with a 'j.' It meant 'hunter'" (39). Thus, like many Americans, Oscar has to be reminded that he should not be ashamed of having German ancestry. Keller also skillfully defuses another point of resistance to the Nazis' ideology: their horrible fashion sense. When Oscar asks Harry if the National League is a neo-Nazi group, Harry replies: "Depends on what 'neo-Nazi means . . . the news media calls us 'neo-Nazis,' and that's undoubtedly where you heard the term. The implications of that to most people are uniforms, swastika banners, and lots of 'sieg heiling.' But that's not us at all. I've got nothing against uniforms and banners, but we don't use 'em" (37). The Aryan chic promoted in both novels is Americanized; Rambo would never have worn one of those horrible brown shirts.

For Oscar Yeager, "History is . . . a record of the development and interaction of various human *types*: of races and ethnic groups above all else" (11). The tendency to classify people into types is innate; according to Larry Hirschfield's *Race in the Making* (1996) typing by occupation or age takes precedence in some cultures over typing by race or gender. Such typing contributes to group loyalty— "the sense of responsibility and human concern are reserved for those like us. At its most extreme, this tendency leads to dehumanizing the enemy, to persuading followers that the enemy is subhuman, a different species. This is what Erik Erickson calls *pseudospeciation*" (Robins and Post 104; emphasis added). Family loyalty, tribe loyalty, clan loyalty, species loyalty—such things cannot be eradicated, nor should they be. But pseudospeciation, the setting up of false categories of what is or is not human, is definitive of the body-count manifestations of racism. Recalling his experiences in Vietnam, Oscar theorizes that Vietnamese and African Americans have an "innate differentness . . . He saw their folkways and their attitudes as products of race-souls wholly alien to his own" (10). For racists, "blood" contains the evidence of difference, of DNA type, of species, and it is the blood of alien "species" that the "hunters" must shed to maintain racial autonomy. Earl Turner writes in his diary, "It is frighteningly clear now that there is no way to win the struggle in which we are engaged without shedding torrents—veritable rivers—of blood" (79).

If nationalism deploys a rhetoric of the family, it also, as we know, writes its story on bodies. This was the national anthem of the Khmer Rouge:

> Bright red Blood which covers towns and plains
> Of Kampuchea, our Motherland,
> Sublime Blood of workers and peasants,
> Sublime Blood of revolutionary men and women fighters!
> The Blood changing into unrelenting hatred.
> (Becker 216, qtd. in Robins and Post 250)

For Hitler, the nation's "substance" was "a substance of flesh and blood . . . a body corporate pulsing through and through with a vital inner life." France is tearing flesh away, Poland is a "national wound that bleeds continuously." The Jew is "a ferment of decomposition in peoples . . . a parasite in the body of other people's pores" that "poisons the blood of others . . . we will not pause . . . until the last trace of this poison is removed from the body of our people." Like the marauding blacks in Pierce's novels, Jewish youths conspire to contaminate the racial purity of the German girl: "With satanic joy in his face the black-haired Jewish youth lurks in wait for the unsuspecting girl whom he defiles with his blood, thus stealing her from her people" (Robins and Post 284–85).[23]

In neo-Nazi rhetoric, cancer (a more medically up-to-date metaphor) has taken the place of parasitic blood poisoning. Earl Turner says in response to hearing the phrase "slaughter of the innocents" from one of the whites forced to bury corpses (195), "Talk of 'innocents' has no meaning . . . We must understand that our race is like a cancer patient undergoing drastic surgery in order to save his life. There is no sense in asking whether the tissue being cut out now is 'innocent' or not" (197). This rhetoric is reiterated by a Chicago reader on amazon.com's customer comments to *The Turner Diaries*: "This book has the courage to reveal in plain sight who the power brokers in this country are and how to deal with them. In many ways, this is a sad story of many important people being sacrificed, however [sic], sometimes the good cells of the body must die to remove the cancerous ones." Just as "Martians" has become short-wave radio code for racial minorities (Stern 228) and NWO (New World Order) has become internet code for an international Jewish conspiracy, the cancer metaphor has become code for violent acts.

The ending of *Hunter* is somewhat unsatisfactory in terms of standard notions of plot resolution. Though the "Blacks" go on a rampage in the Day of the Long Knives, killing 58,000 people nationwide, this isn't enough to get "the folks in Iowa and the other parts of the country which aren't being affected much by the rebellion" sufficiently riled up; what is needed is a long-term power outage so that "all the food in the refrigerators spoiled and the TV screens were blank" (256–57).[24] We are left with Oscar and his sweetheart Adelaide pondering what the National League should do next. A more definitive closure is reached in the penultimate chapter in which Oscar kills William Ryan, his collaborator within the FBI.

The relationship between law enforcement and the contemporary militia movement is more complicated than the relationship between law enforcement and other radical groups. Police officers with connections to various militia groups do exist, and such connections are more difficult to identify since such people are not visibly marked. But other factors are probably more significant in explaining why FBI response to these groups seems ineffectual. It is true, as an FBI representative stated to Ken Stern, that since the days of the Black Panthers and the American Indian Movement, "lawsuits had opened agents to liability if they were overzealous" (232), but overcautiousness does not account for federal ineptitude in dealing with David Koresh and Randy Weaver. The FBI may be skilled at engendering paranoia, but it does not know how to deal with paranoids.[25] The FBI has also claimed, "explaining why it had not been overly concerned with the militia movement before the [Oklahoma City] bombing, . . . that it was not allowed to surf the Net" (Stern 230). This excuse seems barely believable. More likely, a combination of technological backwardness and, more importantly, lack of evidence of an overt conspiracy to commit specific acts account for such hesitation. Movement leaders are sophisticated in speaking in code and maintaining a decentralized, cell-based network that is difficult to track; Pierce explains the system in *Hunter* (146–47); this "leaderless resistance" strategy originated with the John Birch Society and was openly discussed at a conference convened in Estes Park, Colorado after the Weaver shootings by the KKK, Militia of Montana, and other groups (Stock 146, 168).

To the extent that Pierce speaks for the new radical right, Oscar's murder of William Ryan represents a political break from the anti-Communist far right of J. Edgar Hoover and the John Birch Society, which never openly espoused anti-Semitism. In fact, the Society's founder attributed any anti-Semitism within the group to "'agents provocateurs' hired by his conspiratorial enemies, the Insiders" (Pipes 130). George Lincoln Rockwell spoke of the Birchers with contempt in the sixties (Bennett 324–25); perhaps they simply weren't angry or aggrieved enough. Robins and Post observe that "it sometimes appeared that the Birchers' only common destiny was fleeing from boredom" (193)—at the height of its popularity, the group seems to have been more a social organization than a warrior society.[26]

In the larger perspective of American history, we can read Oscar's killing of the FBI agent as patricide—Oscar chooses between "good father" Harry Keller who raises his racial consciousness, and "bad father" William Ryan, whom he can never fully trust because Ryan continues to collaborate with the Jewish conspiracy. And in a sense, the new, zealous and terroristic American white supremacism personified by Oscar Yeager is the evil spawn of American institutional and law enforcement practices. As Michael Rogin says in *Ronald Reagan, the Movie*, ever since Tocqueville's time "the criminalization of political differences, the collapse of politics into disease, the spread of surveillance, and the stigmatization of dissenters as social pariahs have all played important roles in the suppression of radical politics" (63). The FBI has engaged in political surveillance since the twenties, and both the COINTELPRO of the FBI and the illegal domestic surveillance network of the CIA under the Johnson administration in the sixties contributed to a situation that deteriorated even further under Nixon: "by his surveillance and intimidation of political opponents and the press, Nixon recreated the hostility to legitimate opposition that lay behind the Alien and Sedition Acts [of 1798]" (78). Since then, Reagan has granted the CIA authority to conduct domestic surveillance (79). These powers are expanding beyond almost anyone's expectation with the Patriot Act and associated measures under the Bush/Ashcroft administration. Such acts attack "the bonds of trust that make political opposition possible" (Rogin 77). Where there is no trust, there is suspicion, and paranoia is merely suspicion carried on by other means. The new radical right is one end product of the paranoid style in American politics.

Though Morris Dees of the Southern Poverty Law Center and Ken Stern of the American Jewish Committee take the radical right movement as a very serious threat, Daniel Pipes has adopted what he calls the "optimistic view," that conspir-acism has a "far lesser role" where democracy is fully established. But Pipes has more recently turned to ferreting out Marxists, revisionists, extremists, and other wrong-thinkers in higher education in *Campus Watch*, so his optimisim about democracy seems to have limits.

The optimists, according to Pipes, also point to the information overload in American culture that "overflows anyone's capacity or attention span" (182–83). This position relies on the multiple voices, intertextuality, and cynicism of the postmodern condition to act as a self-limiting device on anything unidirectional. William Pierce's view of the American people is similar in doubting the capacity of anybody but his fellow technocrats to engage in intelligent analysis. One might hope to expect more from the American people than that they won't get too para-noid because they lack the attention to analyze too much information. On the contrary, the post-September 11 public mood seems entirely vulnerable to new varieties of purges and witchhunts.

Chapter Three

Women's Work?

Child Sexual Abuse Prosecution in the 1980s

In the media-saturated late twentieth century, the performances that carry the immense weight that public executions once carried in the lives of the masses are criminal prosecutions. The nation watched the stately police chase of O.J. Simpson down the California freeways, ushering in the era of the live helicopter's eye view of any freeway chase for which a helicopter-cam happens to be available. An entire network, Court-TV, is devoted to the 24-hour-a-day airing of the excruciatingly slow turning of the wheels of justice, with a surfeit of commentators and commercial products on hand to fill in the gaps in the infrequent excitement. The popularity of the film *Titanic* is not inconsistent with this generalization: as in a prosecution, the plot turns on who will sink and who will swim. Likewise in the more recent "reality" series *Survivor, Big Brother, The Apprentice,* etc. the deserving, and sometimes the not-deserving, will get their comeuppance.

One of the crimes that carries the most resonance is disappeared children. When Polly Klaas was taken from a bedroom window, raped, and murdered, the perpetrator was eventually found and convictd, but thousands more paid as well. Polly Klaas became the poster child for California's three strikes legislation and voter initiative. Even after her father withdrew from the campaign when he realized it went far beyond the incarceration of violent offenders, it was the force of this event in the popular imagination, part of a 300% increase in coverage of violent crime in TV ntework news in the two years prior to its enactment (*Legacy*), that drove the measure through. The image of the stolen, raped, and murdered child is a focal point of a much wider range of anxieties about children. The child as popular icon is idealized as innocent, untouched by original sin. Even though this model is not consistent with Judeo-Christian theology, it persists, perhaps because of a crude conflation of Adam and Eve's fall from grace with sexual knowledge, which helps drive anxiety about the need to protect children from knowledge of sex. But at the same time, our culture does not treat its children well. From one fourth to one fifth of the nation's children live in poverty, and increasing numbers of children are part of homeless families. These chidren are being punished for the sins of their mothers, who represent the stereotype of the "welfare queen" so successfully deployed by Reagan in the early eighties.

A more specific process of demonization was at work during the same period. Twenty years ago, the term 'witchhunt' in American parlance, more often than not, referred to the HUAC hearings of the fifties—the pursuit of Communists, former Communists, and fellow travelers by the House Un-American Activities Committee. Nowadays, an internet search on the word 'witchhunt' is more likely to reveal websites about Satanic ritual abuse and recovered memory prosecutions of the eighties and early nineties.

The collaboration of journalist Debbie Nathan and attorney Michael Snedeker in *Satan's Silence: Ritual Abuse and The Making of a Modern American Witch Hunt* was published at about the same time the HBO movie *Indictment: The McMartin Trial* premiered in 1995 and stands as a the best overview of the range of the child abuse prosecutions and their source in the McMartin "school" of sociological thought. Nowadays, few blink when John Leonard remarks in a review of conspiracy culture texts that alien abduction stories do "less damage to our neighborhoods than the Black Mass fairy tales [hypnotherapists] sanction about tortured tots and bloody bunnies at the local daycare center" (25). But still, there is no consensus—witness the response to Leonard's aside by a social worker from Calistoga, California: "We're not 'regressive hypnotherapists,' but we know bloodied bunnies and tortured tots *have* existed at daycare centers. And, although for different reasons, we can't tell you why we know, any more than the abductees can tell you how they know what happened to them" (O'Neill).

Nathan and Snedeker argue that the source for the ritual abuse hysteria is to be found in the economic stresses of the movement of women into the workforce: a "massive social speedup" in which "childrearing seemed more arduous, draining, and conflictual, and the tensions women felt were vented through the devil-child movies' use of increasingly resonant symbolism" (34).[1] A number of other scholars have weighed in on the phenomenon and its historical precedents. David G. Bromley, a sociologist and co-author of *Strange Gods: The Great American Cult Scare*, argues that the recent satanism scare is rooted in "an institutional crisis: incompatibility between family and economy, which confronts individuals with contradictory behavioral imperatives" (Bromley, "Satanic Cult Scare" 55). Citing parental loss of control over socialization of children in the two-wage earner economy, Bromley points out that childcare workers occupy a "pivotal point of tension between convenantal and contractual spheres" of social control. Furthermore, he says "they were accused of satanic activity rather than child molestation because the tension emanated from structural tension and nor ordinary, individualistically based deviance." Thus a fantasy narrative has been created: "the narrative warns that the capacity of covenantal family to recreate itself is at risk. The heroic figures in the narrative were the therapists and their allies" (65).[2]

In the early modern witch hunts, the "heroic figures" were the judges and magistrates who took control of village narratives based in folklore and gossip and transformed them into elite texts of juridical discourse. Brian Levack asserts that the judges and magistrates did eventually do the right thing, despite all the damage they managed to cause first: "the decline of the European witch hunt was much more the work of lawyers, judges and magistrates than of theologians or philosophers" (236). Likewise, magistrates in Salem eventually failed in "attempt[ing] to fit this ancient crime into a rational intellectual framework" (Boyer and Nissenbaum 11).

All this is consistent with Keith Thomas and Alan MacFarlane's theories about witchcraft prosecutions in early modern England: that they were a response to socioeconomic pressures related to the shifting of economic activity to urban centers and the breakdown of the neighborly charity imperative of the village community. Anthropologists view such scapegoating practices as "subversion myths (which) appear in time of acute social stress, and typically contain several elements. Most basic is a conspiracy narrative, in which the plotters are usually racial and cultural outsiders. Or they may be members of the culture's powerful elites."[3]

But are scapegoating practices *always* the result of unusual social and economic stress? In ritualized form, the use of a scapegoat is practically universal. George Bataille has constructed a hypothesis of sacrifice based upon an economic model of surplus in *The Accursed Share*. Bataille's transhistorical and transcultural observations present the concept of excess as a fundamental problem of economies that produce more than they can consume. The sacrificial approach is described by Bataille as follows:

> The victim is a surplus taken from the mass of *useful* wealth. And he can only be withdrawn from it in order to be consumed profitlessly, and therefor utterly destroyed. Once chosen, he is the *accursed share*, destined for violent consumption. But the curse tears him away from the *order of things*; it gives him a recognizable figure, which now radiates intimacy, anguish, the profundity of living beings (59).

Joseph Roach, a scholar of early modern theatre and performance, applies Bataille's model to women and children: "In the resulting semiotics of superabundance and sacrifice . . . the heaviest burden of signification was born by the frailest of their accoutrements: women as both consumers and the consumed; children, as both the auguries of surrogation and its realization in the fullness of time . . . " (125). In other words, a scapegoating role is often assumed by a woman—the "tragic mulatto," for instance—who literally embodies the fetishized excess of an economic surplus in the "performance of waste." Though Bataille does not discuss the witchhunts of the early modern era, his theory has resonance for the persecution of women in a variety of contexts. Roach's remarks on women and children are particularly interesting in the context of the "recovered memory" controversy because he views the prominent role of women and children in the "production of theatrical nationhood" as deriving "at least in part from their role as caretakers of memory" (Roach 127).

The hypotheses of economic stress and economic superabundance may seem contradictory and mutually exclusive, but this is not necessarily so. Take, for instance, the case of Margaret Kelly Michaels, a twenty-two year old aspiring actress from Pittsburgh, the focus of the Wee Care prosecution in a New Jersey suburb. The families who brought their children to Wee Care may have been stressed by the need for both parents to work—the sort of economic factor discussed by Keith Thomas in his analysis of witchcraft prosecutions in the context of the loosening of the ties of small villages as workers migrated to urban areas. The families could likewise feel stressed by the destabilization of the maternal role brought on by the fact of the working mother—a sort of inherent maternal conservatism resisting change.[4] But Kelly Michaels also served as a prime example of "surplus" in that she was young, unmarried, an immigrant from the hinterland without community ties, and of ambivalent sexuality; all in all, a "frail accoutrement" of late twentieth century culture and an ideal candidate for sacrificial lamb in a community courtroom ritual.

Most, but not all, of the defendants in the day care sexual abuse prosecutions were women. But the center of them all was always the children: the objects of maternal nurture, whether the surrogate day care provider was male or female. Thus the psychology of maternality was always at issue. Parents undergoing stress of any kind were ripe for regression to paranoid thought patterns which are grounded in the paranoid-schizoid position of early infancy.[5] Larger cultural factors contributed to the development of the state apparatus that was to come down upon the heads of day care workers. When the war on poverty initiated by Johnson in the sixties was effectively countered by the rise to power of the Reagan administration, funding for the still relatively young social work industry shifted to concerns palatable to middle as well as low income classes: self-actualization types of psychotherapy and advocacy for battered women and victims of incest, for example. These things were good developments in themselves, but new and untested theories and techniques accompanied their growing popularity. Anther factor was the sensational appeal of child sexual abuse to the media. In earlier decades, sexual topics could not have been discussed openly, but now that they could, child abuse was as good for ratings as any other sexual topic. These factors, added to societal stress over the changing role of women at home and in the workplace, "conspired" (though not in any planned or orchestrated sense) to reassemble an old cluster of fear around maternal nurturance into a narrative that shifted blame from the mother to the surrogate mother—the day care worker.

Blame was shifted to the surrogate mother as blame was deflected from other real perpetrators of child abuse. The increase in child poverty had many causes, but few were equipped to do anything about it. Social workers and counselors were either privatized or interpellated into the law enforcement system. In private practice, as aforesaid, they tended to pursue individualized approaches to therapy popular at the time: meditation, New Age healing, etc. If they remained in the public sector, they operated more and more as adjuncts to law enforcement. The only way to get attention for a problem was, again, an individualized approach: if children were at risk, they were seized and placed in institutional settings and foster homes where child sexual abuse went undetected or was ignored. [6] The other place where child abuse was ignored and abusers protected was the Catholic Church. Priests in any theocracy hold great power, but a celibate priesthood is fairly unique in the Catholic Church. As therapists are now saying, such a profession unfortunately attracts those whose sexual proclivities are not easily satisfied in mainstream culture, and tends to arrest the sexual development of even those who feel a genuine religious calling. Perhaps scholars of the early modern witch-hunts will be reevaluating their historical analysis of the witch purges. The existence of sexual abuse within the priesthood that has been recently revealed is not necessarily a new phenomenon.

The association of witchcraft specifically with sex and nursing is one which seems to be peculiar to Judeo-Christian based culture.[7] In English and mainstream American literature and popular culture, at least, our concepts of the witch are traceable to the *Malleus Malificorum*, which in turn is based on a Christian dialectic of good and evil as represented by God and Satan. According to the *Malleus*, witches made pacts with minions of Satan, met in covens to perform rites which often involved group sex with a devil or a male witch, flew through the air, and nursed their familiars with blood suckled through witch's tits found on various parts of their bodies. Satan, according to the *Malleus*, would possess either entire male bodies or just their sexual organs to have sex with female witches as an 'incubus.' The text describes the mechanics of this in great detail, including, for example, the storing of penises in a nest in a tree (the largest one belonging to the local priest).

The *Malleus* has become notorious in feminist criticism for its misogyny; this characteristic, perhaps more accurately described as gynophobia, is consistent with the Judeo-Christian creation myth in which Eve, persuaded or duped by Satan, tempts Adam into the original sin of eating fruit of the tree of knowledge of good and evil. But the perverse eroticism of the witch of the *Malleus* and the witch as constructed at the village level over the centuries since the publication of the *Malleus* and other demonology texts of the late sixteenth and early seventeenth centuries goes beyond the scapegoating of Eve. It involves a complex psychology of regression to a preverbal infantile stage in the face of a threat to autonomy or agency.

The compendium of anthropological evidence summarized by Keith Thomas and Alan MacFarlane in their authoritative works on witchcraft contain no evidence of reports of witches suckling familiars with blood in any other cultures. Thus it seems highly unlikely that this aspect of the discourse reflects any survival of pagan magical or religious practices. Rather, it probably developed from a gynophobic notion among the demonologists, perhaps traceable to anti-Semitic ideas about baby sacrifice,[8] into a popular mode of proof due to fact that some sort of wart, mole, skin tag, insect bite or tumor could usually be readily found.

Witch's tits were an important form of evidence in the New England witchcraft scare of the late seventeenth century as well. Often found under the arm or in the genital region, sometimes these skin protruberances caused controversy among the women inspectors. When Goodwife Knapp was hanged at Fairfield, Connecticut in 1653, women surrounded the corpse and

> proceeded to 'tumble the corpse up and down'; then 'several . . . said they could find none (i.e. no marks),' and a heated discussion ensued. A certain Goodwife Staples seemed particularly upset: "wringing her hands and taking the Lord's name in her mouth, . . . [she] said, 'will you say these are witch's teats? They are not.'" Witnesses would later remember that she 'handled the said teats very much' and 'pulled them with her fingers . . . as though she would have pulled them off.' Presently Goody Staples 'called upon Goodwife Lockwood to come' and reiterated her protest: 'Will you say these are witch's teats? I . . . have such myself, and so have you, if you search yourself.' Goody Lockwood answered tartly: 'I know not what you have, but for [my]self, if any find any such things about me, I deserve to be hanged as she was.'

Soon an official searcher, Goody Odell arrived, and "they all wondered, and goodwife Staples in particular, and said they never saw such things in their life before" (Demos 181).

Demos remarks that in terms of clinical psychology the perverse witch-nurse paradigm "expressed a prominent strain of 'orality'—a cluster of 'primitive' concerns centering on the 'bodily zone' of the mouth and its intrinsic 'modalities'" (179). Many witchcraft accusations, in England and New England, arose from the death of a baby soon after some sort of neighborly disagreement. Infant mortality was high to begin with; babies could take sick and die suddenly and for no reason apparent in terms of the medical knowledge of the time. The concept of projection is crucial to Demos's psychoanalysis of the New England witch prosecutions. Starting with the infantile model of "the oldest—the oral—instinctual impulses . . . 'I should like to eat this,' or 'I should like to spit this out'" (200), he concludes that the "intrusive, demanding traits" of the witch are projections of victims who are "uncomfortable about similar tendencies in themselves, about their own wishes to intrude, to encroach, to dominate, to attack—their whole assertive side"(200, 210). His discussion of anorexia as a pathology involving low self esteem and a struggle for autonomy in the face of overly controlling parents (164–65) is particularly interesting in light of the perverse nursing paradigm of the witch's tit. The anorexic or bulimic sufferer literally spits out; the accuser "projects," or spits out, psychic bad objects.

The struggle between autonomy and control was played out to the extreme in Puritan society. Everyone was expected to maintain peace and avoid anger. Young men had to struggle throughout their twenties with economic dependence. Children were strictly controlled: "stubbornness and stoutness of mind" must be "beaten down," particularly the expression of anger. Their training would have started at around the age of two, when weaning ordinarily occurred with the arrival of a new baby (Demos 207). Significantly, this age also marks the beginning of verbal development.

As witchcraft accusations were projections of the accusers' own repressed assertive characteristics, so can the entire discourse of the witch be viewed as a sort of regression to an infantile, preverbal stage of development in which fantasies of malevolent nurture can run wild and dream or fantasy becomes indistinguishable from reality. Language takes on aspects, to a preverbal psyche, that seem uncanny from an adult perspective; chanting of repetitive words and phrases is used to achieve a hypnotic or transcendent state, much like a mother's singing to a baby.

But the fantasies of regression to the infantile state are not the 'pure' fantasies of an infant; they are tainted by the entire system of signification extant in the culture of the 'regressor.' Thus images of malevolent nurture are mixed with the demons of the particular repressive culture: in these earlier cases, Satan. The accusers, whether middle aged women, younger men, or young girls, projected the infantile fantasies of their struggle for autonomy onto the witch. The adults in positions of authority, in turn, projected their own "concerns and expectations" onto the accusers.

Given this paradigm, one can see a logical progression to a projection of adult "concerns and expectations" onto even younger children still in the throes of their own infantile fantasies. This is exactly what occurred in the wave of child sexual abuse accusations against day care providers in the 1980's and early 1990's.

In her study of the maternal trope in early modern English witchcraft cases, Deborah Willis asserts that "witch-hunting at the village level . . . may largely have been a form of women's work" (14). This paradigm has certainly been borne out in the ritual child abuse prosecutions. In the seventies much of the interviewing of rape and incest victims came to take place less by male police officers and more by workers in feminism-inspired rape crisis centers (Nathan and Snedeker 202–03). This shift in investigative technique was historically justified by the institutionalized, as well as sometimes personal, insensitivity of the male interrogator to the victim. But unfortunately, many social workers who took over the investigative role lacked adequate training in both investigatory techniques and in relevant psychoanalytic theory. These problems were exacerbated as the role of social workers in the interrogation process became more institutionalized, especially in the situation of interrogating very young children, demonstrating, in the worst case scenarios, a result reminiscent of the pedagogy of medieval Catholic priests: "a mixture of pure spells and orthodox theology as taught to the illiterate."[9]

Before pursuing a discussion of the interplay of the development of sociopsychological theories of child sexual abuse with investigations and prosecutions during the latter twentieth century, it may be helpful to lay out a chronology of fictional and media treatments of child sexual abuse and satanism during the same period.

The first American film to explicitly address the issue of child sexual abuse was *The Naked Kiss* (1964). In it, a former prostitute (by virtue of one twenty-dollar one night stand) realizes her fiance is seducing a six-year old girl in his orphanage. Conveniently for the plot, he confesses all before she actually sees anything, certain that due to her impaired status as marriage material she will agree to serve as cover for his perversions. Instead, she kills him, but does not go to prison as would most certainly have happened in real life. Instead, the judge dismisses the charges when the child finally corroborates the story (in the vaguest of terms), and the fallen woman is free to leave town with her head high, casting an accusing gaze at the townspeople who weren't smart enough to figure it out.

Nevertheless, the media was not much concerned with child sexual abuse in the sixties and seventies, though as aforementioned, plenty of it was going on in juvenile detention centers and in the Catholic Church. On the other hand, the release of *The Exorcist* (1973) and the other "deomon child" films cited by Nathan and Snedeker breathed new life into old narratives of demonic possession. Seven years later in a book called *Michelle Remembers* (1980), "Michelle" narrates her recovered memories to psychiatrist Lawrence Pazder, covering a full range of ritual satanic practices supposed to have occurred during a five-month period of imprisonment when she was five years old. Independent investigation into records of Michell's whereabouts have shown that the adventure she recalled while in therapy could not possible have occurred (Nathan and Snedeker 45–46).

In 1984, father/daughter incest was addresssed on ABC in *Something about Amelia*, dealing with a "handsome, affluent father who sexually abuses his teenage daughter" (Nathan and Snedeker 197). Meanwhile, Satanic ritual abuse accounts continued throughout the eighties. They reached the zenith of respectability with the 1985 broadcast of "The Devil Worshippers" on ABC's *20/20*. In the following years objections to the conflation of Wiccan practitioners with minions of Satan were addressed by believers with the alleged discovery of the "Wicca Letters," by a San Diego deputy sheriff, supposedly minutes from a convention in Mexico of a plot to take over American day care centers.[10] The marriage of satanism to day care in mainstream media fiction was marked by the 1989 CBS movie *Do You Know the Muffin Man?* which "rehashed details from several ritual cases, but included the wholly fictional climax of parents discovering day-care teachers worshipping the devil amidst piles of kiddie porn" (Nathan 166).

Debbie Nathan, a free-lance journalist, was one of the first to question the narrative with her late-eighties accounts of the Kelly Michaels case in the *Village Voice*. Her coverage led to Dorothy Rabinowitz's 1990 article in *Harpers*. The following year, the Public Broadcasting Network aired Swedish filmmaker Ofra Bikel's *Innocence Lost* on *Frontline* (1991) about the Little Rascals case in Edenton, North Carolina. Two years later came a book debunking the McMartin prosecution, followed by several books addressing various aspects of the false memory issue, some written by forensic sociologists and psychologists.[11]

In 1994, the novel *A Map of the World* by Jane Hamilton was published, recounting the story of a school nurse unjustly accused by a child of sexual abuse.[12] But the watershed event marking the shift in public opinion on these cases was the HBO airing of *Indictment: The McMartin Trial* in May 1995, wherein Ray Buckey, the child-molesting villain of the McMartin trial, was recast as the victim of a hysterical conspiracy theory. Five years earlier, no major television network would have dared question the infallibility of the testimony of ravished, innocent babes. A network like HBO is closely attuned to shifts in the public mood. Such TV dramas and feature films are generally more likely to respond to existing trends in public opinion on controversial issues than to break new ground, and so this docudrama marked a sort of closure on the issue in the public imagination, though the judicial system cannot shift direction so quickly.

To backtrack now to the late seventies, psychiatrist Michael Durfee, at the time head of the Los Angeles county health department's child-abuse program, had organized a group called the Preschool-Age Molested Children's Professional Group. Durfee was a believer in satanic ritual abuse cults, based upon the "informal mentorship of a woman who suffered from multiple personality disorder" and upon his connections with other psychiatrists and graduate students investigating reports of satanic ritual abuse at UCLA's Neuropsychiatric Institute. This group included future McMartin prosecutor Joan Matusinka, who in the early seventies had helped found Parents Anonymous for perpetrators of child physical abuse, and future McMartin investigator Kee MacFarlane, who had been acquainted with child incest victims early on in her career when she worked at a children's group home in Arizona (Nathan and Snedeker 75–77, 13).

This group was well aware of the problems in eliciting coherent narratives from very young children. It was MacFarlane who introduced the use of play therapy, and specifically hand puppets, into the interviewing of suspected abuse victims. MacFarlane and her colleagues sat on the floor dressed in clownlike clothing, spoke in "gentle, high-pitched voices," and initiated discussion about genitals and sex with the innovation of "anatomically correct" dolls sporting breasts, vaginas, penises, anuses, and pubic hair (77–78). In a sense, this practice was not a far cry from Klein's penis-trains and dark-closet wombs, but Klein was playing and MacFarlane's group was not—that is, Klein was reading play in the context of symbol formation and MacFarlane's group seemed unable to interpret toddler play in any way but literally. The social workers' interpretations were motivated solely by their goal of collecting evidence for criminal trials.[13]

The conventional wisdom among therapists and social workers in the early 1980's was the well-known saw that "children never lie." This dogma seems to have originated with the work of psychiatrist Roland Summit of the Los Angeles County Community Consultation Service. He organized the group Parents Anonymous for parents who physically abused their children, and coined the phrase "child sexual abuse accommodation syndrome" to describe the way in which incest victims would falsely recant in order to avoid family fragmentation (Summit, "Abuse"). In a 1983 article Summit proclaimed that children therefore "should always be believed, no matter how illogical and incredible their accusations sound" (Summit, "Child Abuse" 183).

Like Kee MacFarlane's rather prosaic and uninformed application of child play therapy, doctors as well were producing new bad science out of old bad science. The "mixture of pure spells and orthodox theology" perhaps reached its nadir in a pediatrician's office in Bakersfield, California. Dr. Bruce Woodling revived the concept of the "anal wink" from the arcane sexology of the nineteenth century,[14] arguing in a 1981 publication that if the anus dilates when the rectal area is touched with a cotton swab, the patient has been sodomized. Woodling used this procedure in a criminal investigation in April 1982 when he performed the anal wink test on two six and nine year old brothers in Bakersfield, California, 100 miles east of Los Angeles. These boys had been abruptly taken from their home based on a report by three young girls who had been through several months of interrogation and "therapy" and had been removed from their parents' home due to alleged child abuse by their father, Alvin McCuan. The boys' parents, the Kniffens, were friends who were to be called as character witnesses at McCuan's trial; as court proceedings dragged on, the girls described a new scenario: an orgy with the Kniffens, their sons, and another family. Like the Salem witch prosecutions, the circle of accused in Bakersfield grew and grew; soon it came to encompass two Welfare Department workers as well as an assortment of other friends and relatives (Nathan and Snedeker 59–60, 65).

Another child subjected to the same examination, eight years old at the time, later attested that when she denied having been molested, Woodling told her "This examination will tell who's right and who's wrong" and proceeded, in the face of tearful protests, to apply the swabs, insert a glass tube in her rectum, and take pictures. She described the ordeal several years later in the course of an appeal as "the worst thing that ever happened to me." Though a British physician testified at the trial of the girls' aunt and uncle (the McCuans) that the anal wink was "a normal reaction to having an erogenous zone stimulated," the McCuans and the Kniffens were all convicted (186, 188).

The McCuan/McKniffen investigation started with a child abuse report from a psychotic step-grandmother in 1980.[15] The following year her step-daughter and stepson-in-law (the McCuans) were arrested along with another couple he called as character witnesses (the Kniffens), a social worker who got on grandma's wrong side during the investigation (Betty Palko), the social worker's boyfriend, and various and sundry other people (Nathan and Snedeker 64–65). The key investigators had been trained by Roland Summit in Los Angeles (64), and the trial started a couple of months before Judy Johnson accused Ray Buckey and the McMartin school. The first two couples, Alvin and Debbie McCuan and Scott and Brenda Kniffen, spend fourteen years in prison; their convictions were eventually overturned due to "leading questions" during the investigation and "telling the child reports of abuse would help their parents and they could all go home and live together again" ("Judge Frees Two Couples"). Their children have grown up in foster care.

If the anal wink test seems like child abuse, one must also consider the abusive aspects of implanting false memories in children too young to resist suggestibility. The Bakersfield children, though subjected to arduous psychological threats and intimidation to change their stories in addition to the "medical exam," at least were old enough to have some concept of the distinction between truth and fantasy.[16] The same was not true of the preschool children who have been the focus of most of the multiple prosecutions. Even the prominent pro-prosecution studies *Nursery Crimes* and *Behind the Playground Walls* demonstrate that most of the child "victims" displayed symptoms of abuse only after their interrogations had begun.[17] Some of the McMartin children, due to their extreme suggestibility at the age at which they were interrogated, remain convinced that their bizarre narratives actually occurred.

The McCuans and Kniffens had been convicted in 1982. The McMartin case in Los Angeles that was to fuel the nationwide day care sexual abuse panic started with a 1983 accusation against Ray Buckey, an "odd-looking young man" with "longish" hair, grandson of the school's founder and son of the director (Eberle 15). At one point in the investigation the police claimed to have uncovered thirty-six suspects and "as many as 1,200 victims" (Rabinowitz, "From the Mouths of Babes" 56). Kee MacFarlane was the social worker who led the McMartin investigation, later to become an "expert" consulted across the nation by investigators of alleged child abuse and Satanic cults. In the McMartin case,

> After repeated interviewing produced statements about bizarre sex rituals in airplanes, hot air balloons, underground tunnels, graveyards, and funeral parlors, MacFarlane told the press that the McMartin preschool was part of a national network of kiddy pornographers and Satanists operating out of day-care centers (Nathan 137).

The first trial didn't start until 1987 and lasted until 1990, finally ending in acquittals and a hung jury. On June 5, 1990 a California victims rights initiative was passed by voters which along with two court decisions, *California v. Jones* in the California Supreme Court (June 28) and *Maryland v. Craig* in the U.S. Supreme Court (June 27), broadened admissibility of testimony from young children. The first court decision provided that it was unnecessary for a child to testify to time, place or details of abuse for the evidence to be admissible, and the second allowed closed circuit video testimony of children out of the presence of the defendant(s). The second McMartin trial ended within a month after these significant changes in the law, producing a hung jury and eventual dismissal.

Since then, the entire grounds of the former preschool have been excavated in a search for the tunnels the children testified to; nothing was found but Indian artifacts. The woman who made the initial complaint, according to an assistant District Attorney who resigned and later testified for the defense, was suffering from a psychotic episode at the time of the initial complaint; she has since died of alcohol poisoning (Nathan 150). Nevertheless, many of the children and their parents still firmly believe all the lurid incidents testified to actually occurred. The children, of preschool age at the time of the initial investigation, were young teenagers by the time of the second trial. They had been indoctrinated with the investigators' version of events for years in the name of witness preparation.

Between 1983 and 1988 ritual child abuse investigations were initiated in more than one hundred U.S. communities (Bromley 61); of those, about fifty under-went criminal trials (Nathan 152). Perhaps the biggest year for day care abuse allegations was 1984. In January, *Something About Amelia* appeared on ABC, dealing with father/daughter incest who sexually abuses his teenage daughter" (Nathan and Snedeker 197). That spring, a mother in a Jordan, Minnesota trailer park reported that her child had been abused by the trash collector. The other children in the park were interviewed, and said they had been abused by the mother who accused the trash collector. Her sister and brother-in-law mortgaged their house to bail her out, and two months later they were charged. Several dozen people protested outside the courthouse, and three of the protesters, an automo-bile painter, his wife, and a policeman, were arrested for child abuse, along with the policeman's wife and another couple (Rabinowitz, "From the Mouths of Babes" 56). Eventually, the charges of ritual abuse and murder were dropped against the two dozen adults who had ultimately been charged, but "80 percent of the community's residents continued to believe in the veracity of the children's stories that were the primary evidence in the case" (Bromley 61).

Part of what was fueling public concern about child sexual abuse was increased attention to rape and incest. Jeffrey Masson's *The Assault on Truth: Freud's Suppres-sion of the Seduction Theory* was published in 1984, representative of criticism of Freud for dismissing women's complaints of childhood abuse as Oedipal fantasies.[18] At the same time, as feminists fought for better prosecution of rape cases, new reporting systems counted almost 43,000 cases of abuse annually, mostly by fathers and male relatives. A significant and oft-cited study by feminist sociologist and anti-pornography activist Diana Russell, *The Secret Trauma: Incest in the Lives of Girls and Women* (1986), concluded that more than half of all women have suffered from child sexual abuse, but the media usually failed to explain that she included any unwanted touching, even from boyfriends. Her definition of incest was also fairly broad, covering any sexual contact between relatives, however distant, of over five years' age difference. From this she concluded that one in five women were incest victims (Nathan 154–55).

Such statistics, filtered through the media to the general population, helped to fuel the panic about child sexual abuse. At the same time interview theories and techniques developed for incest victims came to be applied to investigations against day care providers and other persons outside the home. The "child sexual abuse accommodation syndrome," was a theory based on a child's reluctance to testify, or tendency to recant, to avoid breaking up a family home. But the "any means necessary" technique to get a child to admit abuse has little relevance if the child has no competing motivation to save the family home. Furthermore, the day care defendants didn't match known profiles even of female incest perpetrators, who tended to be "emotionally disturbed, abuse drugs, and were themselves incest victims. When molesting their children, they would tend to do it nonviolently, by fondling them during diaper changes, for example; and they often feel ashamed and turn themselves in" (Nathan 163).

As 1984 wore on, cases surfaced in Chicago in April, Reno in May, Memphis in June, and by the end of the summer, fourteen day care centers in New York and "dozens" in Southern California. Ritual abuse, pornography production, and animal sacrifice were alleged in Michigan, Ohio, Massachusetts, and Florida as well as New York and California. Another case, later to result in the Supreme Court's 1990 decision *Maryland vs. Craig* to allow videotaped child testimony, started when a preschool teacher was charged in January 1985 with assaulting her charges with a screwdriver, taking nude pictures, and killing a rabbit in front of them (Nathan and Snedeker 107–08).

Later in 1985, Margaret Kelly Michaels was arrested for multiple counts of sex abuse against twenty 3–5 year old children at the Wee Care Day Nursery in an Episcopal Church in Maplewood, New Jersey (a New York suburb). Children later testified at trial that in 1984–85 she had inserted sharp objects, such as knives, forks, spoons, and even a lightbulb into their anuses or vaginas . . . licked peanut butter and jelly from their bodies . . . sodomizing the boys and . . . forcing them to eat her feces and drink urine . . . play[ing] 'Jingle Bells' on the music-room piano naked (Nieves, "Woman Upheld").

After being sentenced to 730 years in 1988 (Rabinowitz, "From the Mouths of Babes" 52), Michaels was eventually released after her conviction was reversed by an appeals court and the prosecution, though never admitting her innocence, eventually decided not to retry the case due to lack of evidence (Nieves, "Prosecutors Drop Charges"). Michaels had spent five years in prison by the time of her release; when the charges were finally dropped she planned to marry a journalist she met while in prison and return to Pennsylvania to write a book about prison life.

The Michaels case illustrates, though it is not alone in this regard, the importance of the in-and-out and feces motifs earlier remarked in connection with Klein's studies. It is also important because, since tape recordings were made of at least some of the child interviews, compelling evidence exists of the coercive and unrelenting nature of these interrogations.

Furthermore, there is a bellwether aspect to the way this case was treated in the media. Initially, it attracted little attention: just one more of many such cases. The reporters who brought the Michaels case to national attention had not covered the original trial and conviction. Debbie Nathan had covered a similar case in El Paso, Texas in 1986 and was one of the first journalists to question the validity of such prosecutions.[19] She constructed her reports for the *Village Voice* on the Michaels case from interviews and court transcripts. A reporter for a CBS-affiliated TV station in the area, Dorothy Rabinowitz became interested in the case from reading Nathan's reports and brought it into the mainstream media with an article in *Harper's* in 1990.[20] This article created something of a stir, and prompted a refutation from a reporter, Lisa Manshel, who had actually covered the trial and was convinced of Michaels' guilt. Her article appeared in the *Washington Journalism Review* in the summer of 1991. All the media controversy, in other words, took place prior to the appeals court reversal, the appellate process not being known for its speed.[21]

Nathan and Rabinowitz seem to agree that the original defense lawyers erred by failing to introduce character witnesses on Michaels' behalf—a decision made because they didn't want to open the door to evidence of two brief lesbian relationships Michaels had had while in college (Rabinowitz, "From the Mouths of Babes" 62). Manshel on the other hand seems to have been influenced by rumors leaked by the prosecution to the press during the trial to the effect that Michaels' parents were molesters and even that her father "had called Wee Care every day to make sure that she was initiating the children in the practices of pederasty" (Rabinowitz, "From the Mouths of Babes" 63). Rabinowitz argues that these stories "had enormous impact on the press, for they meshed nicely with current dogma—and the press is nothing if not up on the latest dogma—which holds that children who are molested become molesters themselves" (63). Nothing along these lines was ever introduced at the trial. Michaels' family is described by Rabinowitz as "a talkative, bookish lot, given to heated debate on art and politics, which might explain Kelly Michaels' rather extraordinary command of the language—a faintly formal, old-fashioned eloquence that made her seem, at times, the child of another era" (55). She sounds like a person, in other words, who would have seemed slightly bizarre to police investigators in suburban New Jersey: an artsy type of ambiguous sexuality who talked funny.

Manshel's rebuttal of Rabinowitz points out that "trial testimony was filled with statements about abuse—verbal, behavioral and pictorial—made by the children long before an investigation was initiated" (18). The investigation started when a four-year-old having his temperature taken rectally at a doctor's office said "That's what my teacher does to me at school" (19). Many of the "statements about abuse," however, involve such things as "nightmares, biting, spitting, bed-wetting, masturbation, or . . . any sort of noticeable changes in behavior"—what the social worker in charge of a Sexual Assault Unit told the parents to look for (Rabinowitz, "From the Mouths of Babes" 56–57). Most objective parents uninfluenced by advice from "experts" would recognize that these are all part of normal toddler development. These were the same sorts of problems that Klein's patients had, and Klein considered them relatively normal. She believed that all children should undergo psychoanalysis as part of their education because "anxiety can be alleviated only by forcing suffering and guilt into consciousness" (Grosskurth 165, 168). Certainly, some children are more anxious than others, but no small child is entirely free from anxiety.

Despite the many points Manshel raises, an overall picture of the investigatory process In the Michaels' case—representative of the problem of suggestibility in all such cases—can be seen in the following interview transcript of a four-year-old boy. It is important to remember, also, that by the time the investigators start transcribing interviews there have usually already been previous conversations.

FONOLLERAS: A lot of other kids have helped us since we saw you last.

LUKE: I don't have to. No!

F: Did we tell you Kelly is in jail?

LUKE: Yes, my mother already told me.

F: Did I tell you this is the guy who arrested her, put her in there? Don't you want to ask us any questions?

LUKE: No!

(Fonolleras handed Luke an anatomically correct doll.)

F: What color did Kelly have down there? Brown like her head? Did she have hair under her arm?

LUKE: My daddy do.

At this point, Luke began to shriek, and there are indications that he was kicking Fonolleras. Fonolleras offered him a piece of cake and asked him if he would like to see Investigator Mastrangelo's badge. Mastrangelo then said to Luke, "So your penis was bleeding?" Luke laughed.

F: Did Kelly play 'Jungle Bells' with clothes on?

LUKE (screaming): No, I saw her penis! I peed on her!

F: You peed on her?

LUKE: No, she peed on me!

At this time Luke told Fonolleras that he wanted to stop. But Fonolleras urged him to continue. He asked more questions about Luke's penis, about whether he put it in Kelly's mouth.

F: Whose mouth did you have to put your penis in?

LUKE: Nobody.

F: Did anybody kiss your penis?

LUKE: No. I want to go home.

F: Did she put this fork in your bottom? Yes or no.

LUKE: I forgot.

F: Did she do anything else to your bottom?

LUKE: That's all she did.

There followed a series of "I forgot" and "I don't know" responses. Finally, tiredly, Luke said "Okay, okay, I'll try to remember." He then said—in an obviously playful, make-believe tone—"She put that in my heinie."

F: The fork?

LUKE (shrieking): Yes!

There were more questions, and more no's from Luke. Fonolleras then said, in a disappointed tone, " I thought you were going to help me." The session ends with Luke shouting, "It's all lies!" (Rabinowitz, "From the Mouths of Babes" 58)[22]

In retrospect, most people connected to the legal system, whether police investigators, social workers, clinical psychologists, or lawyers, would (one would hope) be horrified at the leading and overbearing nature of the questions asked of this child in the face of his responses. But in the mid-eighties, the field was relatively new and untried. The investigators were not acting in bad faith, but they clearly did not know what they were doing, reckless as such incompetence may have been.

But if the investigators didn't know what they were doing, neither did the prosecutors and the judges. In the El Paso case that Nathan had covered, for example, the prosecutor relied heavily on the aid of Kee MacFarlane, the McMartin social worker with the Satanist/pornography conspiracy theory. The judge remarked after the trial that "he hates these cases, 'never had anything like them before and don't know what to do with them. I just let Debbie (the prosecutor) shear the law off the page. An appeals court can rule later on what the law is.'" (Nathan 140). What the appeals court ruled more than a year later was that defendant Michelle Noble's right to confront her accusers had been violated by showing the jury videotaped interviews of the children (this was prior to *Maryland v. Craig*). On retrial, the hysteria had abated and in a different atmosphere, the defense showed some of the same videotapes, cited by a juror as "'tasteless' proof of how they had badgered the children" (Nathan 146).

The case with the closest chronological parallel to the rise and fall of satanic day care abuse in TV fiction was the Little Rascals Day Care case in Edenton, North Carolina. *Do You Know the Muffin Man?* had been aired in fall of 1989, just about the time that accusations among parents in Edenton began to snowball. The 1992 conviction of Robert Kelly in the Little Rascals case (two years after the end of the McMartin trials) was overturned by a state appeals court in May 1995 ("North Carolina").[23] The pro-defense HBO film *Indictment: The McMartin Trial* aired May 27, 1995. But the appellate reversals had more to do with the lower court's sloppiness than a shift in judicial attitudes. One reason for the Little Rascals reversal was that the prosecution was allowed to introduce therapists' notes into evidence during closing argument, without allowing for cross-examination about them. Juror interviews had indicated the notes were crucial in obtaining the conviction (Bikel). A co-defendant, cook Dawn Wilson, was prosecuted because she refused to testify against the other day care workers under a grant of immunity. Her conviction was reversed because the judge had improperly allowed cross-examination about her use of cocaine and marijuana ("North Carolina"). The effect this sort of fishing expedition had on Dawn Wilson would seem to vindicate the Kelly Michaels' defense decision to keep character evidence out of the case.

In San Diego, Dale Akiki, a child care volunteer at Faith Chapel, was acquitted in 1993 after a 7 1/2 month trial and 2 1/2 years in jail. Akiki is yet another odd looking or otherwise socially marginal defendant; he "suffers from a rare genetic disorder that has left him with droopy eyelids, a clubfoot, limited use of his elbows and a head grotesquely enlarged by the buildup of fluid." Prosecutors contend he dunked children's heads in toilets, tied them up, took nude photos, kidnapped them to a nearby house, and killed animals. Specifically, children testified that Akiki "brought an elephant and a giraffe to class, killed the elephant in front of his startled audience and slaughtered a rabbit as a way of warning his 3- and 4-year-old subjects not to reveal his heinous crimes" (Granberry, "Is Trial," "Former Preschool Worker"). Witnesses also said Akiki conspired with his wife and another sitter to subject the children to "rituals of mayhem, involving urine, feces, water torture and animal mutilation." (Granberry, "Case Illustrates Flaws"). The prosecution, however, never produced any physical evidence at the time of trial (Granberry, "Ex-School Volunteer Acquitted").

The Akiki case is fairly recent, though the alleged incidents date to 1988–89, and its outcome marks the beginning of the backlash. The San Diego County District Attorney lost the 1994 election due in part to public outrage about this case and another in which a five-year old girl was coerced into naming her father as a rapist. An alert appellate defense attorney obtained DNA testing on the girl's underwear after the father had already been in jail two years—the semen proved to belong to someone else, a known molester. The child, Alicia Wade, had told both a doctor and a police detective that someone had climbed in her bedroom window while she was sleeping and taken her away, giving a detailed description of the man. But such authorities apparently "believe the children" only according to their own assumptions of probability; the doctor found the child's story so "unrealistic" she did not even write it in her report. The child stuck to her story throughout thirteen months of isolation from her family before finally telling the authorities what they wanted to hear, that "Daddy did it." Suspicion had been focused on the father because he was in the Navy and a recovering alcoholic, and apparently that was enough because "child welfare authorities believe military families are susceptible to the tensions and instability that contribute to abuse" (Wilkins).

As with the early modern witchcraft prosecutions, the weight of the evidence in the cases has ultimately failed to fit into any rational intellectual framework. In 1994, The National Clearinghouse on Child Abuse and Neglect Information published the results of a five-year study concluding that no evidence exists of organized satanic child abuse in or out of day care environments (Goodman). The tedious weight of juridical epistemology seems to have finally countered the hysteria, aided by the requirement that all interviews with children be videotaped, thus exposing the more egregious harrassment, coercion, and intimidation that has been going on in much of the investigation process. Nevertheless, it is unclear that such prosecutions are over. Over two dozen "poor and uneducated" pentecostal church members were prosecuted for a child sex abuse ring in Wenatchee, Washington in 1995 (Nathan and Snedeker 246). Though one civil lawsuit against the prosecutors for official misconduct, filed by those who had been acquitted, failed to obtain a verdict of liability because jurors decided that the prosecutors had acted in "good faith," another defendant later settled for $290,000 in 1999.[24] The appellate process has been excruciatingly slow, especially for the Bakersfield defendants who spent fourteen years and their children's entire childhood in prison, and sometimes it does not work at all. At the time Nathan and Snedeker's study went to press in early 1995, fifty-one were still incarcerated, some serving lifetime terms. At last count, about fifteen people are still incarcerated in at least nine states plus Ontario, Canada on unlikely sexual abuse convictions (Manning et al).[25] Since the exposure of sexual abuse in the Catholic Church, it is not politically expedient for governors to override the appellate process. Thus in 2002 Massachusetts Governor Jane Swift pardoned five women executed in the Salem witch trials over four hundred years ago, but refused to commute the sentence of Gerald Amirault, of the Fells Acre Day School case (Pollitt). Amirault, incarcerated since 1986 was finally paroled and released April 30, 2004.

The road from incest investigation to the day care prosecutions offers fascinating insight into the misapplication of psychoanalytic theory to the real world: Melanie Klein's brilliant understanding of the dark and frightening world of the infant psyche transposed into an instantiation of phantasy into the preschool child's perception of reality.

Melanie Klein was the first psychotherapist to initiate play therapy into the field of child psychology. Her competitor Anna Freud preferred to assume a pedantic role with young children, but Klein played with them and provided her young patients with their own personal sets of toys, kept in individual drawers in her office. Klein has been roundly denounced by postmodern "anti-Oedipus" theorists Gilles Deleuze and Felix Guattari for imposing an Oedipal construct upon one of her early and best-known patients: "'screaming' Daddy, Daddy at poor little Dick,"[26] but little Dick was not an ordinary patient—any present day diagnostician would immediately identify him as autistic—and Klein's methodology with Dick seems to have had marked success in terms of bringing him up to a level of social interaction that seems comparable to the best achievements of contemporary therapists with autistic patients.[27]

Klein's accounts of interactions with her young patients reveal the extent to which these two-to-four year old children are preoccupied with feces, but also the relationship of what Freud would have called "anal" preoccupations to the theme of putting things in and taking things out of bodies. Most of her patients came to her from upper middle class families; many of them were the children of other therapists. Their problems tended to be problems with feeding, bedwetting, nightmares, etc.—the sort of problems modern-day therapists often identify as symptoms of sexual abuse, but which any parent knows can occur in entirely "normal" children. One of Klein's most interesting little playmates was three-year old Trude, suffering from "night terrors and incontinence of urine and feces." Trude asked Klein to lie down and pretend she was asleep so Trude could "attack me and look into my buttocks for feces (which I found also represented children)" (Klein 48). Discussing Trude in another essay, Klein says she came out of the particular corner which she called her room, stole up to me, and made all sorts of threats. She would stab me in the throat, throw me into the courtyard, burn me up, or give me to the policeman. She tried to tie my hands and feet, she lifted the sofa-cover and said she was making 'po-kacki-kucki'.[28] . . . Another time she wanted to hit me on the stomach and declared that she was taking out the 'a-a's' (faeces) and making me poor. She then pulled down the cushions, which she constantly called 'children,' and hid herself with them in the corner of the sofa, where she crouched down with vehement signs of fear, covered herself up, sucked her thumb and wetted herself. This always directly followed her attacks on me (61).

Klein concluded that Trude, whose mother was pregnant, wanted to rob the children from her mother's body (said children being represented by feces) and kill her mother. She says Trude's fixation on her mother was "peculiarly strong" for a two years old, resulting from these feelings of hostility and aggression (61). This seems plausible enough, considering the potential intensity of sibling rivalry, but what makes it interesting in the context of the child abuse prosecution testimonials is the feces and in-and-out motifs that are a mainstay of such testimonials.

The same sorts of preoccupations appear in accounts of some of Klein's other patients. Six-year-old Erma also wanted Klein to lie down and produce feces; in Erma's case Klein was supposed to be a baby and after this play-acting Erma, rather than becoming guilty and fearful as Trude did, "played the part of a cruel teacher who knocked the child about" (66). Rita, at age two, put an elephant next to the baby doll's bed to prevent the baby from getting up and going to the parents' bedroom to attack them or steal from them (62). On one occasion Rita "blackened a piece of paper, tore it up, threw the scraps into a glass of water which she put to her mouth as if to drink from it, and said under her breath 'dead woman'" (49). Thus feelings of hostility and aggression toward a parent alternate with feelings of guilt and anxiety for the parent's well-being.

One of Klein's pertinent conclusions from these experiences was that "anxiety about attacks on the inside of the body is of great importance in men as well as women" (50). Though Klein's concerns with castration fears and the Oedipus paradigm were generally more grounded in Freudian theories than contemporary feminist psychoanalysts would deem necessary, her adherence to Freudian thought (despite her reputation among her peers as an iconoclast) does not necessarily detract from her salient insights into the young psyche. Is it possible that some of her patients had been sexually abused? Klein's attitude toward child sexuality was somewhat casual; at one point she offhandedly refers to an interpretation that "some sexual activity seemed to have occurred between herself [a seven-year old girl patient] and her friend, and that this had made her very frightened of being found out and therefore distrustful of other people" (39). She describes all sorts of sex play among young children as "typical" (82). Klein seems not to consider the possibility of incest or other sexual abuse in any of these cases, but is, overall, willing to a fault to attribute her patient's problems to incompetent nursing, insufficient parental affection, and (the most likely sounding cause) abusive toilet training.[29]

Besides the feces, urine, and in-and-out of the body motifs, a number of other psychologically interesting motifs appear in some of these cases. Klein would have identified the underground tunnel story of the McMartin case as a symbol of the mother's birth canal given that she identified much less obvious sites such as cupboards and dark hallways in these terms (103). The "bloody bunny" motifs referred to by the social worker in her letter to *The Nation* (noted in the beginning of the chapter) appeared in the McMartin and Akiki cases. Like Douglass Durham's mock crucifixion of the white man, the bloody bunny has a pagan, anti-Christian connotation associated with Easter: a blasphemous distortion of the only officially sanctioned sacrifice in the Christian religion. With the bloody bunny, "mere" sexual abuse crosses over into the Satanic ritual paradigm that Kee MacFarlane proselytized across the country. The fork in the Michaels interview by Detective Fontelleras has a Satanic resonance as well, it being hard to account for otherwise: why else would Kelly Michaels put a fork in Luke's "heinie?" These motifs mark the interrogator's overlay on existing preoccupations of the children. Forks have to do with food; toddlers eat food at day care—they also defecate and urinate at day care, and all these bodily functions comprise a large portion of the interaction between the child and the day care worker throughout the day. Moreover, food and bodily excrement have a primary significance in object relations theory: as the actual "objects" that go in and out of the body, they bear a resonant association with objects as internal or external imagoes that represent the child's significant others.

These sorts of dynamics exist in the adult mind as well, though at a more sublimated level. In series of leading questions such as those by Detective Fontelleras, adults write their own psychological constructs upon the bodies of children. Most of the abuse prosecutions discussed above involve at least a subtext of satanic ritual abuse theory. This part of the McMartin case was dropped by the prosecution because the prosecutors doubted the jury would believe it. This did not keep MacFarlane, however, from proselytizing the SRA theory across the country, serving as an expert witness, and even publishing an article in the University of Miami Law Review. A parallel to this strategy can be seen in the prosecutorial rumormongering about Kelly Michaels' father. Only a belief in ritualistic activity (or at least, as MacFarlane claimed in the El Paso case, a child pornography ring) could support the multiplicitous nature of the charges involving cooks, policemen, friends and relatives.

The paradigm of Satanic sacrifice involving bloody animals, bloody babies, lactation (the witch's tit), and sexual intercourse have resonated for adults for centuries. Given the existence of published contemporary "accounts" such as *Michelle Remembers*, it became all too easy for overzealous but well meaning caseworkers such as MacFarlane to apply the imprimatur of official sanction to the model and find it wherever they looked. Otherwise, faced with the even more fantastic stories about airplane rides and underground tunnels (McMartin), women with penises (Wee Care), the cooking of babies in microwaves (Little Rascals), and elephants and giraffes in Sunday school, they would have known when to stop. The response to such stories was not to question the rest of the so-called "evidence"—despite the standard courtroom jury instruction that a witness whose testimony is false in part may be false in its entirety—but to selectively choose child witnesses so that the patently impossible stories would not come before the jury.

One of the problems with obtaining convictions in the mass day care prosecutions, as time went on, was the circumstance that most day care situations were fairly public environments with parents coming and going, often unannounced, throughout the day. Day care centers without such public access have been forced to adopt such policies to protect themselves, perhaps the only positive aspect to emerge from these prosecutions. In those cases resulting in conviction, jurors were able to suspend any rational disbelief that someone could have carried on in such a way without being noticed. One of the biggest strengths for the prosecution was that these children would go home every night to a parent or parents fully aligned with the prosecution theory; the story line would be reinforced at dinner, bathtime, playtime, bedtime (or in the case of Mary Ann Barbour, all night long). Any prosecution instructions to parents not to discuss the case with the children were likely to be ignored; it is clear that this was the case with at least one of the Little Rascals mothers interviewed by Bikel. The children were, of course, separated from further contact with the accused day care workers, and by the time of trial their young memories of the actual person had been replaced by the fictional person, if they could remember who the perpetrators were supposed to be at all. At one point in an interview of a Little Rascals child, the child pointed to a picture of the sheriff as one of the defendants; this identification was, of course, selectively ignored (Bikel).

Separation of defendants from family support has also been material for the prosecution in obtaining the few adult confessions that have been obtained in these cases.[30] In the Country Walk case in Dade County, Florida, seventeen-year-old Ileana Fuster was intensively reprogrammed by her defense attorney and several psychiatrists and psychologists during her one-year pretrial incarceration until she finally agreed to testify against her husband Frank Fuster (the original damning evidence against Frank Fuster was a throat swab test on a child that showed positive for gonnorhea; the test used has since been shown to be unreliable in producing a one-third rate of false positives).[31] Ileana was a Honduran immigrant without extended family or any other support from the "outside." Her confidant was "Mom Shirley," the chaplain at the jail (Shirley Blando, who tended to believe Ileana's protestations of innocence). One psychologist described Ileana as "an extremely needy child"; the psychologist said he could "get her to respond in any way that I pushed her."[32] Prosecutor Janet Reno obliged Ileana's need for the emotional support she had been deprived of by visiting her frequently in jail and holding her hand during her "confession" depositions (Nathan and Snedeker 169–77).[33]

In *The History of Sexuality*, Michel Foucault describes the approach of nineteenth century physician Jean-Martin Charcot in separating patients from their families:

> he sought to detach the sphere of sexuality from the system of alliance, in order to deal with it directly ... Charcot noted on several occasions how difficult it was for families to 'yield' the patient whom they nonetheless had brought to the doctor, how they laid seige to the mental hospitals where the subject was being kept out of view, and the ways in which they were constantly interfering with the doctor's work (112)

Charcot, like too many contemporary practitioners of the "healing" professions, assumes uncritically that the institution of medicine knows best: the family "system of alliance" must sometimes be broken for the better good of the patient. Though it may be done with good intentions, and some family "alliances" are undeniably abusive, the practice marks the site of contest between the apparatus of the state and the domain of the family. Certainly the family is itself an model that performs some of the ideological work of the state, but it can also, and sometimes should, be a site of resistance.

Where the focus of investigation is the home rather than the more public day care center, separating the child from the family has been key to obtaining evidence against parents, though these children, usually beyond the preschool age, are less suggestible than toddlers. Alicia Wade was taken away from her parents for two years until she agreed to accuse her father. Children who produce stories that both the parent figures and the authorities want to hear—Bobbie and Darla McCuan's cooperation in acceding to all the products of grandma Mary Ann Barbour's fevered imagination—sometimes get to stay home (with grandma Barbour, who had succeeded in getting them removed from their parents' home). But for the Kniffen boys of Bakersfield, who thought they were doing what they were supposed to just like Bobbie and Darla, the outcome was more disastrous. Brian Kniffen, now an adult, was six when the police took away his parents. He says his mother told him "Go with these people and do what they say. Then everything will be alright [sic] and we'll be back home." Investigators likewise told him that he would have to testify that his parents sexually abused him in order to be reunited with them; this statement by investigators was one of the primary reasons for the eventual reversal of his parents' convictions.[34] Brian did what he was told and his parents were in prison for fourteen years. Cutting off the lines of communication between Brian and his parents was essential to obtaining his testimony. His mother, at least (after fourteen years in prison), now knows better than to trust the authority of the state without question.

Certainly abuse does go on within family environments, where it is much easier to conceal than in a day care center. Increased attention to the problem of incest was a positive development in the seventies that somehow went wrong. There are cases where a child should be removed from the family environment, and making such a determination is not an easy task. But as Nathan and Snedeker point out, preventative strategies are more desirable than after-the-fact responses: not just "laundry lists of taboo body parts" but broader institutional steps to remediate poverty and the economic inequality of women that sometimes keeps them, with their children, in an abusive environment (251). Demonizing the day care workers went the wrong direction in engendering a paranoia that puts some children right back into an authoritarian and/or impoverished home environment where there may be a greater risk of abuse. This is even more troublesome when one considers that sexual abuse is not the only, nor even the worst, kind of physical abuse. We must not let puritanical and unrealistic notions of childhood "innocence" blind us to the fact that coercive sexual abuse is *not* a fate worse than death by shaking or bludgeoning.

The fallout of the ritual abuse prosecution hysteria has been pervasive and insidious in other ways as well. They broke up many marriages and families. If performing the investigation was "women's work," so, in the words of Nathan and Snedeker, "believing the children" was "women's work" as well. As investigations went on and on, the mothers of child witnesses became obsessed, introjecting the supposed harm on the child into themselves, utilizing therapy sessions to talk about negative sexual experiences from their own youths, and becoming alienated from their husbands (Nathan and Snedeker 120–123). Young children who had been taught to believe they had been abused became "severely disturbed," developing a variety of dysfunctional behaviors (123–126). Pre-school children indoctrinated with "good-touch, bad-touch" seminars came to believe that even being bathed by a parent was "bad" (127).[35] Teachers stopped hugging children. Professional day care workers changed careers; already working for minimum wage with minimum respect, many were driven out by parental suspicion, rising insurance premiums, and the costs of remodeling facilities to provide panoptic surveillance to protect themselves. Classist attitudes about low-wage workers helped fuel this outcome: a handout at an FBI-sponsored seminar on satanist ritual abuse in 1985 said that "while satanist men and women were generally intelligent, they were also 'working class' . . . 'underachievers' whose interest in the occult reflected their 'mediocre lifestyles'—which included the fact that they worked for minimum wage caring for other people's children" (130). Like the use of racial profiles in traffic stops, such notions among law enforcement are not likely to be published in criminology journals or given other official sanction. But they are present, nevertheless.

As in the early modern period when workers were moving from the countryside to urban areas, familial economies were stressed in the latter twentieth century. But there is another parallel between the recent prosecutions and the European witch-hunts. As juridical texts proliferated in the early modern period, Willis documents a shift from the village level demonization of the mother figure and her familiars to the elite texts in which male aristocrats place the malevolent mother in service of a male devil. Likewise, progression of fantasy demons from surrogate mothers to Satanic fathers parallels the course of child development as the child moves from phantasies about the "bad mother" to an entry into the world of the Law of the Father.[36] In a similar way, the focus of child sexual abuse prosecutions has shifted from real-life, guilty incestuous fathers, to day care mother surrogates, and back again to the father figures of the "recovered memory" cases. The latter-day Wenatchee prosecutions revolve around a pentecostal pastor as supposed ringleader of sadistic orgies in the church basement: Satan rises again to lead the coven. But even as the demon figure became male, the iconography metonymically sidestepped the sorts of abuse more likely to occur among paternal and paternalistic leadership figures. Orgies at church, like orgies in a day care center where people are often coming and going, would seem to cry out for discovery. Even without an innocent bystander walking in, the more people are involved, the more likely someone would talk about it. Abuse is much more likely to occur in private, a "secret" with a "trusted friend."

When sexual abuse by Catholic priests became public in Newfoundland, families of then-grown abused children said that their world was turned "upside down." They questioned the validity of their marriages, their sacraments, their confessions and penance. Since these supposedly sacred acts had been performed by priest using the trappings of religion to ensnare children, the sacred ceremonies were for these families transformed into black masses, Satanic rituals (Scheper-Hughes). And so Satanic ritual abuse has in fact been taking place in the eyes of Catholic believers; the Satanism hysteria is not so much a matter of seeing things in the shadows that do not exist, but of seeing cultural reflections mapped onto the bodies of more vulnerable scapegoats.

Janet Reno has serendipitously facilitated a further shift in the course of millenial American demonology. The "good mother" District Attorney who held Ileana Fuster's hand as Ileana confessed to Satan-praying, bird-slaughtering, and father-diapering (Nathan and Snedeker 108, 176) became for the moment, as Attorney General, the nation's official witch-burner in the case of David Koresh's coven of Christian fundamentalists in Waco, Texas on April 19, 1993. Acting on the heels of the breakup of the Soviet Union, Reno's act displaced the communist menace onto child abusers: she destroyed the village in order to save it. Perhaps Janet Reno has became the kind of "good mother/bad mother" the country could deal with because she is not a real mother. She had no "nanny problem" like the previous nominee Zoe Baird, nor any of the other personal peccadilloes likely to surface with sufficient investigation into the background of any working mother. The nation-as-family at that moment, with the good/bad Reno mother and the ineffectual Clinton dad, had the industrialized psychological counseling industry as spiritual advisor. But for some of those driven back to the bosom of the personal family as the only protection against the onslaught of outsiders, this model becomes the enemy against which isolation and insularity is a defense. Both the fear of perverted day care workers and the fear of doctrinaire social workers can contribute to such a retreat into insularity.

Looking at witchhunts across the centuries, analysts such as Levack, Demos, and Bromley all agree that major panics about such subversive activity occur in waves. True as this may be, the waves do not occur at random. It is likewise unlikely that sexual abuse of children by Catholic priests just started in the latter twentieth century. Whether it occurs in waves is perhaps unknowable. But the historical moment at which child sexual abuse achieved the status of a moral panic in the late twentieth century was marked not only by entry of more women into the workforce, but an accompanying moral panic over crime. It was not only women, and men in the "feminized" occupation of child care, who took the heat. The young, particularly youth of color, have been punished not just by child poverty but by their own burden of accursed demonization. The icon of young innocence transforms, around the age of onset of puberty, into the icon of the dangerous delinquent. As color of the icon concomitantly changes from white to black, the focus of suspicion shifts from the nurturer to the insufficiently nurtured.

Chapter Four
Motherhood and Treason
Pynchon's Vineland *and the New Left*

'Frailty, thy name is Woman!'
—Hamlet

Putting all fantasy aside, for what will Thomas Pynchon be remembered in one hundred years? Will it be for his role in the vanguard of the American postmodernists, or will it be as a historical novelist? His aspirations as interpreter of history have become clear with the publication of *Mason & Dixon* (1997) in which his narrator the Reverend Wicks Cherrycoke opines:

> History is not Chronology, for that is left to lawyers,—nor is it Remembrance, for Remembrance belongs to the People. History can as little pretend to the Veracity of the one, as claim the Power of the other . . . a Past we risk, each day, losing our forebears in forever,—not a Chain of single Links, for one broken Link could lose us All,—rather, a great disorderly Tangle of Lines, long and short, weak and strong, vanishing into the Mnemonick Deep, with only their Destination in common.
> —The Rev. Wicks Cherrycoke, *Christ and History* (MD 349)

Within this tangled web, Pynchon attempts no more than to bring to light occasional linear fragments. In *Vineland* (1990) his chosen filament is the history of the New Left and Pacific Coast counterculture. The book's opening epigram from blues singer Johnny Copeland—"Every dog has his day, and a good dog just might have two days"—echoes Hamlet's defeated concession to fate: "Let Hercules himself do what he may/The cat will mew and dog will have his day." In *Vineland* the dog is Brock Vond and he does have two days: the Nixon era and the Reagan era.

It is no longer any secret that the FBI operation COINTELPRO, initiated against the Communist Party U.S.A. in 1956 and against the Socialist Workers Party in 1961, expanded during the sixties well beyond the parameters of even politically motivated surveillance to rely on the use of informants and agents provocateurs to fuel, in the words of FBI Special Agent James O'Connor, "the paranoia endemic in these circles and to further serve to get the point across that there is an FBI agent behind every mail box" (qtd. in Davis 10).[1] At its worst, COINTELPRO encouraged New Left activists to plant bombs and provided them with assistance in doing so "in such a way that they would misfire and kill those who were doing the bombing" (151). Even after COINTELPRO officially ended in 1971, compelling evidence existed of a law enforcement conspiracy to produce a state of social unrest and paranoia sufficient to enable the government to round up dissidents, place them in secured facilities, and declare a state of martial law for an indefinite period (Davis 150–151).[2] Thus Pynchon's passages in *Vineland* about the concentration camp from which DL rescues Frenesi are more than mere figments of Pynchon's paranoid imagination. Something is, in fact, rotten in Denmark.

After Nixon's resignation such surveillance operations were impaired by the scrutiny of the Church Committee investigation (Senate and House Select Committees on Intelligence Activities), only to be renewed under Reagan in connection with CISPES (Committee in Support of the People of El Salvador) and related U.S. religious and other activist organizations (Gelbspan). Pynchon's novel, probably set in 1984 for the date's Orwellian resonance rather than for any historical significance specific to that year, focuses more on drug enforcement harrassment of the northern California counterculture than on the Central America movement. Nevertheless, the reempowerment of Brock Vond coincides historically with the more repressive role that the FBI, in conjunction with the Drug Enforcement Administration, reassumed in the early 1980s.

When a novelist who had already achieved fame for his elaborations of paranoid thought systems and their metaphysics in *V* (1961), *The Crying of Lot 49* (1966), and the Joycean *Gravity's Rainbow* (1973) turns for his subject matter to a law enforcement culture of sustained surveillance and proliferation of paranoia, one can reasonably expect a *tour de force* that will be taken seriously by Pynchon's diverse and widespread readership. Unfortunately the contemporaneous rise of postmodern theory, insofar as it takes its cue from the French poststructuralist questioning of the determinacy of textual meaning beyond self-referentiality, has sometimes distracted critical attention, even among those concerned with the politics of postmodernism, from more historicist-driven readings of *Vineland*. The elaborate systems Pynchon constructs do invite such postmodernist readings, but the novel is also important as an exercise in cultural memory. Remembrance may belong to the people, but Pynchon, as more than one critic has noted, is writing not just for those who lived through the sixties and post-sixties upheaval but also for subsequent generations that were not there (Hayles 14, Hite 149, 153 n32).

Linda Hutcheon argues that Pynchon's fiction collapses into "the ultimately closed, self-referring system." Claiming that its "intertextually overdetermined, discursively overloaded" nature" engenders "conspiracies that invoke terror in those subject (as we all are) to the power of pattern," she concludes that this "paranoia in the works of contemporary American writers" is "paradoxical" in that its "totalizing plotting is inscribed within texts characterized by nothing if not by overplotting and overdetermined intertextual self-reference" (17). Her point seems to be that the conspiracy plot of the text is itself conspiratorial in terrorizing (in the Lyotardian sense) the reader with the semblance of realism. But allowing that this may be true, the text is not thereby a closed system. Such a text, like any dystopean science fiction novel, functions as a warning and thus participates in politics rather than simply creating an aesthetic, unrelated simulacrum.

Baudrillard's concept of the simulacrum—that "the highest function of the sign is to make reality disappear, and at the same time to mask this disappearance" (188)—is pertinent here, though problematic in its characterization of this function as "highest." It is not Pynchon's project to make reality disappear; he cares deeply about history. As Terry Ceasar has pointed out vis a vis Baudrillard's statement, Pynchon "has refused to 'mask' either his own disappearance or that of his sign. Indeed, the fact that he has, on the contrary, just disappeared . . . guarantees not only his 'sign' but some reality outside it, to which it refers" (183). But on the other hand, *Vineland* does mask the disappearance of reality in unexpected and sometimes undesirable ways. The narrative may so distract the reader with improbable acts of transfenestration, a Japanese deus ex machina, and the walking dead as to mask the distortion of the history of the New Left that proceeds unnoticed or perhaps doubly masked by Pynchon's feminist good intentions. Specifically, it is the 'simulacrum' contained in the character of Frenesi Gates that, perhaps unwittingly, fulfills Baudrillard's expectation.

In general, Pynchon's expansion of the FBI's surveillance and infiltration of leftist political groups into a secret police infrastructure complete with its own highway system and underground detention camps is not so much paranoid fantasy as mere hyperbole. His depiction of the service and subservience of academia and the media to the capitalist real estate speculators and their police state are genuine political critiques—neither part of a "realist" Jamesonian master narrative nor part of a "postmodern" closed self-referential system. The feminist film collective is a bit romantic, perhaps according women a greater significance in the pre-feminist New Left than they actually had, but with good authorial intentions. But with Frenesi's hypersexuality and seduction by Brock Vond, the novel inserts a Mata Hari fantasy into the text that is jarringly inconsistent with both the subservient position of women in the New Left and with the actual psychological profile of the typical FBI informer.

In the novel Frenesi Gates, a California red-diaper baby from an IWW background, is a filmmaker with the feminist film collective 24fps. She is recruited by Brock Bond as an informant while imprisoned in the aforementioned underground detention camp. The reader eventually learns that prior to marrying Zoyd Wheeler and giving birth to Prairie she had brought about the death of Weed Atman, math-professor-turned-radical-leader at the College of the Surf located in a fictional region "bracketed by the two ultraconservative counties of Orange and San Diego" (204). Pynchon is having a bit of fun with the geographical location at the expense of the Marines, since this site is actually occupied by the Camp Pendleton Marine training base. But the death of Weed Atman is no joke; like the underground detention camp, it is merely hyperbolic in its historical reference.

The "jacketing" of problematic radicals by the FBI—"putting a jacket on them" by having FBI undercover operatives plant rumors that such persons are undercover agents—was a common technique and resulted in more than one shooting incident such as the one in which fellow activist Rex shoots Weed when Frenesi accuses him of being an informer. Sometimes the result of the "snitch jacket" was merely exile, as incurred by an unwitting activist at the Message Information Center in San Diego who had the bad luck to witness two separate arrests. The actual undercover informant at the Message Information Center (most likely Howard Berry Godfrey, discussed below) seized upon the opportunity to sow suspicion and was able to report to the FBI that the target was now "completely ostracized by members of the Message Information Center and all of the other individuals throughout the area . . . associated with this and/or related groups."[3] Along with the "snitch jacket," the FBI utilized the spread of insulting disinformation. For example, two Black Panthers were killed at UCLA and several months later, one Panther was killed and two were wounded in San Diego as a result of derogatory cartoons the FBI had been surreptitiously circulating and attributing to the Black Panthers and Ron Karenga's United Slaves Organization (Churchill and Vander Wall 42). But the FBI targeted activist college professors in particular, more often with anonymous letters to colleges and donors rather than with bullets. The best-documented case was the firing and subsequent blacklisting of Arizona State University philosophy professor Morris J. Starsky in 1970; FBI records obtained by the Socialist Workers Party over a decade later established that the FBI had sent anonymous letters containing "blistering attacks" to all five members of the faculty Committee on Academic Freedom and Tenure (Davis 59–60, Blackstock 175–176). But shots were fired into the house of San Diego State economics professor Peter G. Bohmer in 1972 by Howard Berry Godfrey, head of the counter-intelligence unit of the SAO (Secret Army Organization), a right-wing paramilitary group in San Diego and undercover informant for the FBI. A young woman in Bohmer's house was seriously wounded; Bohmer was not injured but was subsequently fired by the college president based upon reports supplied by the FBI. Despite three hearings vindicating Bohmer, state chancellor Glenn Dumke rejected the third hearing's findings and upheld Bohmer's dismissal. (Blackstock 15–16, Citizens Research 161–162).

Thus the Weed Atman shooting echoes incidents documented in the historical record of the southern California New Left: there were undercover informants, snitch jackets, shootings, and neutralizations of university professors. The only element Pynchon adds to the mix is the sexualizing of the undercover informant's relationship to the FBI. What were real informants like? If FBI informants who have achieved a degree of notoriety are at all representative of the "typical" informer, they would most likely be male and from unstable backgrounds like those of Louis Tackwood, a black Los Angeles street hustler held hostage to law enforcement by his criminal record (Citizens Research 61–70), [4] and Douglass Durham, the former Des Moines police officer fallen from grace when he beat his wife to death (Churchill and Vander Wall 220). Godfrey, the San Diego agent provocateur, was formerly a member of the right-wing Minutemen before (according to Godfrey) the Minutemen were "destroyed by Communists in the Justice Department" (Citizens Research 162). On the other hand, many of the "confidential informants" referred to in FBI files were actually undercover FBI agents.[5] Female FBI informants investigating the New Left did exist, but there is little evidence that they played a prominent role.[6] One reason was the inherent sexism of the FBI: there were few women agents and those who did exist "were a pretty straitlaced bunch" (331) according to former undercover agent Cril Payne, who asserts a further reluctance on the part of the FBI to recruit women as informants because "they were generally considered emotionally unsuited for such work" (204). The two female informants described by Payne who knowingly provided information to the FBI were both recruited from the "straight" world and sent underground. One was a bored WAVE from the Naval base at Whidbey Island and the other, "Spacey Tracey," had dated Payne before he went undercover; Payne describes her, prior to being "opened up," as "a naïve little Southern belle from Georgia. Very proper and a little slow." Spacey Tracey was later recruited as an informer by another agent, but became a "convert . . . gone over to the other side." (187, 184–85). This is not to say that FBI agents did not have sexual relationships with women in the underground. Judging from Payne's account, they went at it with gusto. But the agents were undercover, unlike Brock Vond, and the women provided information unwittingly.

The role of Frenesi Gates in Pynchon's text exemplifies his fascination with the sexual power of fascism, the S/M scenario. This theme was fully explored in *Gravity's Rainbow*. As Hite has pointed out, Frenesi has "Katje Borghesius's odds weighing turncoat mentality" and "Greta Erdmann's association of submission and abasement with transcendence" (140). But this aspect of Pynchon's work is ultimately even more depressing to the feminist reader than the *Gravity's Rainbow* denouement of annihilation from above. If the dialectical model of sexual dominance and submission is as accurate a model of the psychoanalytic workings of power as some Foudcauldians assert, the implications for the viability of political resistance or change are somewhat grim.[7] It is these implications for the viability of political resistance that make it important for readers to recognize that in Frenesi Pynchon is not representing a psychologically true picture of the relationship between the state and resistance groups other than in the sense that she functions as a fictive bridge for homoerotic contact.

From Frenesi's point of view, "Men had it so simple. When it wasn't about Sticking It In, it was about Having The Gun, a variation that allowed them to Stick It In from a distance" (241). But even Foucault himself does not give sexuality such a totalizing role in power relations: "Sexuality is not the most intractable element in power relations, but rather one of those endowed with the greatest instrumentality: useful for the greatest number of maneuvers and capable of serving as a point of support, as a linchpin, for the most varied strategies" (103). Even in *Vineland* there are other power strategies at work besides the sexual, most notably the vulnerability of parenthood exemplified in Zoyd's relationship with Prairie. But Brock Vond's sexual power over Frenesi overshadows this aspect of the text. As other critics have noted, Frenesi's sexual fascination with Brock Vond invokes the line from Sylvia Plath's "Daddy": "Every woman adores a fascist." But even in *Vineland* every woman does not adore a fascist—only Frenesi and possibly her daughter Prairie.[8] The narrator implies this predilection has been "spliced in a DNA sequence" (83) and if so, the gene has been passed on to Prairie who is saved only by improbable deus ex machina in the final pages. Having had her surfeit of family reunification, she takes her sleeping bag off into the clearing in a thicket where Brock Vond tries to sweep her up into his helicopter just when Reagan pulls the plug on the whole operation. Later, finally going to sleep, she whispers, "You can come back . . . It's OK, rilly, Come on, come in. I don't care. Take me anyplace you want" (384).

Molly Hite has written an excellent analysis of Frenesi's relationship to Brock Vond and the ways in which this aspect of the text are informed by two seminal, if one will pardon the expression, feminist texts: Sandra Gilbert and Susan Gubar's *The Madwoman in the Attic* (in this case, the female bats in Vond's belfry) and Eve Sedgwick's *Between Men*. Sedgwick's work is well known for its exploration of homoeroticism between male characters in fiction, particularly as performed through the body of a woman with whom they are both in some way involved. Indeed, the Sedgwickian implications of the relationship are hard to miss in the tender post-coital scene in which Brock tells Frenesi not to wash, knowing that she will be later consorting with Weed Atman: "You're the medium Weed and I use to communicate, that's all, this set of holes, pleasantly framed, this little femme scampering back and forth with scented messages tucked in her little secret places" (214). If that were not enough to get the point across, Frenesi's former female lover (and arguably the novel's heroine) DL later explains to Prairie, "this is some-thing else between men . . . Maybe your mom's only in there to make it look normal and human so the boys can go on discreetly porkin' each other" (265–66).

Hite argues that as in *V* and *Gravity's Rainbow*, Pynchon is "forcing under-standing of and even empathy for conventionally inconceivable acts" (140). Nevertheless, she duly notes that Prairie's fantasized submission to Brock "strik[es] a deeply problematic concluding note that suggests complicity may be as ingrained and inherent as mortality" (141), interpreting the DNA line about Frenesi's genes as support for this sort of species, as well as familial, flaw. Hite sees DL as a link between Frenesi and Prairie "who presents the possibility of alternative construc-tions" (143). But overall, Hite wants to absolve Frenesi and Prairie of their sins:

> In *Vineland,* complicity is a fact of life, but it is not inevitable any more
> than it is always advertent . . . Technology has brought government and
> corporate surveillance to such a pitch that snitching has become
> outmoded, if not redundant. On the other hand, in *Vineland* complicity

> is not by definition total and does not by definition rule out resistance. In contrast to *Gravity's Rainbow*, where the only possibility for opposition seemed rooted in a prehistoric, or pre-Western historic, purity, associated with primal Nature . . . , *Vineland* suggests that originary purity was always a delusion (147).

Hite's discussion is on target as far as identifying a central dilemma in the text, but she seems to conclude that the capacity for betrayal is a sort of original sin, perhaps by way of a sex-linked gene, for which forgiveness is the only answer.[9] N. Katherine Hayles likewise has followed this sort of redemptive theme in her essay aptly titled "'Who Was Saved?': Families, Snitches, and Recuperation in Pynchon's *Vineland*." The title question is the question Hector asks Zoyd, implying the ultimate failure of the sixties revolution.

Hayles articulates the subtly unsettling nature of the family reunification ending of *Vineland,* recuperative in the negative sense of "recovering, often obliquely or underhandedly, traditional values whose falsity has been demonstrated"(24–25). She will allow "the realization that apparently totalized structures have fissures that can be exploited for progressive purposes," but ultimately concludes that "at a time when the nation seems more conservative and capitalistic than ever, what is saved is not the vision that the sixties represented but a few moments of grace" (28).

Both Hayles and Hite try hard to find something good to say about Frenesi's betrayal of everything her family and her chosen profession stands for. Would even Sylvia Plath have gone so far for love of a fascist? Even if one were to apologize for Frenesi's acts by attributing them to the hostage syndrome, it is difficult to assent to Hite's characterization of her as "the most fully feminine character that Pynchon has created to date." Certainly, as she goes on to say in the rest of the sentence, Frenesi is "the character who most fully exposes the feminine as a necessary construction of the neo-fascist They-system" (Hite 140). But why give tacit assent to such a construction? Is Hite implying that femininity cannot exist outside such a construction, on its own terms?

In an earlier essay on Pynchon's women in *Gravity's Rainbow*, Marjorie Kaufman gives Pynchon credit for writing what one could call an equal opportunity novel (apparently in response to the question she was asked to write about) in that there are a variety of women characters who are "as 'round' as the male" (199). Yet she points out that among the many female characters, "The mothers are destroyers: They belong to 'Them'." Kaufman maps out a convincing patttern originating in Pynchon's earlier novel *V*:

> Thus for the child to love the Mother "They" made, it must love death-in-life and must hate or fear the fragile self that would oppose her. To love Mother is to love tyranny and oppression and wish to emulate its power, or to love the submission and humiliation the oppressor demands (211, 213).

This is indeed the tension that informs the relationship between Frenesi and her daughter Prairie; it offers a better explanation for Prairie's fascination with Brock Vond than the DNA hypothesis. But the Bad Mother is not Pynchon's invention. She is an old, old, story.

The story of Hamlet informs *Vineland* in several ways. Like the fall of the royal family of Denmark, the subject of *Vineland* is a story of national tragedy: leadership that loses the trust of the people through failure to keep its own house in order; leadership foundering in a morass of suspicion, accusation, and intrigue; leadership running out of places to bury its skeletons. Weed Atman, heir apparent of the new generation, has been killed through treachery before the novel begins, but his ghost still roams the pages seeking "karmic adjustment." Brock Vond, the usurper, is "porkin'" Frenesi, the queen of the underground, and it is fitting (the national graveyard being as full as it is) that Brock's ultimate fate lies in having his bones removed as he is carried off into the spirit world by Yurok ghosts.

The analogies of Pynchon's characters to Shakespeare's are not entirely consistent, but then, ambiguity and ambivalence in familial relationships abound in both texts. Hayles's commentary on the interchanges between the snitch system and the family system in *Vineland* illustrates the resonance of the themes of family and treason here. In *Hamlet,* Claudius murders his brother the king and marries "my sometimes sister, now my queen"; thus Hamlet becomes "a little more than kin and less than kind" to Claudius. The tension of uncertainty in familial hierarchy is echoed in *Vineland,* where the queen has a daughter rather than a son, and Prairie's biological paternity is unclear. Her biological father could be Weed Atman or possibly Brock Vond, but almost certainly not the father who raises her, Zoyd Wheeler, because he apparently meets Frenesi after she is already pregnant. Frenesi seems as much of a mother as a wife to Zoyd during their brief marriage in her emotional inaccessibility and his comparative naïveté. Certainly in the way he pines for her during the years after she has long since disappeared, Zoyd is behaving in a somewhat infantile manner, idealizing her memory almost beyond belief.

Like Hamlet, Zoyd performs the appearance rather than the reality of insanity with his annual transfenestration ritual. This ceremony of jumping through a window in order to maintain his mental disability status with the feds (and thus his stipend) is an arrangement imposed by Brock—symbolically, it can be read as a ritual castration in the sense that it keeps Zoyd separated from Frenesi. On the other hand, Zoyd's official career as a maniac hardly robs him of power against Brock since he never had any to begin with. Like Hamlet, Zoyd is ultimately unable to act: Brock is eventually done in by an utterly random deus ex machina (the Reagan administration withdraws the budget, leaving Brock literally hanging in midair).

The psychoanalyst who wrote *Hamlet and Oedipus,* Ernest Jones, approved T.S. Eliot's summary of Hamlet's mental state: "Hamlet's 'madness' is less than madness and more than feigned" (Eliot 146, qtd. in Jones 66)—a description that could also be applied to Zoyd, whose life, aside from parenthood to Prairie, has degenerated from impotent rage to chronic depression.[10] Jones notes that others have diagnosed Hamlet as a victim of "melancholia, and the likeness to manic-depressive insanity, of which melancholia is now known to be but a part, is completed by the occurrence of attacks of great excitement," though Jones himself, getting technical, asserts that Hamlet's moods oscillate too rapidly for this diagnoses and calls his disorder, instead, "a severe case of hysteria on a cyclothymic basis" (67–68). Jones was an early mentor of Melanie Klein, and his book on Hamlet, published in 1949, was a reworking of a paper he had written in 1908 undertaken in order to incorporate Klein's research on infant phantasies (Grosskurth 156). Nevertheless, though Jones utilizes Kleinian terminology in discussing the "splitting" of the mother image into an "inaccessible saint" and a "sensual creature accessible to everyone" (86), his overall picture of Hamlet's conflict is much more grounded in Freudian thought than Kleinian thought. He sees Hamlet's paralysis as based in repression of childhood Oedipal jealousy of Hamlet's father and incestuous thoughts about his mother; thus "the thought of incest and parricide combined is too intolerable to be borne" (70).

Kleinian psychoanalysis overall has been much more focused on the role of the mother than of the father; indeed, overzealous practitioners have been vulnerable to criticism for a universalizing of mother-blaming. But to take Jones's critique a step further, one could say that Hamlet's paralysis has more to do with his mother's acts than with repressed jealousy of his father. Compare Marjorie Kaufman's interpretation of Pynchon's destroying mothers: "for the child to love the Mother 'They' made, it must love death-in-life . . . to love Mother is to love tyranny and oppression and wish to emulate its power" (213). Hamlet's mother has committed treason, wittingly or not, by marrying the usurper/oppressor. Hamlet loves his mother, but he cannot kill the oppressor without hurting her—and she does, in fact, die as a by-product of his revenge. Frenesi's collaboration with the oppressor poses the same problem for both Zoyd and Prairie: neither can act against the usurper/oppressor without endangering her. Moreover, Frenesi's treason is entirely knowing. She may have been merely weak, a victim of the hostage syndrome, when Brock first seduced her ("Frailty, thy name is Woman!")—but there was no mistaking him for an ally.

The protagonist's impotence in both these texts—as in the early sixties film *The Manchurian Candidate*, produced in the heyday of Freudian psychoanalysis—is ultimately the mother's fault. In this context, whether the Bad Mother is a symptom of Oedipal or pre-Oedipal conflict is less to the point than why mother is so bad. Is Kaufman too kind to Pynchon in asserting that his women are no more evil than the men of the "They" system? Her essay was written before *Vineland* was published. Pynchon displays erudition on feminist issues in this novel, but a feminist reader cannot be happy with the feminizing of the turncoat upon which the plot turns.

Critics can agree that *Vineland* is a novel about loss of innocence. But they differ as to the implications of this observation. According to Hite, as aforestated, the novel suggests that "complicity is a fact of life, but it is not inevitable . . . and does not by definition rule out resistance ... originary purity was always a delusion." (147–148). Hanjo Berressem's analysis of the Frenesi-Brock relationship echoes Hite's allusion to flawed primal Nature. He correctly asserts that "the moment of the conception of betrayal (of Weed Atman) is the 'primal scene' and thus the central moment in *Vineland*" (*Pynchon's Poetics* 222). But Berressem's Lacanian analysis of Brock as master and Frenesi as hysteric leads to an implicit infantilization of the sixties movement. He describes *Vineland* as

> a book about the tragedy of growing up, as well as the tragedy of childhood ... *Vineland's* ultimate tragedy is that whereas growing up entails the loss of innocence from *within*, staying a child entails the loss of innocence from *without*, because as a child one is inevitably co-opted by the dominant culture. *Vineland* constantly thematizes this fateful complicity of innocence with power (230).

Berressem asserts that following Lacanian principles, revolutions such as the sixties movement "are started in the name of the pleasure principle, or real *jouissance*," a disavowal of the Name-of-the-Father doomed to failure (234). Frenesi, with her

> dreams of universal love and harmony, is caught in the hysteric's position and thus 'hystericized' by and in a phallocratic, Western society ... The tragic moment of *Vineland* is related to the fact that this position, rather than providing a 'counterforce' to the discourse of the master, is its perfect accomplice (218).

In another essay, discussing the thematics of eighties media in the novel, Berressem goes even further:

> *Vineland* as a historiographic metafiction mirrors the subject's inevitable ideological complicity in its writing ... In showing its own complicity with the media and its full immersion in them, it becomes a direct figure of this complicity ... Pynchon shows that historiographic metafiction cannot be used as an objective, analytic tool, because it has itself 'always already' lost its innocence ("'Forward Retreat'" 369).

Certainly *Vineland* is about the media and its complicity with the state apparatus, but one should not go so far as to say that Pynchon sees his own work as an extension of the state apparatus. Berressem's argument here illustrates the eventual inadequacy of Lacanian theory and concomitant aspects of postmodern critical theory to the task of accounting for agency and resistance in the adult world. So long as everything is "always already" accounted for, nothing ever changes. But things do change; all disavowals of the Name-of-the-Father are not doomed to failure. The United States got out of Vietnam. Nixon resigned.

Women became filmmakers. Single parents and blended families gained more acceptance. The counterculture survived in the Pacific coast region—the name "Vineland" carries all the nuanced connotations of a new frontier. The "mild herd creatures" whom Brock Vond sneers at (echoing Fredric Nietszche)[11] may still be with us, watching TV, but they may still inherit the earth.

There are more fruitful avenues than Lacan in psychoanalytic theory for discussion of power and desire in a political context. Pynchon acknowledges the anti-Oedipus paradigm by way of his allusion to Deleuze and Guattari: Prairie's boyfriend's band The Vomitones uses Deleuze and Guattari's *Italian Wedding Fakebook* at their command performance at the Italian gangster wedding. Deleuze and Guattari's real-life *work Anti-Oedipus: Capitalism and Schizophrenia* departs from the traditional psychoanalytic model of desire as sexual to a more holistically constituted subject as "desiring-machine" whose desire is

> produced, coded, and invested in the social field within different types of social organization . . . Thus the position of the family in relation to the economic, political, and cultural field is radically altered . . . desire is invested in two opposing ways: in paranoid investments, wherein desire inscribes itself on large 'molar,' statistical aggregates that are unifying or totalizing, and in schizophrenic investments where the flux of desire remains "molecular." (Johnston 80–81, 83).

Deleuze and Guattari's analysis bears some relationship to Wilfred Bion's analysis of large-group paranoia, which in turn evolves from Melanie Klein's work. Klein's concept of the fundamental nature of the "paranoid schizoid position" of infancy informs Hite's comment on *Vineland* that "originary purity was always a delusion." The paranoid schizoid position is the pre-Oedipal situation of the infant who desires to orally consume its mother's body or some reasonable facsimile thereof.[12] Thwarted, at least partially, in that desire, the infant develops aggressive fantasies toward the mother followed by guilt about the aggressive fantasies. The aggression is projected onto the mother so that the infant experiences paranoia in addition to guilt. The rest of psychic growth and development is concerned with making reparations for this primal combination of guilt and paranoia. This model of the infant psyche is relevant to the situation of an adult's response to trauma if one accepts the hypothesis that paranoid thought patterns may involve a regression to the infantile paranoid schizoid position. One can go further and apply the concept to the responses of larger groups to trauma and reconstructed memory.

Klein's work is most commonly applied in the contemporary clinical realm in the context of "object relations" theory, which loosely describes therapy to improve the way the patient relates to other people, particularly in families and other close relationships. In *Vineland*, the closest any of the characters come to redemption from guilt and paranoia is the Gates family reunion at the end of the novel. Like the family reunification scene at the end of Alice Walker's novel *The Color Purple*, the family, though the site of past trauma, is also the only possible site of redemption, reconciliation, and thus relief from psychic guilt. The guilt may be real guilt for real misdeeds, as in Frenesi's case, or psychic guilt (Zoyd and Prairie) resulting from the complex processes of splitting (idealization vs. aggression) that accompany trauma and loss.

The larger backdrop of characters in the novel, the "mild herd animals" of the sixties detention camps and the Thanatoids watching TV while awaiting karmic readjustment through the miracles of Japanese technology, are in a more problematic situation. As one Kleinian social psychologist explains, "the love and concern available in individual relationships is not available to the large group"; thus large groups become "morally impoverished." and "appeal to myths of rugged individualism" is "dangerous. For it encourages solutions—an actual or imagined withdrawal from public life—that can only make public life less manageable, an outcome that can only encourage further withdrawal" (Alford 19, 103). Does such moral impoverishment lead to a need for sociopolitical order, even fascism, as Brock Vond believes? The question is left unanswered in the text, but the developing relationship between bisexual wonder woman DL and Takeshi, the Japanese wizard of karmic adjustment, offers a hint of promise to the lost Thanatoids.

The Kleinian analyst whose work with group processes of paranoid or persecutory thought formation is best known is Wilfred Bion. Bion describes three basic patterns of group organization or aims: fight-or-flight groups, dependency groups (looking to one person as leader), and pairing groups that engage in an ambivalent witnessing of the romantic relationship of a pair. A given group may shift frequently from one aim to another.[13] In *Vineland* all three patterns appear at one time or another. The film collective fps is probably the most functional fight-or-flight group in the text, despite Frenesi's betrayal. The dependency group is best articulated in Brock Vond's opinion of the "mild herd creatures" in whom he sees "not threats to order but unacknowledged desires for it . . . Brock saw the deep . . . need only to stay children forever, safe inside some extended national Family . . . men who had grown feminine, women who had become small children, flurries of long naked limbs, little girls naked under boyfriends' fringe jackets" (269). This infantilization approximates the psychological regression every fascist dreams of, and the subtext lurking behind the distancing between Brock's voice and the narrative voice is the presidency of Ronald Reagan and the childishness of the TV culture over which he presides. Finally, the ambivalent witnessing of romantic pairing is split into two pairs: the Zoyd/Frenesi axis of persecution, masochism and unrealistic idealization and the Takeshi/DL axis of bionic woman-power and the wonders of Japanese technology. The idealistic hope articulated by this pairing is undercut by the ambivalence of the two characters themselves: they fend off consummating their relationship like Mulder and Scully in *The X-Files*.

The theme of attempting to replace the reparative "love and concern" traditionally found in the family with something from a larger group is present in much of DeLillo's work as well. This fundamental need is related to the seeking out of patterns and larger designs that is a feature of "paranoid" literature. As Scott Sanders has said of Pynchon's earlier work, "God is the original conspiracy theory . . . paranoia is the last retreat of the Puritan imagination" (140). This is so not only in Sanders's sense of the substitution of a demonic plan for a divine one, but in the sense that Puritan thought locates the devil within the Puritan subject. The Puritan heritage of the Pynchon family is well known; his ancestor William Pynchon, magistrate at one of the witchcraft trials, "becomes William Slothrop" in *Gravity's Rainbow* (Pearce 3–4).[14] Pynchon's novels are informed by Henry Adams's concept of philosophic tracks—the "visible tracks" of history, as first noted by Tony Tanner in the influential essay on *V* describing "the need to see patterns which may easily turn into the tendency to suspect plots" (153–154). There is, then, a relationship between the construction of pattern in fiction—plotting—and the psychological need for such patterns in real life "to give shape to reality." Perhaps Tom LeClair's model of "systems theory" as the means of looking at postmodern fiction as "aspects of a larger reconstructive impulse" (xi, 8) will provide a useful template upon which to plot models of small and large group reconfigurations and their dynamics of power and desire. Certainly "systems"—the "They-system" and the oppositional, carnivalesque "We-system" described by Pirate Prentice in *Gravity's Rainbow* (638) are central to Pynchon's ontology. As Mark Siegel interprets Pynchon's "creative paranoia,"

> First, some sort of 'paranoia,' an oversensitivity to patterns, is necessary for the investigation of reality . . . Second, we must create a We-system in order to counter Their strategy and to keep our paranoia from devouring us. The We-system . . . does not proceed rationally . . . but it appears to function, at least on one level, simply by violating the behavior that They would predict (19).

Siegel's interpretation of the narrator of *Gravity's Rainbow* as "a contemporary individual trying to invent, to 'assemble' a self" (124) parallels a Kleinian account of ego formation. His use of the term "devouring" is particularly resonant of the Kleinian description of the Other as the "bad breast" threatening to devour or consume the infant. The infant starts with a confusing array of multiple "objects"—psychic building blocks—that must be reduced into a concept of self and other. Through the psychological processes of introjection and projection, a sort of out-with-the-bad and in-with-the-good psychic calisthenics, the infant matures into a concept of self described as the paranoid-schizoid position. This, however, is just an early stage: ego formation in the Kleinian scheme does not really begin until the infant moves on to the depressive position, in which psychic guilt is experienced for the hostile projection of bad objects into the Other ("bad breast" in strictly Kleinian terminology) and the concomitant aggressive phantasies directed toward the Other.[15]

Thus those who perceive Pynchon's novels as somewhat infantile are in a sense correct. Paranoia is the universal state of mind of early infancy. But psychic regression has long been understood as a response to trauma, and such regression can be productive. Where a real enemy exists, the thought processes of paranoia are a useful, if not strictly logical, response. On the other hand, while Pynchon's paranoid explorations may be playfully phantasmagoric, they are not psychotic in the sense of being disconnected from reality. Though the novel may be problematic in its mother-blaming aspect, it is far more than the nostalgic novel for hippie has-beens described by some early reviews.[16] It is a narrative of trauma and recovery, a recovery more successfully negotiated within the novel at the family level than at the large-group level.

Conspiracy theories such as Pynchon's can function as historically specific modes of resistance. The conspiratorial constructions that can be superimposed on witches or immigrants can be more directly aimed at the dominant power structure, as Pynchon is clearly doing. They employ tools—hyperbole, irony, destabilization of the realist paradigm—that are more commonly recognized as tools of ethnic minority writers who are tapping into literary traditions outside the Enlightenment, realist heritage of white American writers. But such literary techniques are emblematic of a larger concept of minority discourse as discourse that resists the dominant paradigm, probing its flaws, seeking out in "apparently totalized structures," as Hayles says of Pynchon, "fissures that can be exploited for progressive purposes" (28).

Be that as it may, conspiracy theories, as resistance or otherwise, are benign neither in origin nor in effect. For readers, *Vineland* may succeed to some extent at destabilizing, through humor, some of the real residual fear of the FBI and government infiltration among many activists. But the novel is too easily misunderstood by those who were never subject to government surveillance and persecution. It is driven not so much by nostalgia as by the sort of disengagement and resort to fantasy often associated with psychological disintegration under torture. When this relationship to real history is ignored or misunderstood by readers, the effect may be mere titillation or, at worst, one more opportunity to blame the mother for everything that went wrong.

Chapter Five

Motherhood and Terror

Silko's Almanac of the Dead

Almanac of the Dead is a difficult novel to read, not solely because of its length. Those who get past the Demerol and cocaine scenarios in the opening pages are just as likely to founder by the time they reach the clitorodectomy description in the first passage about the mutilation video industry. Critical response to the novel tends to focus on this aspect and, indeed, it can hardly be ignored. Janet St. Clair says the novel "portrays a nightmarish wasteland of violence, bestiality, cruelty, and crime" ("Death of Love" 141). Sven Birkerts calls it "a veritable 'Satyricon' of late-century sexual and narcotic practices" (40). John Skow remarks that the novel always portrays white culture as "murderous, corrupt, mad with greed and hideously perverted" (86), but in fact the same can be said of most of the mixed blood and Native characters.

One might be tempted to conclude that male critics in particular are disturbed when women write about such things. But horror and perversion are not totally testosterone-related—one can get a good dose of them from reading Melanie Klein's accounts of the play-fantasies of preschool children from respectable middle-class families. Klein's work, as well as Julia Kristeva's, is illuminative in describing the terror of the prelinguistic state of infancy: the liminal state between nonexistence and self-awareness that constitutes the aftermath of the birth trauma. Silko's novel can be read in the context of disturbed relationships with maternal objects—including the Earth figured as maternal.

Published in 1991 and a decade in the making, Silko's novel has a couple of nasty European-Argentinian aristiocrats masterminding an escape to outer space as revolutionary forces massing in Chiapas commence the march north to the U.S. This facile description hardly does justice to everything going on in the novel, but does help to focus on the significant image of the repressed racialized other returning to threaten the integrity of the boundaries of the national symbolic. This border crossing resonates with the anxiety over psychic borders represented by what Klein calls the "paranoid schizoid position": the psychological liminal state mapped onto the liminal 'state' of Arizona. *Almanac* is a dystopian/utopian novel that in some ways evolves from the revolutionary fantasies of the mid-seventies expressed in Nasnaga's *Indians' Summer* (1975), the post-Wounded Knee, pre-bicentennial novel in which armed Indians reestablish national sovereignty on reservation land. Silko's novel is so wide-ranging, almost eight hundred pages in length, that it exceeds generally acceptable bounds of authorial control, as Silko herself has acknowledged in saying that the spirits seemed to have taken over at some point during the writing process (Irmer).

Silko's term for the world of perversion in which the revolution takes place is "witchery," a concept introduced in her first novel *Ceremony*. Witchery is not gendered female in the southwestern Native tradition, as it is in dominant EuroAmerican discourse. Silko's witches are more often, though not always, male. Witchery is more than the mere practice of witchcraft, though witches and witchcraft are a prominent feature of Native spiritual belief in the American southwest. The term more accurately describes a poisoned spiritual environment offering only limited opportunities for intervention by individual agency. To live in such an environment evokes the powerlessness of infancy—the "paranoid-schizoid position" in Klein's terms, or what Julia Kristeva describes as a liminal world of primal terror—this is why *Almanac of the Dead* articulates so many paranoid narratives and conspiracy theories.[1]

Writing for *Time*, Skow describes Silko as "very angry," writing with "exultant rage" of the "fury of Native Americans from Mexico to Alaska who have had to live for 500 years on what she sees as an infected continent." But this perception of Silko's attitude seem remote from the way that she describes the novel in interviews. Skow's defensiveness evokes Klein's description of the infant's fear of the "bad breast" coming after it in retaliation for the infant's hostile aggressive fantasies: Skow projects hostility into Silko's authorial stance as if she is angry at him. This is not to say that Silko is not angry, but hers is an anger reflected upon in tranquillity. Not all poetry is beautiful; the poetry of horror and destruction can be found in Hindu mythology, for example, and no one claims that it was conceived or written in a state of exultant rage.

How would Silko's novel be interpreted if it had been published under a name like, say, Don DeLillo? Critics might remark that he has applied his postmodern tools—hyperbole, irony, destabilization of the realist paradigm, the paranoid epistemology—to the challenging task of bringing attention to the plight of the Native American—etc., etc. In other words, a white man's postmodern irony is an Indian woman's "exultant rage," just as a loud angry white man is deemed powerful or eloquent while a loud angry white woman is deemed shrill or strident. Silko's novel is as fully a part of the postmodern genre as of the genre of Laguna or American Indian storytelling, and it offers a case study in what the two have in common, employing strategies of irony, hyperbolic excess, and defamiliarization[2] as cosmic figures are radically reconstructed out of mythical time and into the late twentieth century.

Silko's literary erudition should not be underestimated, though there is sometimes a tendency to stereotype Native writers as Rousseau-esque "primitives." On one occasion one of her undergraduate professors, listening to the argument of one critic who could not believe she could have had Joyce's *Portrait of the Artist as a Young Man* in mind when she wrote *Ceremony*, was compelled to inform the critic that she had indeed read Joyce in his class.[3] On the other hand Richard Rorty, discussing *Almanac of the Dead* along with the work of other postmodern novelists (Neal Stephenson, Thomas Pynchon, Norman Mailer) implies that Silko has been reading too much recent European philosophy, or at least that she has too much in common with those who have: "those who find Foucault and Heidegger convincing often view the United States of America as . . . something we must hope will be replaced" (7). Whether or not she is unduly enamored with these particular philosophers, Silko is undeniably well read in European philosophy and literature. She read a Scandinavian version of "The Twilight of the Gods" when she was in fifth grade, a story which she found very foreign and disturbing (Seyersted 5, 42–43); she likes Hume and Spinoza (Silko and Wright), considers Wittgenstein a poet (Barnes 62), and studied post-Einsteinian physics concerning space-time while writing *Almanac* (Coltelli 138). Silko's novel has Nietzschean overtones in the sense that Beaufrey and Serlo seem to have Zarathustran qualities.

Another problem in interpretation of this novel is the tendency to read it from the perspective of a realist tradition in American literature. The text has "realist" aspects in that it is a political novel, its author offering a sociopolitical critique that examines imperfection in excruciating detail. But the author is also writing from the site of a rich tradition of Pueblo (Keres) oral literature, the context of which is obvious in her prior fiction but that critics have tended to overlook or at least minimize in interpreting *Almanac of the Dead*. In this respect, Silko's work is reflective of that of many women writers, particularly women of color, who incorporate folklore and family stories into narrative fiction. Women were the primary storytellers in Silko's family, as they are in many cultures.[4]

Likewise, a familiarity with folklore in general—not solely Native American folklore—affords a better understanding of the tone of the narrative. Hyperbole and irony are staples of the oral tradition in American frontier folklore, and so it should not be surprising that they are features of American Indian folklore as well. Absurd sexual humor as a particular variety of such tropes is pervasive in American Indian folklore, as it is in many folklore traditions. It plays a prominent role in *Almanac of the Dead*, making fun of the enemy's sexual proclivities is one of the oldest forms of rhetorical excoriation. Of course, hyperbole and irony are also staples of speculative fiction. Consider, for example, the sexual excess of Rabbit in Marge Piercy's *Woman on the Edge of Time*—he is friend, not enemy, but the hyperbole is a part of the overall feminist dynamic of the novel. Silko's hyperbole plays on all frequencies, from the narrow-band absurdity of the federal judge with his harem of basset hounds to the wide-band scope of the exodus of Mexican *indigenas* from the accursed ruins of the Aztec empire northward to the United States.

Jean Francois Lyotard has remarked that "capitalism inherently possesses the power to derealize familiar objects, social roles, and institutions to such a degree that the so-called realistic representations can no longer evoke reality except as nostalgia or mockery, as an occasion for suffering rather than for satisfaction . . . This theme is familiar to all readers of Walter Benjamin." (74). The theme is likewise familiar to American Indians such as Silko who view capitalism as a disease of patriarchal European colonialism (at the same time viewing Marxism as yet another product of a fevered European mind). Consider one of the least "Indian" of Silko's settings: the luxury ocean view condominium north of San Diego, one of the playgrounds of degenerate European aristocrats Beaufrey and Serlo. The condo is a sort of restaurant at the end of the universe from which these colonial traders in cocaine and body parts can oversee their transcontinental operations while patronizing the "arts": young David's photography. The scenes that transpire at this condo are realist in the sense that they portray, with convincing verisimilitude, capitalism at its worst: predatory and beyond the bounds of the law. The oversized bathtub, the furnishings, the ocean view—all accoutrements, like the unlimited supply of cocaine, of the successful capitalist—are defamiliarized and mocked through the cocaine, marijuana, and alcohol induced haze through which they are experienced by the young naifs Seese and Eric. Seese, whom I will argue is yet another of Silko's Yellow Woman characters, falls asleep in the bathtub; while almost freezing to death there due to her drug-induced oblivion, she dreams of wandering naked at a ski resort, having lost sight of her aviator father in his dress uniform (49). Seese has many dreams in this condo; it is a cold nest of capitalism's excess wherein she becomes increasingly detached from reality as she suffers over the loss of her kidnapped baby and the suicide of her friend Eric.

Lyotard's critique of the grand narratives evokes a terror of the real: that is, a terror of what Fredric Jameson critiques as the master narrative of realism. Lyotard describes the desire for Hegelian "real unity" as an illusion that brings "terror." He fears "the mutterings of a desire for the return of terror, for the realization of the fantasy to seize reality" (81–82). The genius of Silko's novel lies in its harnessing of the tools of epic narrative, the realist novel, and the science fiction novel,[5] not to fulfill a fantasy to seize reality, but to explore the terror of the real by way of reality's descent into the terror of the liminal: the borderline, abject spaces of psychic and physical disembodiment and disintegration.

Sven Birkerts asserts that Silko's "premise of revolutionary insurrection is . . . naïve to the point of silliness. The appeal to prophecy cannot make up the common-sense deficit" (42). But the "common-sense" question becomes somewhat irrelevant if one approaches the novel with the premise that spiritual or psychic space-time is "real" and it is the corporeal world that is illusion (that is, a floating chain of signifiers). Silko has repeatedly made the point that for her storytelling is a way of making things happen; thus to call the indigenous latino revolution that occurs in the novel "prophecy" (in the sense that it re-tells southwestern tribal prophecies about the disappearance of "all things European" from the continent) is somewhat beside the point.

An entrance into the spiritual world of American Indian ontology can be found by way of psychoanalytic theory, insofar as it explores the liminal states of consciousness that mark the border between being and not-being of individual consciousness or ego. As Bakhtin has noted, "the most intense and productive life of culture takes place on the boundaries" (2), and Silko's novel is a border text, not only geographically, racially, and culturally, but psychologically and aesthetically as well.[6] What Freud calls "dreamwork" can as easily describe the coding of the fragmented passages of the Almanac, a fifth portion of the Mayan Codices which Silko puts in the possession of the two mixed blood Yaqui sisters Lecha and Zeta. Likewise, much of the novel consists of dreams and visions of various characters, and some of the characters are shapeshifting avatars or incarnations of characters from Keresan cosmology. This is what Lecha, the TV psychic, says about Freud (narrated from Seese's point of view):

> Lecha had got herself warmed up. Freud had interpreted fragments—images from hallucinations, fantasies, and dreams—in terms patients could understand. The images were messages from the patient to herself or himself.
>
> Lecha continued with her crackpot theories: Freud had sensed the approach of the Jewish holocaust in the dreams and jokes of his patients. Freud had been one of the first to appreciate the Western European appetite for the sadistic eroticism and masochism of modern war. What did Seese think Jesus Christ symbolized anyway? (174)

This is what Freud says about the "primitive" mind:

> ... It was not until a language of abstract thought had been developed, that is to say, not until the sensory residues of verbal presentations had been linked to the internal processes, that the latter themselves gradually became capable of being perceived. Before that, owing to the projection outwards of internal perceptions, primitive men arrived at a picture of the external world which we, with our intensified conscious perception, have now to translate back into psychology (85–86).

One need not denigrate a Native ontology as quaint or "primitive" (as do not only Freud but many anthropologists) in order to approach its verbal presentations as "the projection outwards of internal perceptions." Likewise, with all due respect to Freud's revolutionary insights, one can proceed much further into the liminal world of internal perceptions by departing from classical Freudian theory and adopting the Kleinian premise that there is no such thing as "primary narcissism." Primary narcissism describes, for Freud, a stage of early infancy "before there is a recognition by the infant of an object, and when the infant's own ego is taken as the object of libidinal love" (Hinshelwood 354). Klein, on the other hand, asserts that an infant engages in object relations with "part-objects" which are "identified with a part of him" (Hinshelwood 355). The infant lives in a world of "phantasy" which is unconscious at least in the sense that it is pre-linguistic; Klein uses the 'ph' spelling to distinguish the term from conscious fantasy.

The connection between object relations theory and Native ontology can perhaps best be explained by way of Julia Kristeva's concept of the abject, informed, in turn, by Mary Douglas's observations in *Purity and Danger* about the function of purification rituals.[7] The source of what Kristeva calls abjection is "what disturbs identity, system, order. What does not respect borders, positions, rules. The in-between, the ambiguous, the composite" (4). The abject is what is "jettisoned" from the subject as intolerably "opposed to *I*': the jettisoned object is radically excluded and draws me toward the place where meaning collapses" (1–2). Kristeva is generally referring here to bodily by-products usually considered disgusting or repellent: urine, feces, vomit, phlegm, blood, and especially menstrual blood. Kristeva's abject is akin to Klein's part-objects: literal or representational parts of the body that must be expelled. Thus the liminal infant psyche (and the same can be said of the borderline personality), must expel these bad part-objects in order to maintain her identity. This fundamental liminal state is one of primal terror: terror of the "immemorial violence with which a body becomes separated from another body in order to be" (10).[8]

Witchcraft among Indians of the American southwest is very much concerned with both the by-products of the body and the insertion of foreign objects into the body: a bad witch puts things into a victim's body, and a healer can get such things out.[9] At one point in *Almanac of the Dead* Mosca, one of the minor characters, is beset by a spirit which has settled in his shoulder, giving him a literal pain in the neck but also relaying information to him (606). Though a minor character in the novel, Mosca is an important character in terms of the connections being drawn herein between the paranoid state and the spirit world of the Keres oral tradition. "Mosca," of course, means "Fly."[10] In both *Ceremony* and *Storyteller*, Fly appears as a messenger to the fourth world, the first four worlds being underneath the world that we live in, which is the fifth world. In the Keres creation story of the Emergence, the people emerge into this world from a hole in the ground. In Silko's story, Fly and Hummingbird have to find tobacco to bring to Grandmother Spider Woman (below in the fourth world) in order to placate her because she is upset with the humans. In *Almanac of the Dead*, the alienated, twentieth-century Mosca flits around in his truck in death-defying trajectories while abusing practically every type of substance except tobacco. Meawhile, he tells his friend Root his theories about witches and ghosts, "Zombies, open graves, and ghost armies traveling in green fireballs" (602). His body is so full of natural electricity that wristwatches cannot keep time on his arm (605). Mosca says that the dead souls of Europeans are unhappy on the American continent because they are outnumbered and because their families do not honor them, so they travel restlessly and cause trouble (603–4). Mosca can identify witches only when he is in a moving vehicle, often by a flash or a glow (601–2) or by eye contact—though the first witch he says he ever saw seems dressed remarkably like a priest, wearing a "long black skirt" (209).

Root calls Mosca a racist (212) and thinks he is crazy and paranoid. Root and Calabazas, the old Yaqui smuggler, laugh at him though they "should have known better" (609). Mosca does not trust anyone and is unable to form close relationships with women. He blames his mother's schizophrenia for his short stature and his inability to trust people: "Mosca's mother had betrayed Mosca when she had conceived him in the swirling rainbows of her deranged blood" (610–11). In this image Silko connects the visionary capabilities of Mosca's mother, an otherwise obscure and invisible figure in the text, to the ways in which such connections with the spirit world can interfere with the ability to be a good mother, as is also the case with Lecha. Mosca has an impaired relationship with his mother, as do the vast majority of the characters in the novel, and virtually all of those whose mother is mentioned at all. This circumstance is significant to Silko's representation of the witchery that has plagued the continent for half a millenium, because without a functioning relationship with his or her mother, each of these characters—Mosca, Root, Lecha, Zeta, Seese, Beaufrey, and Serlo—is condemned, in various respects, to life in the liminal world of terror represented by an improper emergence into (or orientation within) ego consciousness or, if one prefers, the symbolic order. Silko comes from a matrilineal culture and it is consistent with this perspective that she does not perceive the symbolic order of consciousness in terms of the phallus.

Lecha's condition is the key not only to the suffering she undergoes from her psychic powers and her attempts to alleviate this suffering with drug abuse, but also to the psychic significance of drug abuse for other characters. Lecha says she has cancer and spends most of her time in a wheelchair. Whether or not she has cancer, something is gnawing at her insides, and she tries to deaden the pain with narcotics. In the opening kitchen scene her twin sister Zeta is dying all her clothes black with dye "the color of dried blood" (1). Meanwhile, as Lecha's amateur nurse and secretary Seese administers Lecha's injection at the kitchen table, Lecha's son Ferro, "says the needle slips in like a lover's prick and shoots the dope in white and hot … *he* doesn't watch junky orgasms not even for his *own* mother" (2). But white is the color of milk as well as semen, and Lecha's name (milk is 'leche' in Spanish) evokes birth and infancy even as Zeta's name and her "dying" operation at the stove evokes death and the death drive that, in Kristeva's model, the infant psyche struggles against.

Lecha and Zeta, birth and death, are the twin granddaughters of the old Yaqui witch and resistance fighter Yoeme, who was given in marriage as a sort of hostage spy to the diabolical Guzman, the white enslaver of Mexican Indians in silver mines. Their mother Amalia is a sketchily drawn character for whom the twins have no respect; Yoeme says dismissively of her daughter Amalia that as a baby she was "always crying and puking milk" (130)—rejecting her maternal heritage. But

Yoeme had deserted Amalia and the rest of her children when she left Guzman (after he started hanging her relatives) and took refuge with the Indians in the hills; Amalia barely remembers her. Amalia suffers from horrible stomach pains; Yoeme says that the pain is "actually a jaguar that devoured a live human from the inside out" (116). The twins' father is a white geologist from the United States found mummified in a hotel room: "the man had dried up inside . . . crackled, full of the dry molts of insects . . . they had both felt it: somewhere within him there was, arid and shriveled, the imperfect vacuum he called himself" (120). He had been struck by an "ailment" or curse

> common among those who had gone into caverns of fissures in the lava formations; the condition had also been seen in persons who had been revived from drowning in a lake or spring with an entrance to the four worlds below this world . . . witchcraft was not to blame. The white man had violated the Mother Earth, and he had been stricken with the sensation of a gaping emptiness between his throat and his heart.
>
> Zeta could feel an empty space inside her rib cage . . . (121)

If Zeta is now missing a rib, this image offers an interesting reversal of the patriarchal myth of Eve's creation from Adam's rib. But if Mother Earth has taken one of Zeta's ribs, what will be created with it? In a larger sense, departing from Judeo-Christian mythology, these images are consistent with the language Klein, Winnicott and other object relations theorists use to describe the psychic world of internal objects. According to Klein, loved ones are internalized by phantasy as actual objects within the body and when one dies this empty space must be negotiated through a grieving process. Zeta's father dies, and Zeta feels emptiness. But these characters—Zeta, Lecha, their mother, and their father—all have disturbed relations with the maternal, and suffer the consequences of a bad internal object. Lecha additionally suffers the burden of psychic powers, a "gift" from Yoeme, which enable her to find only the dead and not the living. She blames herself for many years, thinking that it is her thought processes which are killing the victims of various and sundry atrocities, but Yoeme eventually confirms her understanding that these events are entirely beyond her control (582).

Lecha's introjection of drugs attempts to compensate for the absence of "good" internal objects. The drug use of other characters is consistent with this model of understanding. Intravenous injection particularly has a violent aspect that resonates with the nature of phantasies involving objects invested with the hostility and aggression originating in the individual's own psychic makeup. Mosca says that a gunshot wound initially feels like "good dope right in the vein" (204). An infant wants to incorporate the Other into itself and conceptualizes the other in binary terms of good/bad, satisfction/deprivation. Phantasies of devouring its primary Other, that is, what Klein and her followers call the breast (whether one calls this a death drive as Freudians and Kristeva do or simply a drive of aggression or undirected want) lead the infant to then fear retaliatory hostility from the object of its desire. Thus is Klein's fundamental "paranoid schizoid position" of early infancy, followed by a "depressive" position when the infant begins to feel guilty about having the hostile thoughts. When phantasies progress to introjection and projection of various good and bad objects, the boundaries of identity become disturbed and indeterminate, as is the case with Lecha. She is literally bombarded with incoming images of dead bodies and body parts which then consume her from within; she alleviates the pain with introjection of narcotics which provide immediate relief and also ward off the incoming images by crowding them out.

Zeta, on the other hand, is concerned with identity boundaries of a different sort. She is a professional smuggler violating the boundaries of the national body, a border which is an abomination to her and her fellow Yaquis as it violates their own geographic tribal integrity. She and her nephew Ferro smuggle a wide variety of artifacts, including drugs and guns, but never people because they perceive it as too risky. Zeta, Ferro, and their fellow *coyote* Calabazas are not, however, the only smugglers in the novel. Practically all of the vast assortment of nefarious villains are involved in it, but drugs and guns are only a backdrop in this broader picture to the brokering of torture and mutilation videos and an international market in body parts for transplant.

Conspiracy theories about an international black market in body organs abound in the third world and in the tabloid media, with some basis in fact.[11] The actual medical practice of organ transplants in recent decades, and the demand thereby created for organs, offers just the sort of psychological catalyst likely to result in hysteria among oppressed or traumatized groups, given the close relationship between the conceptualization of internal objects at the phantasy level and circumstances of impaired power and fear. This is particularly true in poverty-stricken third world communities that, having already been robbed of the world's wealth, have little else to be stolen besides their bodies. Symbolically, sweatshop workers in the global economy *are* being robbed of their body parts: their sweat, their health, their youth, their children. Defining the transaction by the pound of flesh is almost remedial in the sense that price and quantity are at least calculable.

Silko has said that she had originally planned to write a cops-and-robbers thriller about Tuscon drug trafficking (Irmer and Schmidt, 153). But some of the underworld characters came to take on the epic and cosmic proportions consistent with the way that the rest of the book evolved. The priapic paraplegic Trigg (aka "Steak-in-the-Basket") who actually performed a good portion of the "wet end" blood and organ harvest in the basement of his Tuscon enterprise Blood Plasma International, embodies a singular synecdoche for the "Vampire Capitalists" denounced in a different section of the novel. But his evil perversions pale in comparison to the masterminds Beaufrey and Serlo, South American descendants of the European aristocracy. Beaufrey in particular seems to have sprung full-blown from the womb as the incarnation of a Destroyer, representative of those understood by the indigenous people of Chiapas as "humans who were attracted to and excited by death and the sight of blood and suffering . . . The European invaders had brought their Jesus hanging bloody and dead from the cross; later they ate his flesh and blood again and again . . . Typical of sorcerers or Destroyers, the Christians had denied they were cannibals and sacrificers" (475). Beaufrey makes no pretense of being a Christian. The most primary of narcissists if ever there were one, he "had always loved himself, only himself. He could remember lying in a crib sucking on his own hand, perfectly content . . . He felt indifferent toward his mother and father, and the kindest nannies" (533). He teaches himself to read by the age of three and by age eight tells his psychiatrist that his favorite book is about a cannibal named Albert Fish, descended from *Mayflower* blue bloods, who likes to roast the arms and legs of children. Beaufrey views Albert Fish as a "kindred spirit" sharing his "complete indifference about the life or death of other human beings" (534).

Serlo, on the other hand, is assisted by his grandfather to this sublime lack of empathy for other humans. Abandoned by his divorced parents to this grandfather who "did not consider massaging the boy's arms and legs at night homosexuality," Serlo grows up with "fetishes of purity and cleanliness; there were insinuations his sex organ touched only sterile, prewarmed stainless steel cylinders used for the artificial insemination of cattle" (547). Serlo is better connected with the old aristocracy than Beaufrey; he is acquainted with South African researchers who have developed the HIV virus and deployed it into African blood and blood plasma supplies (548). Beaufrey and Serlo are involved in a grand scheme to shoot "alternative Earth modules" into orbit around the earth to "orbit together in colonies, and the select few would continue as they always had" while looking down on the remains of the great unwashed and their contaminated planet (542).

Thus in bringing their lifelong fantasy to fruition, Beaufrey and Serlo would become even more like the dangerous and powerful variety of kachina spirits that they sometimes appear to represent. They seem, likewise, to evoke the Destroyers of which Nietszche speaks:

> The creator seeks . . . such as know how to whet their sickles. Destroyers they will be called, and despisers of good and evil. But they are the harvesters and those who celebrate. Fellow creatures, Zarathustra seeks, fellow harvesters and fellow celebrants: what are herds and shepherds and corpses to him? (Nietszche 135–36)

The two paradigms are not inconsistent. More than men but less than gods, Silko personifies the Destroyers as incarnations or carriers of the supernatural forces that comprise the "reign of the death-eye dog," the title of one section of the novel.

Silko remarked before writing this novel that western European people and "Americans especially" have a "puritanical abhorrence of blood and a tremendous fear of death" (Barnes 60). This observation is consistent with Foucault's assertion in *The History of Sexuality* that Western society in the nineteenth century moved from "a symbolics of blood to an analytics of sexuality" in a transition marked by Sade's deployment of "the blood of torture and absolute power, the blood of the caste which was respected in itself and which nonetheless was made to flow in the major rituals of parricide and incest, the blood of the people, which was shed unreservedly since the sort that flowed in its veins was not even deserving of a name" (148–49). At one point in the novel Seese is forced by the police to sit "with her feet in the pool of Tiny's blood . . . remembering the movie with the blood flowing from the elevator doors, oceans of blood. Tiny had been a huge man, over three hundred pounds." As the blood spoils in the heat and the hours pass, she "wet her pants and smiled as she saw how this had excited the police" (696–97).[12] Silko thus utilizes the semiotics of the abject in a critique of the discourse of sexuality which is, as clearly in this novel as in Pynchon's, enmeshed in a discourse of power and abuse of power. This critique is the reason why male homosexuality plays such a prominent role in the novel. It is not homosexuality which is under fire, but rather the abuse of power and phallocentric race privilege, the "blood of the caste" which in Sade's work "flowed through the whole dimension of pleasure" (Foucault 148).

In the language of contemporary American psychiatry, "pseudohomosexual struggles (in men) appear to be about homosexuality but are more accurately about the sense of masculinity. Ultimately, these conflicts have their origin in fears and wishes about issues of power and dependency" (Bone and Oldham 9). Fortunately, psychiatrists have advanced beyond Freud's attribution of all paranoia to repressed homosexuality.[13] Struggles over "the sense of masculinity" involve, like paranoia, issues about power and dependency, but many issues of power and dependency have nothing to do with masculinity. Why, then, are the major conspirators in Silko's main paranoid plot, the plot of the Destroyers, homosexual? The homosexuality of Ferro points to a connection with an impaired relationship to the mother. There are problematic aspects to the use of homosexuality as a motif for a mother-deficit, but in a novel in which practically all the characters are depicted in terms of hyperbolic excess, any resulting offense should be taken more in the spirit of Juvenalian satire than otherwise.

On the other hand, perhaps Sade is more to the point than Juvenal. Seese and her picaresque adventures are very evocative of Sade's Justine. To the extent that society sees homosexuality as a 'taboo' like incest, it is, as Marcelin Pleynet says of Sade, one of many "'written' crimes [to be taken] as methods of reading . . . Sade is only readable for a reading which thinks through the multiplicitous articulations of textual contradictions and which thinks its own insertion into the order of these contradictions" (114, 119). As we have seen, some critics have "thought" their own insertions into Silko's text and concluded that they are under assault—which, as white males, they perhaps are. Silko, like Sade, demands much of any reader in terms of perseverance, not to mention courage and tolerance.[14]

As she was writing this cops-and-robbers thriller, at a time when CIA involvement in drug traffic with the contras was becoming known, Silko says "I began to lose control of the novel and to feel that all of the old stories came in and I felt the presence of spirits. It was taken over" (Irmer and Schmidt, 154.). Discussing in the same interview the old stories that are retold in her earlier novel *Ceremony*, she says: "the old stories still have in their deepest level a content that can give the individual a possibility to understand. What frightens human beings is to not be able to understand or to see what is happening." The resonance with old stories goes beyond Mosca and the obvious motifs of the stone serpent and the Twin Brothers (the Chiapas Indians Tacho and Feo): *Almanac of the Dead* can be read as yet another retelling of the Yellow Woman story.

Silko's modern Yellow Woman story was first published in a 1974 anthology[15] and republished along with assorted variations and commentary in *Storyteller* in 1981. In the old stories Yellow Woman, also sometimes known as Corn Woman or Kachina Girl, is one of four Corn Mothers, the others being Blue, White, and Red (Boas 218; Allen, *The Sacred Hoop* 226–27); "a wanton, an outcast, a girl who runs off with Navajos, or Zunis or even Mexicans. She is also mother of the little war twins, consort of the sun, granddaughter of the one who plays with stars, somehow (obscurely?) related to Grandmother Spider" (Allen, *Spider Woman's Granddaughters* 182). Franz Boas describes "Yellow Woman" as a generic term for heroines in Keres stories, saying that the Blue, White, and Red Woman only appear when all four sisters are involved in the story (218); Paula Gunn Allen says that the name "Kochinnenako" or Yellow Woman "is in some sense a name that means "Woman-Woman because among the Keres, yellow is the color for women . . . Keres women paint their faces yellow on certain ceremonial occasions and are so painted at death so that the guardian at the gate of the spirit world . . . will recognize that the newly arrived person is a woman" (*Sacred Hoop* 226).

In the stories, generally speaking, Yellow Woman goes to get some water and is abducted by a dangerous kachina but eventually returns to the people. Her various abductors include Buffalo Man, Whirlwind Man, Cliff Dweller, Flint Wing, and Whipper (Ruoff 73). As A. Lavonne Ruoff summarizes the significance of the stories, "Yellow Woman becomes a symbol of renewal through liaison with outside forces": she may bring home a baby, or something else of value, as when her interlude with Buffalo Man results in a new source of meat for the pueblo (73). Silko's Yellow Woman story, in which the girl runs off with a Mexican cattle rustler named Silva, highlights the element of Yellow Woman's sexual desire for the spirit man, spurred on by a combination of variety, breaking away from maternal constraints, and the attraction of danger and power. Silko remarks in the title essay of her 1996 collection *Yellow Woman and a Beauty of the Spirit* that "Yellow Woman is my favorite because she dares to cross traditional boundaries of ordinary behavior during times of crisis in order to save the Pueblo; her power lies in her courage and in her uninhibited sexuality, which the old-time Pueblo stories celebrate again and again because fertility was so highly valued." She also mentions that "in at least one story, (Yellow Woman) chooses to join the secret Destroyer Clan, which worships destruction and death" (70).

This context impels a reconsideration of Seese's role as the major protagonist of *Almanac of the Dead*. Though the narrative shifts among the points of view of various major characters, it opens with Seese's perspective. Seese's defining physical characteristics are thin and blonde (23, 596). Silko has said that Yellow Woman's name refers to "the ritual color of the east" rather than to her skin color ("Yellow Woman" 71),[16] and the similarity between Seese's hair and a corn tassel is hard to ignore. The greatest resistance to a reading of Seese as Yellow Woman arises from the fact that she is a white woman, and one of the few in the novel at that (the only others being Max Blue's wife Leah and Seese's friend Cherie, who are thus, one could suppose, Blue Woman and Red Woman if one succumbs to the temptation to read 'Cherie' as 'Cherry').

Whereas Yellow Woman usually encounters the spirit man while getting water or wandering around by the river, a "place to meet boyfriends and lovers and so forth" (Evers and Carr 29), Seese gets mixed up with David, Beaufrey, and Serlo in San Diego where they cavort in cliffdwelling condos[17] with views of the Pacific Ocean, a place where Spider Woman is sometimes said to have gone (Trafzer). David, the father of her child, is the bisexual protégé of Beaufrey who wants Seese out of the picture. Both Beaufrey and Serlo consider David an inferior plaything, former professional companion of elderly men, having become an art photographer whose fleeting glimpse of fame comes from the photos of his street boy lover Eric taken immediately after Eric's suicide—photos developed in the darkroom that Eric compared to a womb (105). Though David is not quite up to the standards of Beaufrey and Serlo, let alone Buffalo Man or Cliff Dweller, he is fully ensconced in the milieu and practices of the Destroyer clan.

Beaufrey takes pride in his masterminding of the suicides and David eventually goes the same way, but Seese somehow manages to rise above his psychological manipulations and ends up working for Lecha as transcriber of the ancient fragments of the Almanac of the Dead. Her sojourn with the Destroyer clan resulted in the birth of a child; the baby was apparently chopped into pieces by Beaufrey, but Seese nevertheless returns to the Tuscon community somewhat better for wear; she stops using cocaine and takes on a fairly significant role as messenger or storyteller. Though her role in retelling the ancient stories is limited to that of a scrivener or typist, this role is consistent with the concept that the meaning of the old stories stays constant through historical change and variation. Lecha and Seese are mere vehicles for the stories that "ride" them as Silko says the stories "rode" her like the African spirits described in Zora Neale Hurston's book *Tell My Horse*: "when the spirits come they ride you, you become their horse, they use you" (Irmer and Schmidt, 154).

Silko lost custody of her youngest child in a contested divorce trial just prior to embarking on the writing of *Almanac of the Dead* (Silko and Wright 59). This circumstance resonates with the disruption of maternal relations that informs the entire novel. As noted previously, no character in the novel has a functional relationship with his or her mother. Seese runs away from home after her father's desertion and her mother's remarriage; both father and stepfather are military pilots. Her mother was afraid of flying, but her father used to brag that "'Seese is a born flyer, just like her daddy" (54). Seese imagines her father "flying and flying forever" (55), an image that correlates with Beaufrey's and Serlo's fantasies of launching orbit modules into space and thus escaping the corrupted (in their view) body of Mother Earth. But even as Seese "flies" on drugs and money in the world of the Destroyer clan, she has nightmares about "diving into a pool that is too deep" and getting lost in "lines and equations; she could imagine any number of possibilities from all the signs and symbols . . . Now she knows that all of it is a code anyway. The blue sky and puffy clouds seen through the deadly jade water of the nightmare pool was a message about the whole of creation" (43).

Silko has spoken in a similar way about the "codes" represented by the Almanac within the novel, i.e., as a message only partially decipherable. The use of this motif as frame for the novel marks an important intersection between postmodern notions of impenetrability, fragmentation, and intertextuality and the similar ways in which stories operate in oral traditions. The bits and pieces of the Almanac also resonate with Klein's description of the ego in the 'paranoid schizoid' position: "the early ego lacks cohesion, and a tendency towards integration alternates with a tendency towards disintegration, a falling into bits" (179). Kristeva discusses the relationship of this "falling into bits" (here translated as "falling into pieces") as an expression of the death drive (*Black Sun* 17–20), a concept which theorists of the postmodern should find provocative. But it seems clear enough that, for Silko, the message of the fragments is to be reassembled, and lies within a maternal order whether conceived as a properly guided and nurtured emergence into the human world (the Fifth World in Keres cosmology) or as a more "global" concept of the maternal as the nurturing earth. There are many "bad mothers" in the novel, including a spiderlike superannuated cripple who actually eats children, but in terms of object relations theory the terrorizing "objects" are more often male than female, trafficking in weapons, murder, body parts, and a scopophilic gaze with no less a goal than viewing the entire production from orbit. In invoking the signifying system of the infant psyche, replete with hallucination, mutilation, and cannibalization of body parts, the Destroyers of Silko's postmodern fable embody the terror of genocide and the depredations of late capitalism in articulating a "They"-system, like Pynchon's Blicero in *Gravity's Rainbow*, in a post-traumatic recuperative search for meaning out of chaos.

The utility of object relations theory is not, as Winnicott proposed and for which he has been soundly criticized, in a search for the "good enough" mother (Doane and Hodges 19–29), but in understanding the nature of the terror of the paranoid-schizoid state and negotiating a way out of it. Silko's "bad mothers" are emblematic of a world gone wrong; they are not the cause of it. The term "witchery" is gender-inflected not by Silko but by the demonization of women that infects the English language; there may be a better word for what she means in Keres, but the word does not exist in English.

The "witchery" that the novel explores is pervasive but cyclic or, as Silko has repeatedly explained, circular in the sense that space-time is unified and circular. The idea that the dominance of the Destroyers for five hundred years is a phase that will pass is emblematic of late twentieth century Enlightenment critique and of the apocalyptic genre of which this novel is only one example. The novel is also significant in its exploration of the liminal terror of the depths of human consciousness, yet not conceived in terms of regression to an infantile state but in terms of a Native American concept of atemporality akin to what others have said about the "postmodern condition." The human infant occupies the paranoid schizoid position in response to the birth trauma, negotiating the imperatives of survival. Yet as Klein's term implies, the paranoid schizoid position is a situational "position" in relation to existing conditions rather than a phase of development, and the distinction is significant when one attempts to apply this psychoanalytical model to a larger group or mode of discourse. The Oedipal paradigm is inadequate to account for this world of terror because it is grounded in a more fundamental terror of life itself. Perhaps this is but a roundabout way of saying that Silko's novel is more frightening than *Oedipus Rex*. Silko's Destroyers are more frightening than anybody's mother, than even the old woman who eats children in *Almanac*. As metaphorical embodiments of the worst aspects of late twentieth century vectors of power, they articulate a demonology that points at real evil rather than deflecting the gaze of accusation to racial minorities, child care workers, or other relatively defenseless scapegoats.

Chapter Six

Beyond the Foucauldian Complex

*Inscriptions and Reinscriptions of the Power Paradigm
by American Prison Writers*

Prison is the ultimate contemporary site of suspicion. Words, acts, personality, character, genes: everything about the prisoner is suspect by reason of the fact that the prisoner has been adjudicated guilty of a crime.

For penologists of the early twentieth century, imprisonment had four purposes: punishment, deterrence, protection of society, and rehabilitation. However, it is no longer intended, in the popular view, either for rehabilitation or for the mere protection of the free world from dangerous individuals, but primarily for punishment (length or frequency of imprisonment has yet to be shown to have a significant deterrent effect). Such punishment is accomplished by making the experience an unpleasant and undesirable one, that is, "to oppress or harass with ill treatment," the *American Heritage Dictionary*'s definition of 'persecution.' This dictionary notes a common association of the practice of persecution with race or religion, but the essential element here is the matter of classification of the individual as a type: in the case of the prison, the type of the criminal, or Foucault's "dangerous individual." In the final three decades of the twentieth century, the United States pursued a course of vengeance against lawbreakers. Rates of incarceration and lengths of sentences progressively increased until approximately 1 of every 145 people in the United States was behind bars in 2001.[1] When one considers that most prisoners spend only a short period of their lives in jail or prison, it becomes clear that if in some respects prison culture is spatially segregated, in a larger sense it is a central aspect of American culture.

It is thus essential, in examining discourses of suspicion in late twentieth century America, to examine the discourses of the persecuted, those of the two million prison inmates in the United States whose words have been published to the free world. This has yet to be done to any great extent, with the exception of H. Bruce Franklin's *Prison Literature in America: The Victim as Criminal and Artist*, first published in 1978 and revised in 1989. On the other hand, *representations* of prisoners and criminality receive a lot of attention, both by critics and by the general public.

Despite statistical evidence that crime rates have decreased since 1980, it is not just incarceration rates that have increased: media coverage of crime has also increased dramatically.[2] A somewhat irrational construction of criminality is often reflected in such media coverage, as in the nationally televised statement of prominent forensic psychiatrist Park Dietz, in response to a query about the high rate of incarceration: "Yes, two million are in prison and three million are still out there."[3] Mike Reynolds, the force behind the passage of the California three strikes initiative, has stated that criminals are out there "cannibalizing us."[4] To what extent do these statements reflect reality? According to the FBI's Bureau of Justice Statistics, in 1980 the violent crime rate was 47.7 per 1,000 (including murder, rape, robbery, and assault); by 2000 it had decreased to less than half that rate: 22.8 per 1,000, with a significant downward slope since 1993. During the same period, total incarceration in jails and prisons increased from 503,586 in 1980 to 2,033,331 in 2000, with the total number of persons under correctional supervision (including probation and parole) in 2000 at 6,445,100. Some law enforcement personnel might argue that this quadrupling of the rate of incarceration accounts for the dramatic decrease in the violent crime rate, but in 2000, only about 10% of federal inmates and 49% of state inmates were in prison for a violent offense (latest data available for local jail inmates was 1996, and only a fourth of them were incarcerated for violent crimes). In comparison, an estimated 57% of Federal inmates and 21% of State inmates were serving a sentence for a drug offense in 2000 (a fifth of local jail inmates in 1996).[5]

So what does Dietz mean when he says three million are still "out there?" Does he mean three million drug users, petty thieves, or crazed killers? All of the above? What about people who lie on their tax returns or cheat on exams? In one survey of 10,000 American households, 91 percent of respondents admitted to having violated laws for which they could have been incarcerated if convicted (Reiman 96). By that definition, many more than three million are "out there": would he incarcerate them all? Dietz has said he left his private psychiatric practice for the study of serial killers and violent crime because he was bored with listening to his patients complain about their mundane lives, and so his perception of the demographics of crime tends to be somewhat skewed. For years, he has devoted all his professional attention to interviewing murderers, and so it may well be that he thinks three million of us are capable of doing what they have done.

But what about citizen Reynolds' image of criminals "cannibalizing us?" Imagery of eating and being eaten, as discussed elsewhere in this book, bespeak fundamental psychological processes that can be traced back to the emotions of infancy. It is perhaps understandable that Reynolds, whose teenage daughter was shot in the head during a hijacking, would be caught up in such a fundamental emotional state.[6]

A favorite media representation of criminality is embodied in the fictional character Hannibal Lechter: Hannibal the cannibal. The Hannibal films (*Silence of the Lambs, Hannibal, Red Dragon*) are based on fiction by Thomas Harris, who attended FBI seminars on serial crime; John Douglas of the FBI's Behavior Science

Unit has said that the unit's "antecedents . . . go back to crime fiction more than crime fact" (qtd. in Seltzer, *Serial Killers* 16). The "looping" of fact and fiction in representations of the serial killer as a type—a somewhat faceless type, in his analysis—is one of the fundamental premises of Seltzer's book on this topic. This cycle of consumption of representations of criminality and its resonance with cannibalism is reflected in a real-life character like Jeffrey Dahmer. Because of the psychological resonance of the system of exchanges involved in the construction of such killers in fact and in fiction, these representations of the criminal tend to continually and repeatedly deflect attention from the actual demographics of the prison population, even for an expert like Park Dietz.

Critical analyses of mass media representations of criminality often utilize Kristeva's concept of the abject in *The Powers of Horror*, that is, the jettisoned and marginalized elements of that which disrupts the symbolic order. Abjection was discussed in the previous chapter in terms of filth and degradation as represented by the expelling of bodily fluids such as spit, urine, blood, vomit, etc., but it also pertains to people or entire groups of people: the Jew, for instance, in Kriseva's reading of Celine, for whom she argues that anti-Semitism "is a kind of parareligious formation; it is the sociological thrill, flush with history, that believers and nonbelievers alike seek in order to experience abjection" (180). Thus, for example, Patrick O'Donnell's chapter on criminality and paranoia in *Latent Destinies* talks about the criminal subject as "a mirror that reflects the lineaments of the legal subject in a system of surveillance that depends on the advent of the outlaw as well as the disciplining of criminality in order to sustain itself" (112).

Important as the analysis of the "sociological thrill" to be collectively gained from the expulsion of this "mirror" into the spatially delimited geography of the prison system may be, this Baudrillardian game of mirrors does not tell us much about the people who are in prison or about their own discursive practices. The only real-life prisoner discussed in O'Donnell's analysis is Gary Gilmore; the rest of it is about fictional representations of criminals.[7] Even his discussion of Gilmore who, after all, practically everyone would acknowledge, was not your typical prisoner, is really more about Norman Mailer's narrative voice in *The Executioner's Song* than it is about Gilmore himself. O'Donnell is absolutely right in identifying a "connection between felony and paranoia in terms of mediated homoerotic and homophobic exchanges between men that occur within the capital, phallocentric order that adjudicates their criminality" (114), as seen quite dramatically in the Maileresque "bevy of male exchanges of scripts, bullets, sentences, and semen" (124).[8] But he goes a bit too far in asserting that "male violence and its consequences signal that the system of crime and punishment that depends on the consensual, paradoxical abjection and assimilation of criminality is operating smoothly" (127). Gilmore's participation in this cultural order and specifically the production of the "consensual fiction" is far from representative of the American prison population as a whole, the majority of which are not even incarcerated for violent crimes, let alone consenting to the mode of punishment or participating in the construction of a narrative representation for public consumption.[9]

Whatever progress has been made in explaining the dynamics of killers such as Gary Gilmore and Jeffrey Dahmer, it falls far short of explaining what "criminality" means in terms of incarceration practices in the United States. Even as "Gilmore and his story are swallowed whole by the public ... [to] satisfy the hunger for stories that construe imaginary differences within the paranoid regime" (O'Donnell 128), the stories coming from the prisons are rarely even on the table.[10] The *San Francisco Chronicle* carried on a lawsuit for years over a federal prison regulation that prohibited them from running a byline on prisoner Dannie Martin's regular column (Sussman). Prison journalist Paul Wright, editor of *Prison Legal News*, was placed in solitary confinement for having too many stamped envelopes in his cell (Fleming). Internet access for prisoners is seen as a security risk and is extremely rare, and so aside from correspondence run past a censor, even the most educated prisoners tend to be somewhat out of touch with contemporary media and culture. Such circumstances, along with all the other cultural factors involved in imprisonment, may lead to the development of a set of cultural and discursive practices that could result in a body of work that could be called "prison literature."

But is prison literature a genre that can be classified and examined? Insofar as the definition of such a genre would assume the existence of the criminal as a "type" that may be classified and examined, issues arise. Such an assumption should be avoided. Nevertheless, just as human behavior is in large part a situational response to environmental stimuli, so writing by prisoners is shaped by the circumstances of their incarceration to the point that one may find common elements in their writing and call it a body of literature. To a growing extent, prison writers in the United States are aware of each other and have read the work of at least the most prominent prison writers, and so we have an evolving body of work that is intertextual, one of the markers not only of a literature but of a culture.

Bruce Franklin argues in *Prison Literature in America* that prison literature and music for African Americans constitute a continuum of slave literature and music. White prisoners are more invested in the ethos of individualism but become "especially dangerous" if they come to understand, like most nonwhites, that "they are in prison not for what they have done as individuals but for what they have done collectively" (xv). The logical continuation of this realization is that contemporary prison writing often does not clearly reflect the writer's ethnicity: the subject position of 'prisoner' may become more significant than the subject position marked by race. This argument may seem counterintuitive to those who associate prison writing primarily with two of the best known late twentieth century American prison writers, Malcolm X and George Jackson. But even though the racial demographics of contemporary American prisons are extremely and notoriously unbalanced, the subject position of the prisoner is less associated with a particular ethnicity than with the subject position of the slave.

Though many people associate prison writing with the work of political prisoners such as Martin Luther King Jr. or Angela Davis, neither of whom, fortunately, spent substantial portions of their lives incarcerated. Strictly speaking (Martin Luther King Jr. and Angela Davis were jailed rather than imprisoned) other political prisoner/writers in the United States, less well-known for the most part, have served years and remain incarcerated. Mumia Abu-Jamal, Kathy Boudin, Susan Rosenberg, and Raymond Luc Levasseur are among the best prison writers with a political background prior to incarceration.[11]

But the genre of prison writing to be more closely examined in this chapter is that of persons who came to prison without an articulated political understanding of their situation and stayed for years if not a lifetime. Besides Malcolm X and George Jackson, the best known of these is Jack Henry Abbott, who died in prison of alleged suicide in 2001. Abbott's *In the Belly of the Beast* (1981) is a collection of essays that were written in the form of letters to Norman Mailer, who had become involved in correspondence with Abbott while Mailer was writing *The Executioner's Song* about the Gary Gilmore case. Abbott's work has become an *ur*-text among contemporary prison writers; allusions to his work are common. His thesis that prisons create a predatory environment in which prisoners adapt by becoming either violent predators or groveling masochists is reflected by his own inability to adapt to the life in the free world. He was reimprisoned for murder one month after he was paroled in 1981. His account of the altercation with the manager of a café that ended in the manager's death is recounted in a play in his 1987 collection *My Return*.

Like George Jackson, Abbott was initially imprisoned for fairly minor crimes—in Abbott's case, the 'crime' of being an unwanted foster child who eventually graduated from juvenile facilities to a maximum (indeterminate) five year sentence in Utah for bouncing a check at the age of eighteen. Jackson grew up in a stable home environment but was imprisoned, also at age eighteen, on an indeterminate one year-to-life sentence in California for his alleged participation in a robbery of less than seventy dollars. Both prisoners were essentially victims of records of petty juvenile crime compounded by the leadership qualities that in a different time and place might have landed them on student council rather than headed for solitary confinement or death. Their prominent positions within prison society resulted in conflicts which minimized their chances for parole under the indeterminate sentence structure.

Jack Henry Abbott's writing does not purport to be literary—he disavows being a "professional writer" in his letters to Mailer (90)—but *In the Belly of the Beast* informs many of the significant tropes of prison fiction. The tropes with which I am concerned here are those of prison violence and prison sex: more specifically, the sexualization of violence. Responding to correspondence from Mailer, Abbott interrogates Mailer's assertions "that violence is associated with sexuality" (92).[12] It seems ironic that someone with as little experience of women as Abbott would insist upon a contradiction between sex between man and woman as "consecration and expression of love" with sex between men as "desecration . . . what is clear is that when a man sodomizes another to express his *contempt,* it demonstrates only his contempt for woman, not man." Perhaps Abbott idealizes heterosexuality. But it is difficult to contest (unless one wishes to problematize the concept of normality) his observation that "the normal attitude among men in society is that it is a great shame and dishonor to have experienced what it feels like to be a woman . . . such an attitude reflects *strong* feelings in the matter" (93; emphasis in the original).

It is important to understand that Abbott's critique of prison sexuality, like Silko's evil male homosexual characters in *Almanac of the Dead,* is not grounded in homophobia, nor intended as an indictment of homosexuality in general. The prison sexuality he describes, like heterosexual rape and sexual harassment, is more about power and domination than about sex. The psychology of sexual domination is perhaps better understood than the other side, the vulnerability of the oppressed to association of sexual response with relief from pain. Earlier in the book, describing the psychological terrorism he experienced in a psychiatric ward, Abbott says,

> I was so constantly and arbitrarily attacked in my cell there, after a while my desire for physical relief was so powerful and all-pervading that when the guards finally would leave off the attack and exit my cell, I would sometimes achieve an erection out of despair and pain. I could easily . . . have misunderstood to the point of becoming a sexual masochist, or a sadist. I could very easily have confused this act of release with a sexual act of love, could have easily been twisted by this thing.
>   How many prisoners have been? (64–65)

Abbott's primary objective, it seems, is to explain to the free world how prisons engender violence in the imprisoned. He expends pages and pages upon the necessity of killing in prison and of developing the mental fortitude to kill. The ability to kill, for Abbott, is not always predicated on avoiding death, but can also be based upon being punked out (sexually dominated): a fate, for those who do not choose to accept it, worse than death. A full examination of the sociology of sex roles in the American men's prison is beyond the scope of this discussion, but an awareness of its complexity and difference from homosexual cultures in the free world is essential to an appreciation of prison literature.

Though Abbott's published work does not discuss his ethnicity, he is half Irish and half Chinese (xiv)—an ancestry apparent in his facial features, marking him in a way that could not have boded well for him as a child during the years when the evil Fu Manchu embodied American popular culture's attitudes toward the Asian male. Norman Mailer thought he looked like Lenin, but his dark hair, broad cheekbones, and other prominent facial features also echo the stereotypical evil halfbreed of American literature.[13]

On the other hand, Dwight Edgar Abbott's memoir *I Cried, You Didn't Listen* (1991) is a text drenched in caucasian identity, though the title eerily echoes Vine Deloria Jr.'s Native American manifesto *We Talk, You Listen*. He is not related to Jack Henry Abbott, though one must wonder if his name facilitated publication of this book. Abbott was initially turned over to the California Youth Authority when his parent were hospitalized for several months after a serious car accident. His account is one of continuous sexual abuse by both counselors and other children leading to an escalating record of violence, attempted escapes, and associated car thefts. Though lacking the literary merit of some of the contemporary novelists, Dwight Abbott's book provides important insight into a problem that few people have had the courage to write about in an autobiographical voice. One of his objectives in publishing his story was to acquaint sexually abused children and young adults with the existence of a support network; various resources are listed in an appendix. The book demonstrates the dangers of systems based upon trust and legitimation of its own system of authority at the expense of all other voices, the same inherent problem that has been more recently exposed within the system of authority within the Catholic Church. When the voices of those in positions of authority have more credence by virtue of their status than those with less 'legitimate' status, whether as law violators or merely as those with less authoritative status and something to be gained by their assertions, then a situation is set up wherein certain voices will never be afforded legitimacy and certain 'truths' can never be recognized.

Fiction writers in prison are less directly concerned than autobiographical writers with being believed. This is partially a function of audience, and partially a function of fiction itself. Prison writers who are still incarcerated may be "telling it like it is" to the outside world, but considering the difficulties of getting their work published, their work is probably best appreciated by other prisoners who understand the embedded cultural assumptions. For those of us on the outside, prison fiction can nevertheless articulate aspects of prison culture that are difficult to describe in the abstract. For instance, one could assert that interactions between prisoners and guards are often highly sexualized, but such a statement does not explain the why or how, or say what is significant about such a discourse. A story like "Dog Star Desperado" by William Orlando, on the other hand, contextualizes the practice, one might even say, naturalizes it. It is this process of naturalization, the making to seem normal in the sense of "just kidding around," that points to the significance of the practice in its hailing of sexuality into the service of power.

"Dog Star Desperado" appears in the recently published anthology of a quarter century of award-winning writing submitted to PEN's annual prison writing contests, *Doing Time: 25 Years of Prison Writing*, edited by Bell Gale Chevigny with a forward by *Dead Man Walking* author Sister Helen Prejean. This double framing of prison texts by figures of cultural authority in the free world, like Norman Mailer's introduction to Abbott's *In the Belly of the Beast*, works to "legitimize" the texts to the general public, as if to say, "we guarantee that this is the real writing of real prisoners, and that it is worthy of your attention." This strategy is the same one that was used for the same purpose with the slave texts of, for example, Phyllis Wheatley, Frederick Douglass, and Harriet Jacobs. Orlando's story is part of an unpublished novel, demonstrating that without such framing practices of legitimation, such texts are unlikely to reach the general public. The story seems like one written primarily for a prison audience and serves as a good illustration of a theme, the interaction between prisoners and guards, that prison readers are likely to find absolutely relevant to their daily lives.

As the story opens, a group of prisoners are being transported cross-country from the federal penitentiary in Leavenworth, Kansas to another in Lompoc, California. The author does not tell us, but prison readers would know that Leavenworth is a maximum security facility and Lompoc is not; thus the prisoners might well be looking forward to their new home, despite the grim and tedious circumstances of their transport, particularly considering the time of year (November) and the impending climate change:

> Our prison transport showed its age. It looked as knackered as some of the convicts it had aboard—men in bad flesh who'd let themselves go, turning gray with the years and bitter for it. The bus smelled funny. The odor of cigarette butts and rusted apple cores, the odor of stale, brooding sweat. A prisoner smell. We sat in our chains . . . content to look hard and forbidding. Desperadoes all. (7)

The tone is not tendentious, but lightly ironic. In the following paragraph, after just saying the prisoners had "little rap for one another," Orlando introduces us to the oral tradition in prison culture:

> Those that did talk, talked shop. Who was hot and snitchin'. Who got stabbed and good for the motherfucker. Who bugged out. Who busted loose one fine morning in Kool-Aid lipstick, cue-chalk blue eye shadow, and bikini briefs over buns of steel. Gossip and lore. Amazing, I thought, that so little could be so absorbing. Still, absent any stone tablets, this was how they passed on the tribal Decalogue—defining value and boundary. This was how they staked out their claims as regulars, as men, as convicts. Real ones. Very few of us left, they would have you know. Rats and queers taking over. (7)

A mock proposition to the narrator from a giant queen named Wonder Woman is followed by a mock counter-offer by the first-person protagonist in a brief but complex verbal exchange wherein both participants aggressively offer to assume the passive position. Orlando identifies his ethnicity as "half Korean, half black," and this exchange invokes all the elements of African American verbal practices of signifying (elaboration on a common known verbal text) and the dozens (brief and skillful exchange of insults). But this is merely passing time. Soon they arrive at Lompoc and are greeted by a squad of jack-booted thugs—"boots, mirrored sunglasses, guns." The narrator briefly switches from first to second person: "You were a barbarian being whipped to the imperial gates," down the sidewalk, "a flowered gauntlet between annuals gay and nimble in the breeze. A ribbon on a pig" (8).

For the next few pages, the prisoners get to know their new guards, commenting at length on the alleged "round heels" of one of the guards' wives, a guard with whom one of the prisoners has had an unpleasant history elsewhere. As the prisoner describes this prior episode, "Him and the gooners rushed my cell—I was in the hole—and jive tossed me up" (9), a description reminiscent of Abbott's account of arbitrary attacks while in solitary confinement. The guard, however, describes this episode as "dancing" with the prisoner (10).

But the main problem, the crux of the plot in this brief story, is the issuing of some worn-out shrunken underwear to the now-naked new arrivals: "The problem was comic; the problem was grave . . . These were not the loose-fitting boxers of custom. They were jockey shorts. Dainty shorts—shrunken and the brown all faded. They were, in effect, pink panties" (10). This motif references the practice of Arizona sheriff Joe Arpaio, who issues pink underwear to all inmates in the Maricopa County Jail as part of a general shock therapy approach that also includes housing in desert tents and black and white striped uniforms.

An older corrections officer arrives in response to their objections, introducing himself in terms of his sexual assets: "half a dick . . . But I got a split tongue" (11). This repartee continues, functioning as a stalling technique and also as an attempt to defuse the prisoners' anger, since the officer has no authority or intention to accede to their demands for reasonable underwear. The narrator says, "I pondered the exchange. C.O.'s sounded like convicts—even unto sex-talking each other, and they had women. Environment rubbed off" (12). The story ends with the arrival of stormtroopers to forcibly extract this group of naked prisoners from the holding area, an operation foreshadowed by the reference to the previous incident at another prison: "riot-garbed and ax-handle armed. They were dressed to dance" (13).

Though the tone of this story is light, the events described are not. Forcible extractions of recalcitrant prisoners from cells are notoriously brutal, often resulting in broken bones and other serious injuries. Despite the running sexual commentary that seems to indicate that everyone finds prison sex to be a big joke, the shrunken, stained underwear represents such an intolerable degree of infantilization and feminization that the prisoners literally risk their lives to protest it. They stand to gain nothing from this confrontation. Even though the bend-over body cavity search is a routine part of their daily lives,[14] the semiotics of the underwear goes beyond the limits of toleration, such an affront to their dignity that they literally risk their lives in protest. The guards, perhaps particularly the avuncular older guard, seem to be enjoying the interchange, and might argue that the prisoners are enjoying it too. Just as with a case of actual intercourse between guard and inmate in a women's prison, this scenario interrogates notions of consent in sexual interactions in situations where the balance of power is so skewed that to say the situation is inherently coercive would be an understatement.[15]

Gay journalist and advice columnist Dan Savage seems perplexed and unhappy about the particular sort of rough trade arising out of the sexual economy of men's prisons. He visited a weekend getaway for people seeking a "realistic prison experience . . . that includes control, confinement, interrogations, and restraint," with "absolutely no sex," according to the proprietor whom everybody calls the Captain. The clientele seems to be primarily gay males ("no girls allowed"): one of the Savage's three companion "prisoners" says he is straight, but it seems possible that this client ("Rob") is actually an undercover employee of the "Academy." The play-guards are moonlighting from jobs as "real cops, real guards" and very large. Savage describes them as "like the nuns at my Catholic grade school—mean and funny" (35). Rob tells Savage and his companions, "Don't assume that these guys don't get off on this too" (36), and Savage's account seems consistent with this interpretation. The explicit sex talk of Orlando's short story is missing, but the clients are naked during many of the scenarios and the guards seem to be having a good time, though able to shift in and out of the role-playing with ease when necessary (otherwise Savage might have died from an asthma attack, as real prisoners often do).

The arbitrary and thus terrorizing interruptions of confinement recounted by Abbott are echoed here yet again: the "very scary" guards "come and go, which means we prisoners are either bored . . . or terrified. There's no in-between" (35). Savage didn't last out the weekend, due to his asthma attack, and did not find the overall experience enjoyable. He argues that "prison is about power and fear and control and punishment, and as we build more prisons . . . the prison experience will become fetishized and fuel the dominance/submission fantasies of the new generations of sado-masochists" (36).

If fetishization of prison sexuality were no more than a boutique niche market for people with preexisting dominance/submission fantasies, then perhaps it would not be a significant social problem. But these sorts of sexual preferences often arise from a background of childhood abuse. Consenting adults should be able to pursue their interests, and it is not necessary to pass judgment on their reasons for enjoying certain practices so long as nobody is being hurt. Nevertheless, we would not say, for instance, that the fact that a lesbian enjoys bondage scenarios justifies the circumstance that her stepfather raped her when she was twelve. Millions of people in this country are passing in and out of the doors of prisons and jails, as inmates and as guards, and they carry the acculturation of the prison world with them when they leave. Something so simple as inexperience with using a condom is part of the acculturation of prison life. In prison, as in the "Academy" visited by Dan Savage, wardens insist that policy prohibits sexual contact. Accordingly, possession of a condom is considered contraband, grounds for solitary confinement, and so prisoners practice unsafe sex in an atmosphere of disavowal and verbal transference. They do not become different people when they are released. In many cases, they may go home to have unprotected sex with their wives, practicing the same strategies of disavowal that prison encouraged. But this scenario only reflects contamination at the microbiological level. The psychological contamination of attitudes about sex and domination may be even more problematic in the long run. Seven-Up recently ran a television commercial (spring of 2002) containing a joke about prison rape. The commercial was cancelled due to protest from prison activist groups, but the fact that it was made illustrates how the discursive practices of prison sexuality can spill over into popular culture.

In the story "Feathers on the Solar Wind" in the same anthology, another incarcerated writer, David Wood, treats the same theme and yet moves beyond it. There is no disavowal or verbal transference of prison sex. There are no guards either, except for their brief appearance in the opening paragraph, dressed in full protective gear as if for the Black Death, to remove a couple of corpses. The entire story takes place in the AIDS ward of an unnamed prison, sequestered from the politics of the yard and the cell blocks as well as from the intervention of guards. It is as if the patients/prisoners are already dead, housed in a purgatorial holding tank, as Willie says, "feathers on the solar wind . . . floating and dancing on the music of the cosmos before the final incineration" (159). The caretaker in this demilitarized zone is an HIV-infected inmate named Deathrow, "big and black and bald and muscular," still symptom-free, his death sentence commuted to life, a convert to Islam (153–54). Deathrow attends to the bodily functions of the AIDS patients like a penitent monk, standing outside the main action of the story which revolves around a bet.

This is a carefully constructed story with an O. Henry-ending.[16] The five main characters form a pentangle, or perhaps a cosmic wheel. They are introduced in the order in which they join in a poker game: South Philly (white), Willie (black), Jimmie (white by inference), Wyman (black), and Smokey (black by inference). The racial integration, not only of the AIDS ward but of the nature of the social interactions within it, is one of the features that sets the story apart. The characters, or most of them, are beyond the identity politics of prison. The older characters are at peace with who they are and who they have been; the younger ones are not, and therein lies the conflict in the story. Jimmie, with a rash on his face and red cheeks, denies that he's a "fag" and wants to "die like a man." South Philly tells him "this is how a man dies, with the Ninja or Alzheimer's, or cancer. If you wanted to throw yourself on a grenade and save your buddies and die a hero's death, you should've joined the Marines" (155).

It is South Philly, the first of these five characters and a trickster figure, who proposes that they bet on who will die next, since two men have died since midnight and "people die in threes" (157). Willie, a wise old man figure, also feels the urge to "dance with Death":

Sirius is high in the sky tonight," Willie mumbled, "and the natives are restless."

"Sirius?" South Philly asked. "What's that?"

"Sirius, the Dog Star, the harbinger of death . . . putting out carbon molecules . . . Maybe if we get enough carbon molecules, we can all be made whole again." (160)

Though he is the first to object to the bet and had also declined to join in the poker game, Smokey eventually bets first, on Willie, who then bets on Wyman, who then bets on South Philly, who then bets on Jimmie. There is one person left on whom to bet, Smokey, and Jimmie refuses to bet. The bets form a pentangular pattern with the last connection undrawn:

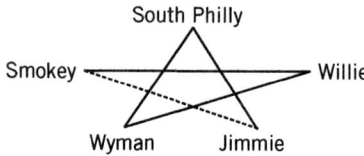

If one were drawing diagrams while reading the story, one might still guess that Jimmie will die, since he is the one exhibiting the most anxiety and now the one to refuse to complete the connection. But Jimmie and Smokey both face death in the shower, in the form of a ghost. Jimmie sees his newly dead cellmate (Daniel Martin Pinkston, probably a writer's joke on prison journalist Dannie Martin/Red Hog) whom he had infected with the disease. He asks the ghost for forgiveness, and the ghost tells him he must forgive himself. Smokey, on the other hand, sees the ghost of his brother who died in the electric chair after Smokey "turned state's evidence" on him. Smokey slits his own throat because, as Willie explains, "he wasn't capable of forgiving himself" (163).

If prison writing passes on, in Orlando's words, the "tribal Decalogue," then this story is passing along more than just a lesson about confession and forgiveness. Prison sex is maybe a sin, or maybe an act of love, which seems to bring on its own consequences. Betraying a brother, on the other hand, is unforgiveable. Like Judas, Smokey cannot live with his culpability.

The rule against snitching has for decades been perhaps the strongest shibboleth among prisoners, or so it would seem from reading American prison literature. It represents the sort of "honor among thieves" that is a necessary part of the social contract among outlaws, and thus the institution of law enforcement and corrections has a great interest in breaking it down. Orlando's offhand remark, "rats and queers taking over," seems dismissive but is not devoid of truth. Dannie Martin, for instance, as one of the "old school" of prisoners, comments at length on the change in demographics and values within prison culture over the past twenty years. Martin, a bank robber by trade, served years in federal penitentiaries and started publishing a column in the *San Francisco Chronicle* in the latter eighties while still incarcerated.[17] He points to the influx of youth in the system as primarily responsible for the changes in values among prisoners. Willingness to inform on each other is only part of it. The older prisoners, Martin contends, have little respect for the younger ones because of their immaturity and lack of professionalism at breaking the law. During the eighties, the federal prisons filled with drug offenders due to the enactment of mandatory minimum sentences. Many of these prisoners barely qualify as "criminals" at all if their convictions were for drug possession, at least within the worldview of old-timers like Martin. Their youth makes them vulnerable to sexual exploitation due to their comparative physical attractiveness and naiveté. If they were involved in gang culture or street life, their self-imposed rules of conduct, or lack thereof, are often anathema to older prisoners. Even former Los Angeles gang leader Kody "Monster" Scott,[18] speaking of California state prisons, acknowledges that younger gang members often seem to be operating totally without the sort of scruples that enable people to get along with each other in prison.

Within the drug culture, a watershed moment may have occurred in 1976 when rock star Gregg Allman turned state's evidence to avoid incarceration on cocaine charges. Such behavior would have seemed unthinkable in the sixties, but Allman's arrest was no doubt considered a great coup of undercover drug investigation as the forces of law and order circled the wagons for the bicentennial, and it is likely that all the powers of the state were brought to bear upon obtaining his cooperation. Whether due to his problems with drug addiction or his new public status as a "fink,"[19] his career never fully recovered, though he has continued to perform without apparent attempts at retaliation from former associates.

A few years later, the new mandatory minimums precluded consideration in federal cases for any sort of extenuating circumstances. The only way out is now reserved for defendants with information to trade. Often those who serve the longest sentences on federal drug charges, even life terms, are not only those who refuse to testify against others but those so far down the chain and out of the loop that they have no information to trade and not even the wherewithal to fabricate it. Such an atmosphere creates a sense of pervasive injustice among those caught up in the system and the old saw "do the crime, do the time"—which law violators might otherwise accept in principle—becomes meaningless. If in the old days, snitches had to be put in protective custody in order to keep them from being killed by other prisoners, now there are so many snitches in prison that such retaliation would be impractical if not impossible. Thus systems of trust and allegiance within prison are critically impaired; no one can really trust anybody. Not only is discussion of past misdeeds with a cellmate unwise, but even revealing enough personal information to enable someone to construct a believable lie can also carry serious consequences.

From a law enforcement point of view, this state of affairs may seem advantageous. Convictions are easier to obtain, and though the most culpable party may not end up getting the worse punishment, the statistics look good. Likewise, within prison walls it may seem that having informants everywhere helps keep the peace. But as with other attempts at universalized surveillance, it increases resentment against the power structure and thus merely enforces an unwilling peace. There is no social contract.

Prison writers have a lot of time to think. Accordingly, much of their work envisions a future. David Wood's story about the AIDS ward envisions the final future facing many prisoners, but finds moments of redemption and even beauty there. It has been said of Jean Genet that he "transformed erotic and often obscene subject matter into a poetic and anarchic vision of the universe" (Merriam-Webster 454). A critical approach that universalizes the prison experience as symbolic of humanity's chains is problematic in the sense that it tends to naturalize a social practice that is an abomination to humanity, Nevertheless, it must be acknowledged that the prisons of late twentieth century America are both representative and replicative of the worst features of American culture. As such, the prisoner's vision of our culture is one that must be contended with. It is a vision of a vindictive, racist, homophobic world where sexual and psychological gratification hinge upon power relationships and manipulation, where everyone must be viewed as a potential enemy, where no social contract is inviolable. In this metanarrative, everyone is criminalized because everyone is a potential criminal.

What kind of a culture have we created where one of our best contemporary poets, Jimmy Santiago Baca, had to go to prison in order to learn how to read and write? Perhaps the best we can say of our prisons is that some survive and return to tell us who we are. But we must not romanticize the experience of those who find themselves and their voices behind bars. Prisons are factories designed to produce destruction, not poets. And it is far more than the lives of individual prisoners that is being destroyed.

Epilogue

One might expect that an epilogue to this book would discuss the bombing of the World Trade Center on September 11, 2001. United States culture has now fixed upon a new Other against which to focus its fear. There are people out there who really do hate us, and it would behoove us to examine the reasons why. It could be more productive than interrogating preschoolers about their day care workers, incarcerating our children and ourselves behind privacy fences and in gated communities, herding teenagers into mega-high schools that look more like prisons ever year, and generally trying to limit our contact with each other to our DSL connections and the satellite dishes on our roofs.

What is a "reasonable suspicion?" This legal term of art has come to supplant "probable cause" as the delimitation of the right of privacy. Since the Fourth Amendment only requires probable cause as to searches of our "persons, houses, papers, and effects," our zone of privacy is more attenuated in our cars and our communications; thus the "reasonable suspicion" standard that has come to dominate the scope of border and highway searches. Yet even an individualized "reasonable suspicion" is being increasingly supplanted by the use of profiling, facilitated by law enforcement's utilization of behavioral science and pretensions thereto. Such profiling practices are currently kept in check only by the theoretical limitations of prohibitions on discrimination against "suspect classes": that is, those categories of persons to whom the Fourteenth Amendment grants "equal protection" and against whom constitutional law considers disparate treatment "suspect" absent a compelling state interest. Thus a standard of suspicion encompasses the state's scrutiny of the individual subject from one end to the other.

The point has already been made, and this writer is hardly alone in pointing out, that post-9/11 federal legislation is likely to have far-reaching consequences for civil liberties. As political and legal battles ensue over just how far we are willing to allow government surveillance to proceed, as individuals in a democracy we need to start focusing less on defining our personal networks of suspicion and more on defining personal networks of trust. How to do that is beyond the scope of this book. The most I can hope to have accomplished here is to illustrate some of the ways in which fear of one thing can get transposed into blame on something else.

Silko once explained her early departure from law school with the assertion that "injustice is built into the Anglo-American legal system . . . the only way to seek justice [is] the power of the stories" (*Yellow Woman* 19–20). Though the legal system has undergone occasional scrutiny in the preceding chapters, this book has not been as much an exercise in critical legal theory as some of its early readers may have anticipated. My focus is more on stories, and though some of those stories have been told in courtrooms, the stories that reach a much greater number of people are the stories that are told in American visual media. How much suspicion is ultimately deemed "reasonable" may ultimately depend on how we—and our lawmakers and judges—are acculturated in a society dominated by mass media. Therefore I am going to close with a discussion of a few recent Hollywood films, films that have in common the existence of a corrupt law enforcement conspiracy. At the beginning of the introduction, I cited films that involved not only government corruption but forays into the fantastic and destabilization of the reliability of perception of reality. *The Matrix* and its 2003 sequel have demonstrated that this motif has achieved major cult status. But the anxieties around government corruption and surveillance have continued to be fertile ground for entertainment in the realist mode.

Enemy of the State was released in 1998 the same year as *The X-Files, Dark City*, and *The Truman Show*. Starring "fresh prince" Will Smith as the unwitting protagonist who knows too much (or rather, the conspiracy thinks he does), this film offers a recapitulation of paranoia of the panopticon somewhat astonishing in its sampling of some of the seventies films that are central to Stephen Paul Miller's analysis of seventies surveillance anxiety in *The Seventies Now*. Gene Hackman plays virtually the same character (though with a different name and history) in *The Enemy of the State* that he played in *The Conversation* in 1974. He's still apparently wearing the same pair of glasses, and he seems to be working out of the same office. *Enemy of the State* also invokes shades of *The Parallax View* (1974; investigator set up as assassin) and *Three Days of the Condor* (1975; CIA agent finds out something he isn't supposed to know and "becomes a kind of walking *Pentagon Papers*" who "must enlist the help of common New Yorkers to get his story to the *New York Times* [Miller 91]). Miller points out that both *The Conversation* and *The Parallax View* were filmed pre-Watergate, though they were both released in 1974, demonstrating that "anxiety about surveillance was in the air before Watergate, an anxiety that sustains the affair" (90).

What's new in *Enemy of the State* is that whereas before the Gene Hackman character was an individualistic private-eye who saw himself as an artist, now he is a defrocked CIA agent (they call it the National Security Agency, but it's clearly a stand-in for the CIA), sacrificed in the political fallout following the fall of the Shah in Iran. Also, the "NSA" now has a satellite that can see everything from outer space, right down to the nose hairs. *The Conversation* reflected anxieties about private surveillance, but *Enemy of the State* is explicitly "about" a pending piece of evil federal surveillance legislation that sounds remarkably like the post-9/11 Patriot Act, given that this film was made in 1998. A rogue group within the NSA (its "communications" team seems vaguely similar to the Lone Gunmen of the *X-Files*) has assassinated a congressman who opposes the legislation, the bird-watching videotape that recorded the assassination gets passed off to the unsuspecting Will Smith like a hot potato, and the defrocked spy has to help him escape the bad guys and save the country.

As in *Strange Days* (1999), the "good guys" are a team of one civilian and one "good cop" against the rogue cops. Both films update the genre by placing an African American in a key role: in *Enemy of the State* a male labor attorney, and in *Strange Days* a female police officer. What seems significant here is that where corruption exists within law enforcement, the involvement of someone from within the system is necessary to prevail against it. The "insider" may be an outsider within the law enforcement network, but the "good cop" is totally trained and invested in the standards and practices of the institution of law enforcement. More recent examples of this model include the imprisoned hero-general who marshals the prisoners into an army to unseat the corrupt warden in *The Last Castle* (2001) and FBI agent Clarisse prevailing over a very inept corruption scheme emanating from the U.S. Department of Justice in *Hannibal* (2001).

The implication of these plots is that there is nothing wrong with the system that produces corrupt law enforcement individuals and conspiracies; apparently there will always be a few bad apples corrupted by power, but someone trained within the same power-driven system will always come forth, invested with the almost-superhuman powers required to prevail. Thus the integrity of the ruling order is always recuperated by the individualist hero.

A more interesting though obscure film is *From Hell* (2001), based on a graphic novel of the same name (otherwise known as a comic book, though this one is over 500 pages with annotations) published by "mad shaggy genius of the comics world" Alan Moore and Eddie Campbell in 2000.[1] This variation on the corrupt government theme involves a 100-year flashback to Victorian England and Jack the Ripper. Johnny Depp plays an inspector who loses his job as he gets closer to the truth: that Jack the Ripper is really the agent of a Masonic conspiracy acting in collusion with Queen Victoria to neutralize the threat of an unwanted heir to the throne, the baby daughter of a former prostitute whom the syphilitic and dying Prince Albert has secretly married. The "fresh princess" is spirited away to Ireland to be raised as an Irish peasant, even more clueless than Will Smith about what's really been going on. Depp's character sacrifices himself to her escape by drifting off into permanent opium oblivion in a scene that seems to have been lifted from Julie Christie's death scene in yet another anti-establishment seventies film, *McCabe and Mrs. Miller* (1971). His superhuman powers lay in his clairvoyance, which was so psychologically disturbing as to have led him to opium addiction before this particular investigation began. But his superhuman powers and self-sacrificing individual heroism do not recuperate the integrity of the ruling order.

Mark Seltzer argues in *Serial Killers* that serial killing is a fairly recent phenomenon associated with mass communication and that "Jack the Ripper" (the true killer, if it was one person, was never apprehended) was one of the prototypical cases. In this context, *From Hell's* revisitation of this primal scene should be read as a rather subversive overlay of a late twentieth century suspicion of authority upon the detective genre that was born in close chronological and geographical approximation to the Jack the Ripper case: Doyle created Sherlock Holmes in 1887 and the Whitechapel murders attributed to Jack the Ripper occurred in 1888.

This discussion is anecdotal rather than systematic in nature, as mass media has become so saturated with police stories that it is difficult to argue which are representative or significant among the deluge, including a seemingly inexhaustible number of spinoffs of *Law and Order* and *CSI* (forensic "crime scene investigation") in the fall 2002 and 2003 seasons. As network television is ratings-driven, this trend suggests that viewers have generally positive attitudes toward law enforcement and its capabilities. The newer dramas rely increasingly on forensic evidence to solve cases, and contribute to a growing perception bordering on faith that all crimes are solvable and all criminals will be caught.

Though HBO's dramas are less ratings driven, its lead cop show *The Wire* is a tour de force of surveillance technology, directed primarily against somewhat stereotypic African American drug dealers. On the other hand, the continuing run of *The Sopranos* may articulate not only the continuing fascination of the American public with the gangster-as-abject but perhaps more pertinently an understanding of organized crime as merely capitalism carried on by other means. Paranoia and suspicion are rarely ongoing states in *The Sopranos*; they are efficiently and summarily resolved by death. Anxiety disorder, paranoia's cheap imitation, is treatable with Prozac. Or is it? Tony Soprano's problems seem to reflect problems with the patriarchal order of his culture, just as I have suggested with regard to authoritarian approaches to law enforcement and the policing of the boundaries of the social contract.

Such approaches to law enforcement and policing are not necessarily endemic to a democratic society, though they seem to be endemic to ours. Hiring more women and minorities as police officers and prison guards will not solve the institutional problems, nor will rooting out specific rogue cops or corrupt conspiracies. The beast within American culture is not a conspiracy of aliens masquerading as humans, yet neither is it as simple as the corruption of individuals or groups of individuals in positions of power, nor is it an evil media conglomerate peddling sensationalistic sex and violence. Our institutions are a reflection of us. Changing ourselves is not as simple as passing new laws or rounding up more and more of the usual suspects and imprisoning them.

The crime of choice for daily news coverage lately has not been drive-by shootings, nor serial killers, nor police brutality. It is family murders where one of the parents kills the children and then attempts, successfully or not, to kill him or herself. The frequency of these reports in the news does not necessarily indicate that such acts are increasing, nor that they indicate a significant public safety risk for the rest of us. But they may reflect, in a convoluted and unconscious way, the turning of cultural anxieties inward. Fathers who kill their families sometimes do so to inflict pain upon an estranged spouse. But the motivations can also be more complex. Andrea Yates saw Satan in her children, and saw no alternative but to destroy the family village in order to save it. Her husband the aerospace engineer, like those who ignored the warning signs from subordinates about the foam insulation on the space shuttle, did not understand the magnitude of the problem until it was too late. Whether it is too late for the rest of us remains to be seen.

Notes

Intoduction

1 Richard Hofstadter asserts that the "paranoid style" has in America "been the preferred style of only *minority* movements," thus distinguishing the American experience from the paranoid styles of Hitler and Stalin (7).

2 A body of work is developing to examine this function of law enforcement in the United States. Most of it, though not all, deals with the McCarthy era. Some of the key texts are Frank Donner's *The Age of Surveillance: The Aims and Methods of the American Political Intelligence System* (1980) and *Protectors of Privilege: Red Squads and Police Repression in Urban America* (1990), Ward Churchill and Jim Vander Wall's *Agents of Repression: The FBI's Secret Wars Against the Black Panther Party and the American Indian Movement* (1988, 1990), and more recently Athan G. Theoharis and John Stuart Cox's *The Boss: J. Edgar Hoover and the Great American Inquisition* (1998) and Ellen Schrecker's *Many Are the Crimes: McCarthyism in America* (1998). A complete discussion of this body of work is beyond the scope of this text. I will attempt a more text-based interpretation of the mechanisms of power and surveillance: an application of the hermeneutics of suspicion to the metanarrative of suspicion, a narrative that questions not interpretation but veracity.

3 Contemporary illustrations of what one could call the "beast within" genre are legion—for example, the subgenre of "the judge is guilty" films which include *And Justice for All,* starring Al Pacino, and *Suspect,* starring Cher. A few of the more recent law enforcement corruption films are discussed in the epilogue.

4 Though this book will not attempt a comprehensive examination of American popular culture on these issues, it seems important to mention some of the significant early articulations of "paranoia" and anxiety over surveillance in popular music: The Kinks' song "Destroyer," Buffalo Springfield's "For What It's Worth" (about that thing that "strikes deep"), Black Sabbath's definitive album *Paranoid* along with its title song, and the lighthearted early eighties reprise by Rockwell, "Somebody's Watching Me." The proprietary policy of the music industry on song lyrics is somewhat prohibitive of further comment herein.

5 Richard Slotkin's *Regeneration through Violence* (1973) and its sequels *The Fatal Environment* (1986) and *Gunfighter Nation* (1992) on the mythology of the American frontier have also been important in their analysis of key texts of power and conquest in American history.

6 Though Lacanian thought will not be much discussed in this work, I do not find Kleinian paradigms to be particularly at odds or inconsistent with it. Rather, Lacan's concern is with the development of the Law of the Father, necessarily involved with the advent of language—thus the fascination of literary critics with application of

Lacanian analysis to discursive practices. But insofar as Lacan is concerned with the construction of master narratives, the particular deconstruction of a master narrative manifested in paranoid thought is intimately associated, I believe, with a regression to the realm of the infant psyche, that is, the paranoid-schizoid position. Thus what happens in a psychoanalytic model of ego construction after the mirror stage is less relevant to my argument.

7   One compelling demonstration of such a descent into chaos, particularly in light of my later discussion of the heritage of the American southern frontier, appears in the concluding scenes of the recent remake of *Cape Fear*. The raced (tatooed and feral) figure of the hillbilly/convict played by Robert DeNiro speaking in tongues as he drowns, the death of an avenging angel gone wrong, articulates the sort of association of the Pentecostal tradition with chaos and entropy that some critics have observed in Pynchon's work.

Chapter One. Crucifying the White Man

1   The woman quoted is Troy Lynn Yellow Wood. The two men under indictment are Arlo Looking Cloud, a distant relative of Russell Means, and John Boy Patton, also known as John Graham. In an interview on Canadian television in December 2000, Patton acknowledged being one of the persons who left Denver with Aquash in December 1975; he denied that she was kidnapped, as has been asserted by others. Aquash's cousin Robert Pictou-Branscombe of Arizona, who has been pursuing his own investigation and pressing for federal action, approves of the indictments but thinks that altogether six people were involved in the execution (Abbott, "27-Year Search Ends"; "Second Man Sought"). The Colorado chapter of AIM has issued a public statement essentially supporting Yellow Wood's point of view (American Indian Movement [AIM] of Colorado Position). Looking Cloud was convicted and sentenced to life imprisonment on April 23, 2004.

2   Dill's First Nations website dickshovel.com contains a considerable amount of AIM material as well as information and links on other Native issues.

3   The term "paranoid" appears frequently herein, and most of the time it is being used in the vernacular sense in which it has come to be used to describe any sort of unreasonable suspicion. The usage of the term in more clinical contexts is discussed to some extent toward the end of this account.

4   Durham's divorce settlement in 1977 includes Durham's agreement to make a "good faith effort" to write a book about AIM/FBI experiences with proceeds to go to the respondent (his third wife). #CD (17)-9615, District Court, 5th Dst. (Polk County) Des Moines, Iowa; hearing and decree August 15, 1977.

5   Unless otherwise noted, Giese cites refer to her article "Secret Agent Douglass Durham and the Death of Jancita Eagle Deer: Your Tax Dollar at Work." In *North Country Anvil*. Her later article "Profile of an Informer" in *Covert Action/ Information* (not to be confused with "Anatomy of an Informer," the J. P. Adams account in *Akwesasne Notes*) consists of excerpts from this earlier piece.

6   Tilsen's more detailed interpretation of the tapes was that "there was so much lying, bombast, and distortion that it's just impossible to sort out the truth; you could listen to all those hours of tapes and not be sure of a single thing you heard" (Matthiessen, 121).

7   Marriage records from Douglas County, Nebraska (Omaha) confirm that the 1965 marriage was Durham's third.

8   This account seems exaggerated for other reasons: as a second-generation member of Des Moines' Italian American community confirmed, "No . . . way—he couldn't have been a head of the Mafia because he wasn't Italian."

9   The Durham case before the grand jury was numbered 57663, and the companion case, defendant Pete De Phillips, was numbered 57662. The numbering system is inconsistent with the number on the information (#70–12893), leading to problems in locating the records. Durham stated in his Congressional testimony that another conviction in 1973, related to his AIM activities in Des Moines, was removed from court records at prosecutorial request due to his undercover status. His undercover status most likely had something to do with the disposition of this 1970 case as well, but at any rate there is no documentation that he was convicted of anything.

10 At the time of Giese's death, she was maintaining an extensive and valuable index of Native resources on a website out of Fond du Lac Tribal and Community College in northern Minnesota. The website was, until recently, accessible at http://indy4.fdl.cc.mn.us/~isk/mainmenu.html. Its successor is www.oyate.org (formerly displaying Giese's turtle logo); now more limited in scope.

11 Jancita Eagle Deer was killed when struck by a car driven by a teenager on a back country road at night. No charges were filed and the police investigation was sloppy, but the most questionable circumstance was that Eagle Deer was standing alone in a "disheveled" and disoriented condition in the middle of a deserted country road at night. Apparently Durham was the last person to see her alive (Geise 10–11).

12 See Brand; Matthiessen; Ward Churchill and Jim Vander Wall, *Agents of Repression: The FBI's Secret Wars Against the Black Panther Party and the American Indian Movement*; Bruce Johansen and Roberto Maestas, *Wasi'chu: The Continuing Indian Wars*; Rex Weyler, *Blood of the Land: The Government and Corporate War Against the American Indian Movement*.

13 Johanna Brand's biography of Anna Mae Aquash asserts that *Pax Today* is "now believed to have been a government front for intelligence gathering" (96), but does not document the source of this belief beyond a general reference to the 1975 Rockefeller Commission report; the report referred to CIA involvement with the American Newspaper Guild (Crewsdon).

14 Unless otherwise noted, all Churchill cites refer to Churchill and Vander Wall's *Agents of Repression*. They published a separate work focusing on facsimile copies of government documents, *The COINTELPRO Papers: Documents from the FBI's Secret Wars Against Dissent in the United States*.

15 An excellent and relatively recent account of the Banks/Means trial is John Sayer's *Ghost Dancing the Law: The Wounded Knee Trials*.

16 Sources disagree on the date of the hearing. Churchill and Vander Wall say it was in February 1976 (*Agents* 268, *Cointelpro* 391), but cite as their main sources Weyler and Matthiessen, neither of whom give the date. However, the *Akwesasne Notes* article ("Your Information Might Save Their Lives" 6–7) from early spring 1976 states that the hearing was on December 3, 1974, which makes more sense because Durham had not yet been outed by AIM (though Durant told *Akwesasne Notes* that he didn't find out about Durham until 1976 because he wasn't allowed to receive *AK* in prison). This dating is reiterated in the late autumn 1976 issue of *Akwesasne Notes* ("Judge Finds Murder Trial Humorous" [8–9]) which refers to Durham's testimony at the sanity trial "during the first year of incarceration." Johansen and Maestas say that Durham "posed as an Indian psychiatrist, who testified at a sanity hearing for Skyhorse that he was irrational and dangerous" (118). Weyler says Durham claimed to be "an Indian professor of clinical psychology from the University of Iowa, who knew all about the Indian mind" (171). As with much of the other published discussions of Durham, most of this is traceable to information provided to *Akwesasne Notes* by Giese, who relocated to Ventura, California to help with defense work at some point between early spring and later autumn 1976. Durham was a defense

witness, Durant had previously been in mental institutions, and a court appointed psychiatrist said that "Paul [Durant] believes the CIA or feds are trying to implant a device in his head. That the authorities are trying to get him to turn against his people. That his mail, phone conversations,etc. are monitored. Paul is paranoid" ("Your Information" 7).

17   The cases were United States vs. Mark Fleury, Reginald Dodge, Larry Johns, and Colin Wesaw, # CR74-L-14 (original conviction case # CR73–5160), and United States vs. Manuel Alvarado and Terry Williams, # CR 74-L-12. This motion was post-conviction as to the Fleury case and prior to final judgment in the Alvarado/Williams case. A hearing transcript was found in WKLD/OC records at the Minnesota Historical Society, box # 135. Page numbers refer to this transcript, a copy of a court document.

18   Taikeff was later lead counsel for the defense at the disastrous Leonard Peltier trial; Taikeff has been criticized for failing to get into evidence the FBI's coercion and threats to Myrtle Poor Bear and the death of Anna Mae Aquash. He left WKLD/OC immediately after the Peltier trial (Churchill and Vander Wall 318–9, 452).

19   "I seen a davenport inside the door" (54). This is not Durham's usual pattern of speech. It is a widespread verb form among white rural and working class Americans as well as rural Indians; likewise the usage "davenport" for couch or sofa.

20   See *Des Moines Register* April 27, 1975, June 1, 1985, editorial June 22, 1975; *Council Bluffs Nonpareil* April 28, 1975; *Omaha World Herald* June 2, 1975.

21   Defense attorney Martha Copelman: "By the way, are you Indian, Mr. Durham?" Durham: "No, I am not" (77). One has to wonder what answer Copelman might have received had she asked him if he were "part Indian" at this point in time (prior to the John Birch tour). Concepts of "Indianness" were somewhat fluid during the early seventies when AIM encouraged and welcomed people with partial Indian ancestry, assuming such claims were bona fide. Durham's credibility with AIM had, of course, been destroyed by this time, even though he seems to be sympathetic to AIM at this hearing and speaking to its interests. Given this orientation, even if he believed he had some fractional degree of Indian ancestry, it would have been in bad taste, i.e. impolite to say that he was "Indian" in front of an Indian audience.

22   Flyer for lecture at the Holiday Inn in Bismarck, South Dakota on October 30, "sponsored by local chapters of John Birch Society" in Box 102, WKLD/OC records at Minnesota Historical Society.

23   The most comprehensive books on the subject are Matthiessen's *In the Spirit of Crazy Horse* and Jim Messerschmidt's *The Trial of Leonard Peltier*; documentaries include Michael Apted's *Incident at Oglala* (1991) and PBS's *The Spirit of Crazy Horse* (1990).

24   Despite the discovery of new evidence suggesting alteration or fabrication of key ballistics evidence by the FBI, appellate courts have refused to reopen Peltier's case because of the strict legal standard on criminal convictions: retrial will not be granted on the mere possibility than the outcome would be different, but only upon the substantial probability of an acquittal—a standard of proof few convicted defendants are able to meet.

25   "The *New York Times* published a collection of articles on the Rockefeller Commission report on June 11, 1975 (18–22). Operation CHAOS was only one of several CIA programs reported. The CIA not only had been investigating the Students for a Democratic Society and the Black Panthers, but maintained files on 1,000 American organizations (21). This is the report that also discloses the CIA's experimentation with LSD on unsuspecting subjects and the plot to assassinate Fidel Castro.

26   Years later, John Trudell blamed the FBI, telling Ken Stern he knew the identity of the provocateur: "the feds never pursued this because the guy that made the bombs and taught us how to make bombs was working with them . . . he was definitely

linked a couple of times [with the Weathermen] and he was let go. And any time they even get a suspicion we're doing something, they don't let us go . . . I remember that the people who learned how to make the bombs were always caught, and those who taught them always walked." (Stern, *Loud Hawk: The United States Versus the American Indian Movement* 289–91).

27 This remark dates from 1955, arising from Eastland's support for the right-wing Federation for Constitutional Government (Stern, *A Force upon the Plain: The American Militia Movement and the Politics of Hate* 220).

28 Aaron Two Elk has described Durham's provocateur techniques while in Des Moines: "always right out front, urging everybody to get it on." Two Elk says Durham issued a memo in chapter leader Ron Petite's name "ordering" all AIM members to "carry arms at all times" (Churchill 223–24, 434).

29 The first memo is captioned "internal Security" file # 281785Z (Churchill, 445). The second teletype is reprinted in its entirety at Churchill *Agents* 282–84; a photo reproduction of it appears in Churchill and Vander Wall's *The COINTELPRO Papers*, 277–80.

30 As discussed elsewhere, "object relations" is a psychological term originated by Melanie Klein. It has to do with internalizing significant others as "imagoes" within one's pysche or body. In this mode of analysis, imagining tumors or cancers would be an example of internalizing hostile or aggressive feelings towards significant others.

31 Durham died at the age of 66 in Las Vegas on February 22, 2004. An anonymous but seemingly reliable source says he died of complications of non-Hodgkins lymphoma (http://imdcontentnew.searchease.com/villages/native/news/dill_aquash_ostriches_AIM.asp).

32 Schreber's father was a famous 19th century German doctor who developed, among other childrearing techniques, sadistic body braces and "sleeping belts" to keep children straight and still. (Schatzman 38–40).

33 The notorious 'mail box' quote comes from an FBI newsletter seized by activists who broke into an FBI office in Media, Pennsylvania in 1971. (Davis 10).

34 Durham called himself a 'convert' in the AIM debriefing interview. Durham stated at the Nebraska hearing that the FBI would not tell him who else was an informant "for anything" (36); this is consistent with the usual "need to know" policy, that an agent is only told what he "needs to know."

35 In this respect, a poststructuralist argument has the potential of advancing a fascist agenda to the extent that poststructuralism holds that everyone's acts are constructed by social imperatives. This concept is interrogated by the 2002 Spielberg film *Minority Report*, based on a short story by Philip K. Dick.

36 Many bodies of dead men were buried on the Pine Ridge reservation during these years as well, victims of the same undeclared war perpetrated by the Dick Wilson regime and the FBI against AIM.

Chapter 2. Lynching the White Woman

1 Peter Knight's phrase in opening address at Conspiracy Culture Conference, 1998. See generally Knight's book *Conspiracy Culture: From Kennedy to the X-Files* (2001).

2 Pierce, on the other hand, launches a thoroughgoing critique of modernism (postmodernism is off his radar screen) that attributes its decline in the standards of literature, music, and the visual arts to the Jewish conspiracy (107–112). The radical right of the sixties likewise demonized "modernity" as equivalent to liberalism and thus the handmaiden of Communism (Bell xii).

3 Allen refers to the survival gathering in the context of middle class white women who had attended it in her novel *The Woman Who Owned the Shadows*.

4   Rainbow people are a counterculture group with significant overlap with the dead-heads (followers of the Grateful Dead). Since the late seventies they have held annual "gatherings" on National Forest land where they camp out and share hugs and psychedelics.

5   However, "in northern California, the Pacific Northwest, and the rural Northeast it is not uncommon for gun-toting paramilitary leaders to live next door to latter-day hippies and marijuana growers" (Stock 3–4). The ramifications of national drug policy in placing both these groups on the same (wrong) side of the law are worthy of examination, but beyond the scope of this discussion. I will only briefly note that it is an oversimplification to treat the right-wing paramilitary groups and the drug culture as two discrete entities, just as the left/right political paradigm is inadequate. The testimony that convicted Timothy McVeigh was obtained, in part, in exchange for immunity from prosecution on methamphetamine-related charges. And in 1999, one of the survivors of the Waco firestorm was arrested at the southern California border with fifty-five pounds of marijuana ("Survivor of Waco Blaze Detained").

6   Richard Hofstadter first discussed the problem of Americans' anxiety about social status and national identity in the context of McCarthyism in "The Pseudo-Conservative Revolt—1954" (51–62). The list of demonized groups is not, of course, comprehensive; anti-immigration sentiment has focused on other groups as well. Daniel Bennett's *The Party of Fear* is a fairly good recent treatment of nativist movements.

7   McVeigh's background, however, is consistent with the argument that those attracted to these hate groups are economically and socially marginalized; he grew up in Lockport, New York, a "failing rust belt town" while co-conspirator Terry Nichol's brother was a farmer in "one of the most rural counties" in Michigan (Stock 147). Timothy McVeigh and Terry Nichols met in the army; those who knew McVeigh in the army have described him as a racist. The role of military culture in hate crime is only beginning to be examined. In his 2002 documentary *Bowling for Columbine*, Michael Moore explores the army-town culture in Oscoda, Michigan with which Nichols was connected and where one of the Columbine shooters lived before moving to Colorado. A sharp-eyed student pointed out to me that prison writer Jack Henry Abbott was born at the same military base.

8   Pierce died July 23, 2002. At the time of his death, the National Alliance was expanding its media operations. In 2001, its white power music company Resistance Records absorbed Vinland Records, the US subsidiary of a Swedish white power music company purchased by Pierce in 1999. The NA has produced a video game entitled "Ethnic Cleansing," and sent a group—the Anti-Globalization Activist Network—to the G8 summit protests in Canada in 2002. The fate of the National Alliance after Pierce's death has yet to be seen (Anti-Defamation League).

9   One characteristic of this closed system of thought seems to be its invulnerability to irony. Thus the sixties prank of jokester liberal Leonard C. Lewin's *The Report from Iron Mountain* (a parodic pseudo-report of a secret government study on the desirability of maintaining a state of war for the psychological and economic health of the nation) has been distributed as the real thing among the radical right since the mid-eighties.

10 For further discussion of the relationship between paranoid groups and their leaders see Otto F. Kernberg's "Leadership Styles and Organizational Paranoiagenesis."

11 According to Catherine McNicol Stock, the Order was also known as the Silent Brotherhood and was named after an elite guard in the German arm, the Bruder Schweigen (173).

12 Recently, the Aryan Nations has adopted the acronym AIM, for Aryan International Movement ("Separatists Offer Aid")—a move that cannot conceivably have been

made without awareness that AIM is the acronym for the American Indian Movement. As for Pierce, for Aryans modern-day Indians are under erasure.

13   This factor distinguishes *Hunter* from *The Turner Diaries*, which offers a twisted version of premillennialist Christian theology about the apocalypse (Brodie), most pointedly by setting the time of the final tribulation period as 1991 to 1999; the Second Coming was Hitler's birth (the "Great One") in 1889 (Macdonald 210).

14   Christian Identity theology, originating in the Anglo-Israelism of late-nineteenth and early twentieth-century Britain, holds that Aryans are the descendants of Adam and Eve, Jews are the offspring of Satan via the serpent's seduction of Eve, and blacks are the subhuman "mud people" who already existed before God created Adam and Eve (Robins and Post 182–87). The religious branch of the radical right is treated in *American Militias: Rebellion, Racism & Religion* by Richard Abanes (1996).

15   Of course, "black men" are rarely on the "welfare rolls" as usually defined unless they are either single parents or permanently disabled.

16   Compare Pierce's deputizing of black men from the welfare rolls to retired police officer Gerald "Jack" McLamb's 1993 lecture at the Seattle Preparedness Expo, asserting that "the Crips and the Bloods will be used as SA-style storm troopers to take away guns from Americans who refused to surrender their weapons to federal authorities" (Stern 157).

17   Though Celtic markers are prominent among the radical right, other white European ethnic minorities are drawn to it as well. The surname of Mark Basque, a prominent member of the Militia of Montana (Stern 92), is a reminder of the large Basque population in Idaho and Montana. Serbian Americans are now particularly vulnerable to the spreading of anti-Semitic conspiracy theories; see for example Bob Djurdjevic's website truthinmedia.org.

18   It is worth noting that during this period, England allowed only Lowland Scots to settle in Ulster. Gaelic-speaking Highlanders were excluded because of fears that they would identify with the native Irish rather than the Lowland Scots (Dobson 15). Thus, though the Highlanders present a much more romantic picture of Celtic ethnicity, most Americans with Scots-Irish ancestry are not descended from anyone who spoke Gaelic. Furthermore, not all of the Ulster settlers were Scottish; they included French Huguenots, English Puritans, and dissidents from Holland (9).

19   Pat Robertson, who has "deep Scottish roots," has recently entered into a joint venture with the Bank of Scotland to set up a "virtual bank" in the United States, servicing customers entirely by telephone and the internet (Hiday). Considering Robertson's past railings against the international banking conspiracy, one can only remark, regarding this new Mother Bank from the mother country, that it takes a thief to catch a thief.

20   American Indians are invisible on Pierce's racial map. The most complete laundry list of mongrels and mud people in *The Turner Diaries* includes "Whites, half-Whites, Gypsies, Chicanos, Puerto Ricans, Jews, Blacks, Orientals, Arabs, Persians, and everything else under the sun: the typical, cosmopolitan racial goulash one finds in every American metropolitan area these days" (200). *Hunter* mentions Indians a couple of times, but only in the context of "fighting the Indians and taming the wilderness" (70) and the multiculturalist assaults on the literary canon when "democracy came to the academy and the standards were lowered so that the Hottentots and wetbacks could get degrees too . . . unless a book were written by a militant lesbian, a revanchist American Indian, or a Negress with AIDS who'd converted to Judaism, it was suspect" (144–5).

21   Though some Marxists argue that the relationship of liberalism to late capitalism is entirely consistent with Marxist thought, full consideration of this point would be

beyond the scope of this analysis. One interesting rural perspective can be gained from Ward Churchill's anthology *Marxism and Native Americans* (1982).

22   *Oscar* blushes more than once in *Hunter* because blushing is a signifier of whiteness, as explained in Ridgeway's *Blood in the Face*

23   The foregoing comprise a composite of phrases from various speeches and writings of Adolph Hitler.

24   Stock points out that for Randy and Vicki Weaver, the distance from Iowa to Idaho, i.e. from "the politics of producerism" to "the culture of vigilantism," was shorter than one might think. The Weavers grew up in Iowa and encountered the ideology of the far right in Cedar Falls—ironically, a college town, home of the University of Northern Iowa. In 1983 they joined the Christian Identity movement and moved to Boundary County, Idaho, home of the Aryan Nations and the Order. Though Vicki's family lost their farm to highway development, they remain repulsed by Vicki's beliefs after the FBI shot her in 1993 (144, 149).

25   The FBI used the same techniques with Koresh that had worked with Manuel Noriega. Robins and Post comment on the FBI's handling of the Koresh matter that "they misdiagnosed Koresh as a psychopath, a con man . . . When such an individual is hanging from the edge of the cliff of sanity, you do not subject his hands to merciless pounding with a high-frequency drill . . . Moreover, the government and media's focus on Koresh, the failed rock star who longed for prominence, must have rewarded his grandiose narcissism. He was the center of America's attention" (129).

26   Though scholars tend to speak of the John Birch Society in the past tense or as vestigial organization of Midwestern troglodytes, twenty-one thousand people still subscribed to its newsletter in 1991 (Robins and Post 192). It maintains an up-to-date website, though current membership numbers are not publicized, and a prominent JBS billboard urging the United States to "get out of the United Nations"appears at a major intersection five miles from my home in southern California.

Chapter Three. Women's Work

1   The movies mentioned are *Rosemary's Baby* (1968), *The Exorcist* (1973), *It's Alive* (1974), *The Omen* (1976), *The Devil within Her* (originally entitled *I Don't Want to be Born*, 1976), and *The Changeling* (1979).

2   Bromley cites three characteristics of what he calls countersubversion ideologies: (1) a physical/objective dimension in which subversives are cast as aliens, (2) a moral/normative dimension in which they are cast as "quintessentially evil," symbolized by inversions of the sacred, and (3) a cathectic/subjective dimension in which contact with subversives is corrupting—"irrestistible, inexorable and irreversible" (56).

3   Nathan and Snedeker (34), citing Cohn (xi) and an essay by Veronique Compion-Vincent entitled "The Baby Parts Story: A New Latin American Legend."

4   The idea that women occupied an inherently conservative role in village politics in the early modern period is discussed by Alan Macfarlane in *Witchcraft in Tudor and Stuart England.* Christina Larner goes further in arguing that women tended to attack other women who did not conform to the roles dictated by a patriarchal society in *Enemies of God: The Witch-Hunt in Scotland.*

5   The Kleinian concept of the paranoid-schizoid position is discussed most extensively in the chapters on Pynchon and Silko.

6   See Dwight Edgar Abbott's autobiographical account *I Cried, You Didn't Listen,* discussed further in chapter 6.

7 A more universal feature of the discourse of witchcraft is introjection and projection of objects in and out of bodies, a psychological dynamic consistent with Klein's object relations model.

8 Norman Cohn recounts a baby-eating hysterical pogrom against early Christians in Lyons in AD 177 (3–4).

9 This description was inspired by a "spell" offered as incriminating evidence in the Lancashire witch trials:

> What is yonder that casts a light so farrandly?
> Mine own dear son that's nailed to the tree,
> He is nailed sore by the heart and hand
> And holy brain-pan. (Rosen 366 n22)

10 See Arthur Lyons, *Satan Wants You: The Cult of Devil Worship in America* (149) and Shawn Carlson and Gerald Larue, *Satanism in America* (102). The actual documents have never been made available (Nathan and Snedeker 129).

11 Paul & Shirley Eberle, *The Abuse of Innocence: The McMartin Preschool Trial* (1993); Jeffrey S. Victor, *Satanic Panic: The Creation of a Contemporary Legend* (1993); Lawrence Wright, *Remembering Satan: A Case of Recovered Memory and the Shattering of an American Family* (1994); Richard Ofshe and Ethan Watters, *Making Monsters: False Memories, Psychotherapy and Sexual Hysteria* (1994); Elizabeth Loftus and Katherine Ketcham, *The Myth of Repressed Memory: False Memories and Allegations of Sexual Abuse* (1994).

   See also David D. Bromley and Anson D. Shupe Jr., *Strange Gods: The Great American Cult Scare* (1981), an important earlier work that predated the day care prosecutions, and Elaine Showalter, *Hystories: Hysterical Epidemics and Modern Culture* (1997), a feminist semiotic analysis which includes chapters on recovered memory and satanic ritual abuse.

12 The novel offers a somewhat Freudian and not particularly feminist rationale for the child's accusations: he has observed his somewhat negligent single mother in the primal scene with her boyfriend. It was made into a film of considerably inferior quality to the book in 1999.

13 Elizabeth Loftus, a leading forensic psychologist and authority on suggestibility of witnesses, describes a controlled study in which children willingly reported abusive behavior by a role players with a doll, based solely on suggestive questioning. The control group not exposed to suggestive questioning provided reasonably accurate answers as to what the role player did with the doll (78).

   As for "recovered" memories, Loftus maintains that true memories of sexual abuse are rarely repressed. Loftus herself says that she was abused by a teenage male babysitter as a six-year old child. She never forgot the experience, so she had no need to "recover" it. Nevertheless, one of the repressed memory therapists she encountered as a professional psychologist felt compelled to help her deal with her pain by drawing a figure of the molester, sticking pins in it, and presenting it to Loftus (226).

14 Nathan and Snedeker cite the example of French physician Ambroise Auguste Tardieu, who asserted in 1858 that the rectum of the passive homosexual is funnel shaped whereas the penis of the active pederast is "slender, undeveloped . . . with a small glans, tapering from root to tip like a dog's." (186, 292 n.20).

15 This woman, Mary Ann Barbour, had had a troubled life. She was thrown out of a window by a relative as a child and had a plate in her head from a traffic accident. She ran away from home at age fourteen and was in her third marriage when she reported the alleged abuse of her step-granddaughter Bobbie McCuan to authorities in January of 1980. When Bobbie was not immediately removed from her parents' home (the parents had promised the social workers they would keep the accused, Rod Phelps, away from Bobbie), getting no response from her congressperson or the state

Attorney General, she pulled a knife on her husband and was committed for psychiatric observation. She was released, but later in 1982 as the prosecution progressed, she stopped sleeping again and kept the girls up with her all night, interrogating them and reporting new and increasingly bizarre scenarios of abuse to the authorities. Later, on the witness stand at the trial, she could not recall many of these allegations (Nathan and Snedeker 54–64).

16   Bobbie McCuan would have been seven years old in 1980, the time of the grandmother's initial report leading to Bobbie's first interrogation, though the step-grandmother (Mary Ann Barbour) had been examining her genitals since she was four. There was perhaps reason at the time to suspect a step-grandfather named Rod Phelps, but his name got lost in the confusion of what was to follow (55). The blended and extended family relationships involved in the Bakersfield prosecutions are so complex that it is difficult to follow them even by constructing a family tree.

17   David Finkelhor, Linda Meyer Williams, with Nanci Burns, *Nursery Crimes: Sexual Abuse in Day Care* (132). Lead author Finkelhor was an incest expert who had concluded in earlier studies that women were unlikely incest perpetrators (see note below). On the McMartin case, see Jill Waterman et al., *Behind the Playground Walls: Sexual Abuse in Preschools*.

18   Jeffey Moussaieff Masson followed up this controversial treatise with the publication four years later of the perhaps even more iconoclastic *Against Therapy: Emotional Tyranny and the Myth of Psychological Healing.*

19   Nathan discusses the Texas case in *Women and Other Aliens.*

20   The Kelly Michaels case as well as the Amirault case and a few other latter-day travesties from the day care panic are covered in Dorothy Rabinowitz's *No Crueler Tyrannies: Accusation, False Witness, and Other Terrors of Our Times* (2003). A handful of people remained imprisoned through the end of the nineties, most prominently the Amirault family in Massachusetts—ground zero for the coverup of child sexual abuse by Catholic priests.

21   One of the mothers in the Michaels case, Patricia Crowley, was a local newspaper editor. She published her own credulous account of the case, *Not My Child,* well before the appellate reversal. Most of the mass prosecutions involved the children of similarly influential people, more often children of people connected with law enforcement who were acquainted with people who had been to seminars.

22   The editorial comments in the above transcript are Rabinowitz's, but they are somewhat superfluous to the actual dialogue. Manshel says Rabinowitz's account is "far from accurate"—that the child never said "It's all lies" during an audiotaped interview. But then Manshel says what really happened was that before the grand jury "the youngster started shouting Lies! Lies! Lies! in response to McArdle's (the prosecutor's) questioning. When she then asked, 'Okay. Then what did Kelly do?' he answered quietly, 'No. It's the truth'" (19). At any rate, the exchange she quotes does not seem materially different.

23   New charges have been brought against Kelly based on testimony from an older girl who seems not to have reported the alleged abuse until years into the day care prosecution.

24   The verdict in the civil suit, Roberson vs. Perez, was rendered June 29, 1998 ("A Time Line"). The settlement was announced February 24, 1999 ("Man Says He Settled").

25   This latest count is from a letter to *The Nation* in 2002, signed by Debbie Nathan, Lona Manning, Carol Weissbrod, and Bob Chatelle. According to the letter, updates are available at www.freebaran.org/cases.

26   Here is the actual passage, commenting on Klein's narrative of her session with Dick: "The psychoanalyst no longer says to the patient: 'Tell me a little bit about your

desiring-machines, won't you?' Instead he screams: 'Answer daddy-and-mommy when I speak to you!' Even Melanie Klein." (Deleuze and Guattari 45)

27 Klein found that Dick was interested in "trains and stations and in door-handles, doors and the opening and shutting of them." Klein named a big and little train "Daddy-train" and "Dick-train," and as Dick rolled the little train toward the station, she explained "The station is mummy; Dick is going into mummy." Dick found this theme very stimulating and it seems to have elicited the same sort of communicative breakthrough as Helen Keller having the water run over her hand (Klein, "The Importance of Symbol Formation in the Development of the Ego [1930]" 98–109). For commentary from both an authority on autism and from middle-aged Dick himself, see Phyllis Grosskurth, *Melanie Klein: Her World and Her Work* (187–88).

28 In German, 'popo' means buttocks; 'kacki' means feces; 'kucks' or 'kuchen' means cakes (Klein 232).

29 The object relations school of psychotherapy grounded in Klein's and Winnicott's work has been criticized, not without cause, for the universalization of mother-blaming for all sorts of psychological problems. Overall, one could argue that Klein herself was more interested in absolving mothers of guilt than in blaming them.

30 The only other "voluntary" confession of a defendant besides Ileana Fuster was by Paul Ingram, former deputy sheriff in Olympia, Washington, who confessed after a long period of interrogation marked by sleep deprivation and hypnosis-like procedures (there have been numerous "Alford plea"-type confessions, i.e., guilty pleas based not upon a confession of guilt but upon the admission that the prosecution has sufficient evidence to convict). Ingram dutifully "recovered a memory" of raping his daughters in accordance with the memories one daughter "recovered" with the aid of a pseudo-feminist faith healer at summer camp in 1988 (Ofshe and Watters).

31 Nathan and Snedeker (195), cf. W.L. Whittington et al.

32 An example from Ileana's testimony (later recanted, and the recantation later recanted), about Frank putting snakes inside her and the children: "'Well, I remember a snake,' she answered. 'What about a snake?' asked a lawyer. 'Having bad dreams about it,' she replied." (Nathan and Snedeker 175).

33 Reno has denied visiting Ileana prior to her guilty plea (174), but the depositions transpired in the days thereafter. Nathan and Snedeker cite Jan Hollingsworth, *Unspeakable Acts* (475) on the hand-holding.

34 Brian Kniffen's story "Kniffen Sons Want Parents Back," appeared in the *Bakersfield Californian* July 26, 1996 and in the *FMS (False Memory Syndrome) Foundation Newsletter* (e-mail edition) 5:8 (September 1, 1996).

35 Nathan and Snedeker gleaned such information from grant reports filed with the government by the Clearinghouse on Child Abuse and Neglect Information (245).

36 One could remark that continental psychoanalytic theory itself has travelled a similar Oepidal progression from a focus on the bad mother to a fascination with the phallic signifying system of Jacques Lacan, who was not only familiar with Klein's work, but even offered to translate some of it, and then lost her manuscript (Grosskurth 377, 389–90). See also Burgoyne and Sullivan, *The Klein-Lacan Dialogues* (1997, a collection of essays by contemporary psycholoanalysts).

Chapter Four. Motherhood and Treason

1 This statement appeared in a newsletter dated September 9, 1970, produced by Special Agent James O'Connor of the New Left desk at the Philadelphia FBI field office. The newsletter was one of some one thousand classified documents stolen from the Philadelphia FBI office by an anonymous group calling itself the Citizens

Commission to Investigate the FBI on March 8, 1971. The Citizens Commission disseminated copies of the documents widely among American news media; Davis's source as to this particular document is the *Delaware County Daily Times* March 24, 1971.

Davis's book is a relatively concise and evenhanded account of COINTELPRO operations from 1956 through the 1980s. Many of his sources, however, are secondary. For more complete documentation of sources on FBI surveillance see Chapter 1.

2   The earliest description of the "San Diego conspiracy" to create a massive disturbance at the 1972 Republican Convention was given by informant Louis Tackwood to the Los Angeles-based Citizens Research and Investigation Committee, authors of *The Glass House Tapes*, in September 1971. According to Tackwood the purpose of the plot that later developed into the Watergate scandal was "to create a nation-wide hysteria that would then provide President Richard M. Nixon with the popular support necessary to declare a national state of emergency; the government could then arrest all 'radicals,' 'miliants,' and 'left-wing revolutionaries'" (41–42, 171–80, 42).

3   Davis, 150–51. An independent source indicates that the actual informant would have been Howard Berry Godfrey (Citizens Research 161–163).

4   According to Tackwood's account, he was raised until the age of 7 by his grandmother, during which time he spent 3 years housebound and virtually alone while she worked as a domestic servant, seeing her only twice a week. He then lived with his father and uncle; his father was killed in a drug-dealing dispute when his son was eleven. Tackwood was an extremely precocious child who read books by the age of six, argued interest rates with bankers at age nine, and was forging bank withdrawal slips at age 10. His favorite authors as a youth included Machiavelli, Napoleon, Hitler, Himmler, and Bertrand Russell.

    For an account of a more "ordinary" informant, see William Tulio Divale with James Joseph, *I Lived inside the Campus Revolution.*

5   Defense lawyers have complained for years that the term "confidential informant" in FBI files is a fictitious construct used to conceal both FBI operatives and their purely speculative hypotheses. This assertion is supported by the experience of former FBA agent Cril Payne who, in submitting a Freedom of Information Act request on his own files, found that his investigative reports had been classified as material received from a "confidential security informant" (Payne 344).

6   Davis refers to one female informant, unnamed, who provided over 1,000 names of members of an antidraft group and its fellow travelers in the United Church of Christ (149).

7   The sexual paradigm of fascism is succinctly described in the song by Billy of the Vomitones, Greek chorus to Pynchon's drama, sung at the final family reunion:

> Fuck you, mister,
> Fuck your sister,
> Fuck your brother,
> Fuck your mother,
> Fuck your pop -
> Hey! I'm a cop!
>
> Yeah, fuck you, yuppie,
> Fuck your puppy,
> Fuck your baby,
> Fuck your lady,
> Yes I can,
> Hey! I'm the Man! (356–57)

Critical readers will note that the Vomitones have gleaned much of their earlier material from Deleuze and Guattari's *Italian Wedding Fake Book* (*VI* 97)

8   Pynchon has clearly implied that Prairie and Frenesiare fascists themselves: he sent a copy of the novel to his former creative writing instructor at Cornell with the inscription "Dear Walt, this is what you get for asking, a third of a century ago in class, 'How about a story where the parents are progressive and the kids are fascists?' See? You never know when somebody might be listening" (Hite 140).

9   To be fair to Pynchon, he writes the alternative creation myth of Lilith in the Garden of Eden into the text, with the men screwing everything up instead of Eve. It is Sister Rochelle's story, however, not the narrator's.

10   Hayles implies that Zoyd is feminized by way of his parental role to Prairie and thus "liable to seduction in the snitch system" (17), but this is more a cop's (Hector's) fantasy than Pynchon's, even though the narrator says Zoyd's "virginity" is "technical" insofar as providing information to the government (12). Feminization and castration are equally inadequate words to describe Zoyd's lack of agency.

      One way to read the Zoyd/Frenesi relationship would be as two conflicting alter egos of a political novelist. Zoyd writes apolitical song lyrics; Frenesi attempts to be a serious radical filmmaker but degenerates beyond mere failure to become a traitor to the cause.

11   *Vineland*'s narrator explains: "Brock Vond's genius was to have seen in the activities of the sixties left not threats to order but unacknowledged desires for it . . . Brock saw the deep . . . need only to stay children forever, safe inside some extended national Family . . . men who had grown feminine, women who had become small children, flurries of long naked limbs, little girls naked under boyfriends' fringe jackets . . . the sort of mild herd creatures who belonged, who'd feel, let's face it, much more comfortable behind fences" (269). Compare this passage to Nietzsche's revilement of the "herds and believers" in "Thus Spoke Zarathustra," (part 9 of "Zarathustra's Prologue" Walter Kaufman 135–36). Herds of puerile young people are a concern of Don DeLillo in *Mao II* as well.

12   See generally R. D. Hinshelwood, *A Dictionary of Kleinian Thought* and Juliet Mitchell, *The Selected Melanie Klein.*

13   In the third instance, the group harbors both hostile feelings toward the pair for holding themselves apart from the group and an unconscious desire that the couple will produce a child savior for the group. . Bion's work has been criticized on the grounds that he studied "artificial, taskless" groups out of the context of actual cultural conditions and imperatives (Marcus 93).

14   The trial at which the early Pynchon presided was that of Hugh and Mary Parsons.

15   I prefer the term "Other" to "bad breast" as part of a larger endeavor to de-genderize applications of Kleinian concepts in the field of cultural studies. The good breast/bad breast terminology tends to reinforce a mother-blaming paradigm that (though the problem of mother-blaming is of primary concern in this text) is ultimately beside the point.

16   This attitude can be most clearly seen in the European press, supporting my suggestion that the novel can be usefully viewed as a response to trauma. Europeans did not undergo the trauma of the American New Left and its aftermath. See Wendy Steiner, "Pynchon's Progress: Dopeheads Revisited," *Independent* [London], 3 February 1990, 30; Edmund White, "Flower Power-Broking," *Independent* [London] 4 February 1990; James Wood, "Seriously Unfunny, Truly Unreal America," *Times* [London], 3 February 1990, 38; Nicole Zand, "A la recherche du temps hippy," *Le Monde,* 20 September 1991, 24 (review of French translation). From the American mainstream press, see Pico Iyer, "History? Education? Zap! Pow! Cut!" *Time,* 14 May 1990, 98; Malcolm Jones, Jr., "Pynchon's Shaggy Dog Story," *Newsweek,* 8 January 1990, 66; John Whitworth, "Not a Novel for Grown-Ups," *Spectator* 3 February 1990, 28;

Douglas Keesey, "*Vineland* in the Mainstream Press: A Reception Study," *Pynchon Notes* 26–27 (Spring-Fall 1990): 107–13.

Chapter Five. Motherhood and Terror

1   There are problematic aspects to Klein's terminology: the terms 'paranoid' and 'schizoid' both suffer from overbroad application outside the clinical sphere as well as being markers of some of the most politically charged terrain within psychiatry in terms of sexuality and gender discrimination. Nevertheless, the concept Klein attempts to articulate has value beyond the limitations of language to describe it.

2   'Defamiliarization' is a concept originating in the work of Russian formalist Viktor Shklovsky, referring to a technique of increasing the difficulty of the perception process to sharpen perception by disallowing the 'default' application of conventional codes of representation—as in, for example, Tolstoy narrating from the point of view of a horse.

3   James L. Thorson of the University of New Mexico related this anecdote at the annual conference of the Popular Culture Association and American Culture Association on April 1, 1999.

4   Silko's work is also very reflective of the focus on mother-daughter relationships common in contemporary fiction by women of color. See, for example, Charlene Taylor Evans's essay. I read Silko's mother-daughter relationships, however, as much more problematic than Evans acknowledges, as should become apparent through the course of this essay.

5   Unlike much speculative science fiction, however, Silko's novel is overtly anti-technology.

6   Born in 1948, Silko views herself as an "in-between" person generationally as well as ethnically; she discusses her generational liminality in Coltelli's interview (143, 148).

7   Kristeva discusses Kleinian theory most specifically in her book on depression, *Black Sun*. Abjection is the subject of *The Powers of Horror*; the term "designates a psychic moment under sway of the death drive that occurs before libidinal drives are directed toward external objects. It has resonance with the Kleinian paranoid-schizoid position since abjection is an early position involving both aggression and splitting" (Doane and Hodges (86–87). Though Kristeva has been considered a feminist psychoanalyst due to her focus on the maternal, Doane and Hodges convincingly argue that "far from offering a feminist subversion of the language of Lacan, Kristeva's most recent discussion of the mother in *Black Sun* emphasizes the pathology of nonphallic maternal desire" (54). Nevertheless, I find her concept of abjection useful.

8   What Maximum Bob's wife (on the eponymous 1998 television series) calls "fear of the devouring Mother." "Same old, same old," commiserates her cross-dressing mermaid friend.

9   For example, during the wave of witchcraft accusations recorded by the U.S. Army in 1975 (shortly after the forced removal of the Navajos to Bosque Redondo in New Mexico) one accused witch, Biwosi, had allegedly "sent out spies to gather the saliva and feces of his intended victims as well as soil from their shadows and the manure from their livestock. He buried these items and cast spells. He also shot stones into people's bodies" (Moore 188).
    There are both remarkable similarities and remarkable differences between Keres and Dineh (Navajo) beliefs regarding the spirit world. Attitudes about witches are one of the similarities. Another is the existence of other worlds below this one and a creation story involving the emergence of humans from underground into this world. One significant difference is the Dineh aversion to touching a dead body.

10   Mosca also evokes the tricksterish character of the same name in Ben Jonson's
      Volpone.
11   In March 1998, a lynch mob in a Mexican town in the state of Hidalgo killed two
      men who had attempted to kidnap four school girls. Though the town's attorney
      general found "absolutely no evidence of organ trafficking," bystanders said that
      "after the beatings, one confessed to working for a man in Texas who paid $5,000
      for each kidnapped child." Similarly, an American woman was severely beaten in
      Guatemala in 1994 due to rumors that Americans were abducting local children
      (Stevenson). The "baby parts story" has been in circulation in Latin American for at
      least ten years; it is discussed in a 1990 essay by Veronique Compion-Vincent. For
      a discussion of the reality behind the body-parts story, see Ann Folwell Stanford's
      1997 essay. For an extended more scholarly look at international traffic in body
      parts, see Nancy Scheper-Hughes and Loic Wacquant, eds, *Commodifying Bodies*
      (2003).
12   A thorough analysis of the blood motif and the fetishism of blood in this novel is
      provided by Jane Olsmstead in "The Uses of Blood in Leslie Marmon Silko's
      Almanac of the Dead." Olsmstead points out that contemporary dictionary defini-
      tions of 'fetish' seem to imply that fetish users are 'outsiders,' that is, Others, whereas
      the fetishism in *Almanac* is more often practiced by dominant males.
13   Until recently, homosexuality was a "disorder" with its own listing in the handbook
      of American psychiatry, *The Diagnostic and Statistical Manual of Mental Disorders,*
      published by the American Psychiatric Association and usually referred to as the
      DSM.
14   The problem of the deployment of negative male homosexual stereotypes in *Almanac*
      is fully interrogated by Janet St. Clair in "Cannibal Queers: The Problematics of
      Metaphor in *Almanac of the Dead.*" St. Clair convincingly argues that the "cannibal
      queers" are more metaphoric than stereotypic, invoked as a critique of Euro-America's
      phallocentrism, racism and gynophobia (212). Olsmstead draws similar conclusions
      as to a "critique of the fetishized phallus" in the novel. St. Clair also points out that
      the nefarious characters in question often tend to use sex in the service of consump-
      tion without particular regard to gender (208), thus reiterating my argument that it
      is consumption, rather than sex, that is the primary trope here. As for the under-
      current of "outdated psychoanalytic theories about the elusive or abusive mother"
      (218) she points out that "virtually all the characters . . . hate their mothers" (219).
      It is difficult to argue with St. Clair's gentle suggestion that Silko has "at least some
      moral obligation not to promulgate" negative stereotypes of gay males (216), but
      Silko's characters—for example, "faggots who got hot when they wore a pig's
      uniform" (*Almanac* 456)—certainly pale in comparison to the commodifying of
      similar stereotypes in the recent HBO series *Oz* and other representations of prison
      culture, both from within and without. Homosocial conflations of sex and power are
      further addressed in Chapter 6.
15   "Yellow Woman" was one of several Silko stories published in *The Man to Send Rain-
      clouds: Contemporary Stories by American Indians,* ed. Kenneth Rosen. A good
      overview of Yellow Woman in the context of Keres oral tradition can be found in
      Melody Graulich's and A. Lavonne Ruoff's essays in *"Yellow Woman": Leslie Marmon
      Silko.*
16   Paula Gunn Allen says, on the other hand, that yellow is the color "ascribed to the
      Northwest" (*Sacred Hoop* 226). Matters of sacred significance are often elided for
      public dissemination, similar to the practice of altering sacred rituals when they are
      being performed for a tourist audience.
17   The architecture of the beachfront condo has an eerie resonance with the stories of
      Yellow Woman's abductions by Cliff Dweller and Flint Wing. Seese is essentially

"rescued" from the condo by seeing Lecha on TV; in this instance Lecha plays a
Spider Woman-like role in that Spider Woman often helps people down from a high
cliff "by means of her web" (Boas 218).

Chapter Six. Beyond the Foucauldian Complex

1   This calculation is based upon the Bureau of Justice Statistics' 2001 report of U.S
    incarceration at 1,965,495, a rate of 690 per 100,000, the highest in the world.
    Russia is second with 977,700 inmates, or 676 per 100,000. The rates in most of
    western Europe range from 60–130 per 100,000, according to the Sentencing
    Project.

2   See generally Christian Parenti's *Lockdown America: Police and Prisons in the Age of
    Crisis* (1999). On the late twentieth century history of the political use of tough-on-
    crime narratives, see Katherine Beckett, *Making Crime Pay: Law and Order in
    Contemporary American Politics* (1997).

3   The statement was made on an episode of *Sixty Minutes II* broadcast January 16,
    2001.

4   This statement was made in the introductory portion of *The Legacy*, first broadcast
    on PBS.

5   The foregoing statistics are from the following pages of the Department of Justice
    website: "Key Facts at a Glance: Violent Crime Trends"; "Key Facts at a Glance:
    Correctional Populations"; and "Criminal Offenders Statistics." September 14, 2003.
    http://www.ojp.usdoj.gov/bjs.

6   It is possible, nevertheless, for the fathers of bereaved daughters to be more objective.
    The father and granfather of Polly Klaas, the 12-year old whose abduction and
    murder helped spur the three strikes campaign, withdrew from their association with
    Reynolds and the campaign once they realized the ramifications of the three strikes
    initiative for people convicted of nonviolent crimes (*The Legacy*).

7   O'Donnell mentions DeLillo's construction of Oswald in his novel *Libra* in this
    chapter, but aside from Mailer's book on Gilmore his main topics of analysis are the
    1992 Tarentino film *Reservoir Dogs* and an obscure 1952 novel by former Commu-
    nist Party member Jim Thompson, *The Killer Inside Me.*

8   Sedgwick's model of homoerotic exchange taking place over the body of a woman is
    borne out here in the image of the body (a live one, that is) of Nicole Baker, Gilmore's
    girlfriend (O'Donnell's exegesis refers to Sedgwick's important critical work *Between
    Men: English Literature and Male Homosocial Desire*).
        Gary Gilmore received large-scale media attention in the 1970s when he insisted,
    over the objections of the American Civil Liberties Union, that he be executed by
    firing squad after killing two people in cold blood. The state of Utah was happy to
    oblige.

9   The figure of cannibalistic consumption pursued by O'Donnell originates, appar-
    ently, in a statement by Gilmore's girlfriend involving "climbing into Gilmore's
    mouth" and down his throat to "mend the worn spot in [his] stomach" (O'Donnell
    125, 128).

10 Readers might expect that an analysis of television shows, particularly the recent
    HBO series *Oz*, be included here in a discussion of representations of prison and
    criminality. Such a project could easily turn into another book; one hardly knows
    where to begin. As for *Cops* and *America's Most Wanted*, I will merely note that the
    people being filmed as they are being arrested on those shows are only rarely consen-
    sual participants in a public spectacle (unlike Gilmore). As for *Oz*, there would be
    more to say about it in the context of an analysis of homoerotic soft porn than in this

particular analysis. Though sexual and homoerotic content in prison literature is discussed herein, such content does not seem to be present in these examples primarily for the pleasure of the viewer or reader, as would seem, at least to this viewer, to be the case with *Oz*. This is not to say that *Oz* has no redeeming social value. Like pornography generally, it may have some educational value for the inexperienced and unknowledgeable viewer, as in the sometimes didactic observations offered in Augustus's framing narratives. Nevertheless, I doubt anyone would recommend *Oz* for the purpose of teaching viewers how to function better in a prison environment.

11 Susan Rosenberg and Kathy Boudin have been recently paroled.

12 Just as with the Gary Gilmore case, Mailer's fascination with a connection between violence and sexuality and with the homosocial bond is what led him into correspondence with Abbott, and Mailer's influence in shaping the form of this Abbott's published text should not be underestimated.

13 An early example is Injun Joe in Mark Twain's *Tom Sawyer*, but the evil halfbreed stereotype extends well into the late twentieth century in the character of Blue Duck in the eighties mini-series *Lonesome Dove*.

14 Prison writer Sanyika Shakur, commenting on these searches, says "At first it bothered me a lot. I felt like a diseased piece of meat being examined by some pigs at an auction. A bunch of guys getting their kicks off of watching forty naked men moving into different positions of humiliation at the command of a voice . . . I've never seen one of these searches yield anything . . . Although I know that prisoners do secrete weapons, drugs, and other things in their butts, the pigs haven't ever found anything on the searches I've been involved in. This process is just another ritual designed to degrade" (320–21).

15 A story in Chevigny's anthology that addresses the many complex ramifications of a situation involving sex between a woman prisoner and a guard is "Lee's Time" by Susan Rosenberg. Rosenberg's sentence was recently commuted by outgoing President Clinton. She was a political activist targeted by the FBI for supporting the Black Liberation Army, convicted for possession of weapons and explosives.

16 William Sydney Porter, pen name O. Henry, served four years time in prison. According to Bruce Franklin, when it was learned after his death in 1910 that he was an ex-convict, he had a large influence on the evolution of some prison writers from autobiographical narrative to fiction (Franklin, *Prison Literature* (150–51).

17 Martin's columns are assembled in the book *Committing Journalism: The Prison Writings of Red Hog*, a collaboration with editor Peter Sussman that intersperses Sussman's account of the *Chronicle*'s first amendment litigation with a series of Martin's columns. The federal regulation that prohibited the *Chronicle* from publishing Martin's by-line on the columns remains in effect; by the time the case got to the Supreme Court, Martin has been paroled and thus lost his standing to contest the regulation.

18 Scott adopted the name Sanyika Shakur after his conversion to Islam in prison. His autobiography *Monster* (1993) is published under his new name.

19 "The Fink Has Soul" was the title of a review of his new album in *Hi Fi* 7 (August 1977): 110.

Epilogue

1 The quote is from Rob Lightner, reviewer of the graphic novel for Amazon.com. Moore and Campbell (Campbell is the illustrator) are a fairly prolific and prominent English team in the world of underground or "adult" comics.

Works Cited

Abanes, Richard. *American Militias: Rebellion, Racism & Religion.* Foreword by Roy Innis. Downers Grove, Ill: InterVarsity Press, 1996.

Abbott, Dwight Edgar. *I Cried, You Didn't Listen: A Survivor's Expose of the California Youth Authority.* Los Angeles, CA: Feral House, 1991.

Abbott, Jack Henry, *In the Belly of the Beast: Letters from Prison.* Introduction by Norman Mailer. New York: Random House, 1981.

Adams, John P. "AIM, the Church and the FBI: The Douglass Durham Case." *Christian Century* 92 (14 May 1975): 489–495. Reprinted as "Anatomy of an Informer" in *Akwesasne Notes* Early Summer 1975: 14–16 and "Anatomy of an Informer—Part II" in *Akwesasne Notes* Early Winter 1975: 10ff.

Abbott, Karen. "27-Year Search Ends in Arrest." *Rocky Mountain News.* April 3, 2003.

———. "Second Man Sought in Activist's Killing." *Rocky Mountain News.* April 4, 2003.

Adorno, Theodor et al. *The Authoritarian Personality.* New York: Harper, 1950.

"*Akwesasne Notes* Target of COINTELPRO-Type Disruptive Tactics: California Murder Trial Continues." *Akwesasne Notes* Early Summer 1976: 5.

Alford, C. Fred. *Melanie Klein and Critical Social Theory: An Account of Politics, Art, and Reason Based on Her Psychoanalytic Theory.* New Haven: Yale University Press, 1989.

Allen, Paula Gunn. *The Sacred Hoop: Recovering the Feminine in American Indian Traditions.* 1986. Boston: Beacon Press, 1992, c1986.

———. *Spider Woman's Granddaughters.* Boston: Beacon Press, 1989.

———. *The Woman Who Owned the Shadows.* San Francisco: Spinsters, Ink, 1983.

American Indian Movement (AIM) of Colorado Position on the Arrest of Arlo Looking Cloud. April 3, 2003. dickshovel.com/aimcolora. June 26, 2003.

Anti-Defamation League. "William Pierce: Update." July 24, 2003. www.adl.org/learn/ Ext_US/pierce_up.asp. September 4, 2003.

Auchincloss, Elizabeth L., and Richard W. Weiss, "Paranoid Character and the Intolerance of Indifference." In *Paranoia: New Psychoanalytic Perspectives*, John Oldham and Stanley Bone, eds. Madison, Conn.: International Universities Press, Inc., 1994. 27–48.

Bakhtin, Mikhail, *Speech Genres.* Ed. Carol Emerson and Michael Holquist. Austin: University of Texas Press, 1986.

Bambara, Toni Cade. *Those Bones Are Not My Child.* New York: Pantheon, 1999.

Barnes, Kim. "Background to the Story: A Leslie Marmon Silko Interview." In *"Yellow Woman": Leslie Marmon Silko.* Ed. and introduction Melody Graulich. New Brunswick, NJ: Rutgers University Press, 1993. 47–65. Originally published in *Journal of Ethnic Studies* 13:4 (1986): 83–105. Subsequently republished in *Conver-*

sations with Leslie Marmon Silko, ed. Ellen L. Arnold. Jackson: University of Missis-sippi Press, 2000. 69–83.

Bataille, Georges. *The Accursed Share: An Essay on General Economy. Volume I: Consumption.* Trans. Robert Hurley. New York: Zone Books, 1988 (1967).

Baudrillard, Jean. "Beyond the Vanishing Point." In *Post-Pop Art*, Ed. Paul Taylor. Cambridge: MIT Press, 1989. 171–89.

Becker, Elizabeth. *When the War Was Over : Cambodia and the Khmer Rouge Revolution.* New York: Simon and Schuster, 1986.

Beckett, Katherine. *Making Crime Pay: Law and Order in Contemporary American Politics.* New York: Oxford University Press, 1997.

Bell, Daniel, Ed. *The Radical Right: The New American Right, Expanded and Updated.* New York: Doubleday, 1963.

Bennett, Daniel. *The Party of Fear: From Nativist Movements to the New Right in American History.* Chapel Hill: University of North Carolina Press, 1988.

Berressem, Hanjo, "'Forward Retreat': Thomas Pynchon's *Vineland.*" In *Historiographic Metafiction in Modern American and Canadian Literature*, eds. Bernd Engler and Murt Muller. Paderborn/Munich: Ferdinand Schoningh, 1994. 357–51.

———. *Pynchon's Poetics: Interfacing Theory and Text.* Urbana: University of Illinois Press, 1993.

Bikel, Ofra. *Innocence Lost,* 1991; *Innocence Lost: The Verdict,* 1993; *Innocence Lost: The Plea,* 1997; all produced for Public Broadcasting Service *Frontline.*

———. *Snitch,* produced for Public Broadcasting Service *Frontline;* aired January 12, 1999.

Bion, Wilfred. *Experiences in Groups.* London: Tavistock, 1959; New York: Basic Books, 1961.

Birkerts, Sven. Book review, *Almanac of the* Dead. *New Republic* 205 (4 November 1991) 19: 39–42.

Blackstock, Nelson. *COINTELPRO: The FBI's Secret War on Political Freedom.* 1975. New York: Vintage Books, 1976.

Blum, Harold. "Paranoia and Beating Fantasy: Inquiry into the Psychoanalytic Theory of Paranoia." *Journal of the American Psychoanalytic Association* 28 (1980): 331–362.

———. "Paranoid Betrayal and Jealousy: The Loss and Restitution of Object Constancy." In *Paranoia: New Psychoanalytic Perspectives*, John Oldham and Stanley Bone, eds. Madison, Conn.: International Universities Press, Inc., 1994. 97–114.

Boas, Franz, ed. *Keresan Texts.* Volume VIII Part 1. New York: Publications of the American Ethnological Society, 1928.

Bone, Stanley, and John M. Oldham. "Paranoia: Historical Considerations." In *Paranoia: New Psychoanalytic Perspectives*, John Oldham and Stanley Bone, eds. Madison, Conn.: International Universities Press, Inc., 1994. 3–15.

Boyer, Paul S. and Stephen Nissenbaum. *Salem Possessed: the Social Origins of Witchcraft.* Cambridge: Harvard University Press, 1974.

Brand, Johanna Brand. *The Life and Death of Anna Mae Aquash.* Toronto: Lorimer & Co., 1978.

Brodie, Renee. "The Aryan New Era: Apocalyptic Realizations in *The Turner Diaries.*" *Journal of American Culture* 21:3 (1998) 13–22.

Bromley, David. "The Satanic Cult Scare." *Society* May/June 1991:55–66.

Bromley, David and Anson D. Shupe Jr.. *Strange Gods: The Great American Cult Scare.* Boston: Beacon Press, 1981.

Burgoyne, Bernard and Mary Sullivan, eds. *The Klein-Lacan Dialogues.* London: Rebus Press, 1997.

Bywater, William. "The Paranoia of Postmodernism." *Philosophy and Literature* 14 (1990): 79–84.

Carlson, Shawn and Gerald Larue *Satanism in America*. El Cerrito, CA: Gaia Press, 1989.

Ceasar, Terry. "'Take Me Anyplace You Want': Pynchon's Literary Career as a Maternal Construct in *Vineland*." *Novel* (Winter 1992): 181–99.

Churchill, Ward, and Jim Vander Wall. *Agents of Repression: The FBI's Secret Wars Against the Black Panther Party and the American Indian Movement*. 1988. Boston: South End Press, 1988, 1990.

———. *The COINTELPRO Papers: Documents from the FBI's Secret Wars Against Dissent in the United States*. Boston: South End Press, 1990.

Churchill, Ward, ed. *Marxism and Native Americans*. Boston: South End Press, 1982.

Citizens Research and Investigation Committee. *The Glass House Tapes*. New York: Avon, 1973.

Clayton, Bruce. *Life After Doomsday: A Survivalist Guide to Nuclear War and Other Major Disasters*. Boulder, Colorado: Paladin Press, 1980.

Clearinghouse on Child Abuse and Neglect Information, *National Center on Child Abuse and Neglect Compendium of Discretionary Grants: Fiscal Years 1975–1991*. Washington, D.C.: U.S. Department of Health and Human Services, National Center on Child Abuse and Neglect [NCCAN].

Cohn, Norman. *Europe's Inner Demons*. New York: Basic Books, 1975.

Coltelli, Laura. *Winged Words: American Indian Writers Speak*. Lincoln, NE: University of Nebraska Press, 1990.

Compion-Vincent, Veronique. "The Baby Parts Story: A New Latin American Legend." *Western Folklore* 49.1 (1990): 9–25.

Crewsdon, John M. "Triumph and Defeat: The C.I.A. Record." *New York Times* 11 June 1975: 22.

Crowley, Patricia. *Not My Child: A Mother Confronts Her Child's Sexual Abuse*. New York: Doubleday, 1990.

"Customer Comments" on *Blood in the Face*. www.amazon.com. Date of access March 24, 1999.

"Customer Comments" on *Hunter*. www.amazon.com. Date of access October 13, 1998.

"Customer Comments" on *The Turner Diaries*. www.amazon.com. Date of access March 11, 1999.

Davis, James Kirkpatrick. *Spying on America: The FBI's Domestic Counterintelligence Program*. New York: Praeger, 1992.

Davis, Mike. *Ecology of Fear: Los Angeles and the Imaginatio of Disaster*. New York: Vintage, 1999.

Dean, Jodi. *Aliens in America : Conspiracy Cultures from Outerspace to Cyberspace*. Ithaca, NY: Cornell University Press, 1998.

Dees, Morris with James Corcoran. *Gathering Storm: America's Militia Threat*. New York: Harper Collins, 1996.

Deleuze, Gilles and Felix Guattari. *Anti-Oedipus: Capitalism and Schizophrenia*. Trans. Robert Hurley, Mark Seem, and Helen R. Lane. 1972. Minneapolis: University of Minnesota Press, 1983.

DeLillo, Don. *Mao II*. New York: Viking, 1991.

Demos, John Putnam. *Entertaining Satan: Witchcraft and the Culture of Early New England*. Oxford/New York: Oxford University Press, 1982.

Dill, Jordan S. www.dickshovel.com/dur. June 26, 2003.

Divale, William Tulio, with James Joseph, *I Lived inside the Campus Revolution*. New York: Coles Book, 1972.

Doane, Janice and Devon Hodges. *From Klein to Kristeva: Pschoanalytic Feminism and the Search for the 'Good Enough' Mother*. Ann Arbor: University of Michigan Press, 1992.

Dobson, David. *Scottish Emigration to Colonial America, 1607–1785*. Athens: University of Georgia Press, 1994.

Donner, Frank J. *The Age of Surveillance: The Aims and Methods of the American Political Intelligence System.* New York: Knopf, 1980.

———. *Protectors of Privilege: Red Squads and Police Repression in Urban America.* Berkeley: University of California Press, 1990.

Douglas, Mary. *Purity and Danger: An Analysis of Concepts of Pollution and Taboo.* 1970. New York, Praeger, 1966.

Eberle, Paul & Shirley, *The Abuse of Innocence: The McMartin Preschool Trial.* Buffalo, NY: Prometheus Books, 1993.

Eliot, T.S. *Selected Essays.* London: Faber, 1932.

Erickson, Eric. *Identity, Youth, and Crisis.* New York: Norton, 1968.

Evans, Charlene Taylor. "Mother-Daughter Relationships as Epistemological Structures: Leslie Marmon Silko's *Almanac of the Dead* and *Storyteller.*" In *Women of Color: Mother-Daughter Relationships in 20th-Century Literature,* Elizabeth Brown Guillory, ed. Austin: University of Texas Press, 1996. 172–87.

Evers, Larry and Denny Carr. "A Conversation with Leslie Marmon Silko." *Sun Tracks* 3.1 (Fall 1976): 29–30.

Finkelhor, David, Linda Meyer Williams, with Nanci Burns. *Nursery Crimes: Sexual Abuse in Day Care.* Newbury Park: Sage Publications, 1988.

Fisher, Linda. "Hermeneutics of Suspicion and Postmodern Paranoia: Psychologies of Interpretation." *Philosophy and Literature* 16 (1992): 106–114.

Fleming, Scott. Message to PrisonAct listserve. June 13, 2000. http://prisonactivist.org/pipermail/prisonact-list/2000-June/002884.html

Foucault, Michel. "The Dangerous Individual." In *Michel Foucault: Politics, Philosophy, Culture: Interviews and Other Writings 1977–1984.* Trans. Alan Sheridan et al. Ed. Lawrence D. Kritzman. New York: Routledge, 1988.

Foucault, Michel. *Discipline and Punish: The Birth of the Prison.* 1975. Trans. Alan Sheridan 1977. New York: Vintage/Random House, 1995.

———. *The History of Sexuality: Volume I, An Introduction.* 1976. Transl. Robert Hurley. New York: Vintage/Random House, 1990.

Franklin, H. Bruce. *Prison Literature in America: The Victim as Criminal and Artist,* expanded edition. New York: Oxford, 1989.

Franklin, H. Bruce. *Prison Writing in Twentieth Century America.* NY: Penguin, 1998.

Freud, Sigmund. "'A Child Is Being Beaten': A Contribution to the Study of the Origin of Sexual Perversions." *The Standard Edition of the Complete Psychological Works of Sigmund Freud.* Trans. and ed. James Strachey et al. London: Hogarth Press, 1953–74. 17:175–204.

———. *Three Case Histories: The 'Wolf Man,' The 'Rat Man,' and The Psychotic Doctor Schreber.* Ed. Philip Rieff. 1963. New York: Colier, 1977.

———. "Totem and Taboo." *The Standard Edition of the Complete Psychological Works of Sigmund Freud.* Trans. and ed. James Strachey et al. London: Hogarth Press, 1953–74. 13:64

Gelbspan, Ross. *Break-ins, Death Threats and the FBI: The Covert War Against the Central America Movement.* Boston: South End Press, 1991.

Giese, Paula. "Secret Agent Douglass Durham and the Death of Ancita Eagle Deer: Your Tax Dollar at Work." *North Country Anvil* 17 (March-April 1976): Special Supplement 1–13.

———. "Profile of an Informer." *Covert Action/Information Bulletin* 24 (Summer 1985): 18–19.

Gilbert, Sandra M. and Susan Gubar. *The Madwoman in the Attic : The Woman Writer and the Nineteenth-century Literary Imagination.* New Haven: Yale University Press, 1979.

Glassner, Barry. *The Culture of Fear: Why Americans Are Afraid of the Wrong Things.* New York: Basic Books, 1999.

Goodman, Gail S. et al. . *Characteristics and Sources of Allegations of Ritualistic Child Abuse.* Washington, D.C.: National Clearinghouse on Child Abuse and Neglect Information, 1994.

Granberry, Michael. "Case Illustrates Flaws in Child Abuse Trials." *Los Angeles Times* 29 November 1993: A3.

———. "Ex-School Volunteer Acquitted of Child Abuse Charges." *Los Angeles Times* 20 November 1993: A29.

———. "Former Preschool Worker Cries on Stand in Denying Molestation." *Los Angeles Times* 22 October 1993: A3.

———. "Is Trial of Church Volunteer Accused of Abusing Children a Witch Hunt?" *Los Angeles Times* 28 June 1993: A3.

Graulich, Melody, ed. *"Yellow Woman": Leslie Marmon Silko.* New Brunswick, NJ: Rutgers University Press, 1993.

Grosskurth, Phyllis. *Melanie Klein: Her World and Her Work.* Cambridge: Harvard University Press, 1986.

Hall, Stuart, Chas Critcher, Tony Jefferson, John Clarke, and Brian Roberts. *Policing the Crisis: Mugging, the State, and Law and Order.* London: MacMillan, 1978.

Hamilton, Jane. *A Map of the World.* New York: Doubleday, 1994.

Hayles, N. Katherine. "'Who Was Saved?': Families, Snitches, and Recuperation in Pynchon's *Vineland.*" In *The Vineland Papers: Critical Takes on Pynchon's Novel.* Eds. Geoffrey Green, Donald J. Greiner, and Larry McCaffery. Normal, IL: Dalkey Archive Press, 1994. 14–30.

Hiday, Jeffrey L. "Pat Robertson as Virtual Banker Stirs Very Real Controversy." *North County Times* (San Diego County, California) 9 April 1999: D6.

Hinshelwood, R.D. *A Dictionary of Kleinian Thought.* London: Free Association Books, 1991.

Hirschfield, Larry. *Race in the Making: Cognition, Culture, and the Child's Construction of Human Kinds.* Cambridge: MIT Press, 1996.

Hite, Molly. "Feminist Theory and the Politics of *Vineland.*" In *The Vineland Papers: Critical Takes on Pynchon's Novel.* Eds. Geoffrey Green, Donald J. Greiner, and Larry McCaffery. Normal, IL: Dalkey Archive Press, 1994. 135–153.

Hofstadter, Richard. *The Paranoid Style in American Politics and Other Essays.* Cambridge: Harvard University Press, 1964.

Hollingsworth, Jan. *Unspeakable Acts.* New York: Harper & Row, 1986.

Hutcheon, Linda. "Historiographic Metafiction: Parody and the Intertextuality of History." In *Intertextuality and Contemporary American Fiction.* Ed. Patrick O'Donnell and Robert Con Davis. Baltimore: Johns Hopkins University Press, 1989. 3–32.

Incident at Oglala. Director Michael Apted. Carolco International N.V. & Spanish Fork Motion Picture Company ; produced by Arthur Chobaninan. 1991. Carolco Home Video; Van Nuys, CA: LIVE Home Video (distributor), 1992.

Irmer, Thomas and Matthias Schmidt. "An Interview with Leslie Marmon Silko." *Alt-X.* http://www.altx.com/interviews/silko (1995). Republished in *Conversations with Leslie Marmon Silko,* ed. Ellen L. Arnold. Jackson: University of Mississippi Press, 2000. 146–61.

Iyer, Pico. "History? Education? Zap! Pow! Cut!" *Time* 14 May 1990: 98.

Jackson, Carlton. *A Social History of the Scotch-Irish.* New York: Madison Books, 1993.

Jackson, George *Soledad Brother: The Prison Letters of George Jackson.* New York, Coward-McCann, 1970.

Jameson, Frederic. *The Political Unconscious: Narrative As a Socially Symbolic Act.* Ithaca: Cornell University Press, 1981.

Johansen, Bruce and Roberto Maestas. *Wasi'chu: The Continuing Indian Wars.* New York: Monthly Review Press, 1979.

Johnston, John. "Ideology, Representation, Schizophrenia: Toward a Theory of the Postmodern Subject." In *After the Future: Postmodern Times and Places.* Ed. Gary Shapiro. Albany: State University of New York Press, 1990. 67–95.

Jones, Ernest. *Hamlet and Oedipus.* London: Victor Gollancz Ltd., 1949.

Jones Jr., Malcolm. "Pynchon's Shaggy Dog Story." *Newsweek* 8 January 1990: 66.

"Judge Finds Murder Trial Humorous." *Akwesasne Notes* Late Autumn 1976: 8–9.

"Judge Frees Two Couple Imprisoned Fourteen Years in Child Molestation Case." *San Diego Union Tribune* 14 August 1996: A5.

"Justice Agency is Scored for CIA Accord." *New York Times* 11 June 1975: 21.

Kaufman, Marjorie. "Brunnhilde and the Chemists: Women in *Gravity's Rainbow.*" In *Mindful Pleasures: Essays on Thomas Pynchon.* Boston: Little, Brown, 1976. 197–227.

Kaufman, Walter, ed. and transl. *The Portable Nietzsche.* New York: Viking, 1954, 1968.

Keesey, Douglas. "*Vineland* in the Mainstream Press: A Reception Study." *Pynchon Notes* 26–27 (Spring-Fall 1990): 107–13.

Kelly, Michael. "The Road to Paranoia." *New Yorker* 71.17 (19 June 1995): 60–75.

Kernberg, Otto F. M.D. "Leadership Styles and Organizatinal Paranoiagenesis." In *Paranoia: New Psychoanalytic Perspectives,* John Oldham and Stanley Bone, eds. Madison, CT: International Universities Press, 1994. 61–79.

Kifner, John. "Security Chief for Militant Indian Group Says He Was a Paid Informer for F.B.I.," *New York Times* 13 March 1975. 31.

Klein, Melanie. *The Selected Melanie Klein,* ed. Juliet Mitchell. New York: Macmillan, 1986.

Knight, Peter. Opening address at *Conspiracy Culture Conference,* King Alfred's College, Winchester, England, 17 July 1998.

Knight, Peter. *Conspiracy Culture: From Kennedy to the X-Files.* New York: Routledge, 2001.

Kristeva, Julia. *Black Sun: Depression and Melancholia.* 1987. Transl. Leon S. Roudiez. New York: Columbia University Press, 1989.

———. *The Powers of Horror: An Essay on Abjection.* 1980. Translated by Leon S. Roudiez. New York : Columbia University Press, 1982.

Lakoff, George: *Moral Politics: What Conservatives Know that Liberals Don't.* Chicago: University of Chicago Press, 1996.

Lamberto, Nick. Article in *Des Moines Register* 27 April 1975.

Larner, Christina. *Enemies of God: The Witch-Hunt in Scotland.* London: Chatto and Windus, 1981.

LeClair, Tom. *In the Loop: Don DeLillo and the Systems Novel.* Urbana: University of Illinois Press, 1987.

Leonard, John. "Culture Watch: Alien Nation." *The Nation* 3 June 1998: 23–28.

The Legacy: Murder & Media, Politics & Prisons. Michael J. Moore, Director. 1999.

Levack, Brian P. *The Witch-Hunt in Early Modern Europe.* London/New York, 1987.

Lewin, Leonard C. *Report from Iron Mountain: On the Possibility and Desirability of Peace.* Introduction by Victor Navasky. 1967. New York: Free Press, 1996.

Loftus, Elizabeth and Katherine Ketcham, *The Myth of Repressed Memory: False Memories and Allegations of Sexual Abuse.* New York: St. Martin's, 1994.

Lyons, Arthur. *Satan Wants You: The Cult of Devil Worship in America.* New York: Mysterious Press, 1988.

Lyotard, Jean-Francois. *The Postmodern Condition: A Report on Knowledge.* 1979. Transl. Geoff Bennington and Brian Massumi. Minneapolis: University of Minnesota Press, 1984.

Macdonald, Andrew (aka William Pierce). *Hunter.* Hillsboro, WV: National Vanguard Books, 1989.

———. *The Turner Diaries.* 1978. New York: Barricade Books, 1996.

Macfarlane, Alan. *Witchcraft in Tudor and Stuart England: A Regional and Comparative Study.* New York: Harper & Row, 1970.

"Man Says He Settled Wenatchee Sex Case." *Seattle Times* 24 February 1999. http://archives.seattletimes.com.

Manning, Lona, Debbie Nathan, Carol Weissbrod, and Bob Chatelle. "'Satanic' Innocents in Jail." *The Nation* 274:17 (May 6, 2002) 2.

Manshel, Lisa. "Reporters for the Defense in a Child Abuse Case." *Washington Journalism Review* July/August 1991: 17–21.

Marcus, Eric R. "Paranoid Symbol Formation in Social Organizations." In *Paranoia: New Psychoanalytic Perspectives,* John Oldham and Stanley Bone, eds. Madison, CT: International Universities Press, 1994. 81–94.

Masson, Jeffrey Moussaieff. *Against Therapy : Emotional Tyranny and the Myth of Psychological Healing.* New York: Atheneum, 1988.

———. *The Assault on Truth: Freud's Suppression of the Seduction Theory.* New York : Farrar, Straus and Giroux, 1984.

Matthiessen, Peter. *In the Spirit of Crazy Horse.* 1983. New York: Viking Press, 1991.

Merriam-Webster's Encyclopedia of Literature. Springfield, Massachusetts: Merriam-Webster, 1995.

Messerschmidt, Jim. *The Trial of Leonard Peltier,* foreword by William Kunstler. Boston: South End Press, 1983.

Miller, Stephen Paul. *The Seventies Now: Culture as Surveillance.* Durham, N.C.: Duke University Press, 1999.

Mitchell, Juliet, ed. *The Selected Melanie Klein.* New York: Macmillan, 1986.

Moore, Alan, and Eddie Campbell. *From Hell.* Washington, D.C., Mars Import/Eddie Campbell Comics, 2000.

Moore, William Haas. *Chiefs, Agent, and Soldiers: Conflict on the Navajo Frontier, 1868–1882.* Albuquerque: University of New Mexico Press, 1994.

Nasnaga. *Indians' Summer.* New York: Harper and Row, 1975.

Nathan, Debbie. *Women and Other Aliens: Essays from the U.S.-Mexico Border.* El Paso: Cinco Puntos Press, 1991.

Nathan, Debbie and Michael Snedeker. *Satan's Silence: Ritual Abuse and the Making of a Modern American Witch Hunt.* New York: Harper/Collins, 1995.

Nicol, Bran. "'Just Because I'm Paranoid, It Doesn't Mean I'm Not Being Persecuted': Paranoid Logic in Contemporary Theory, Fiction, and Film." Paper presented at *Conspiracy Culture Conference,* King Alfred's College, Winchester, England, 17 July 17 1998.

Nietzsche, Fredric. "Thus Spoke Zarathustra." *The Portable Nietzsche.* Transl. Walter Kaufman. 1954. New York: Viking, 1968.

Nieves, Evelyn. "Prosecutors Drop Charges in Abuse Case from Mid-80's." *New York Times* 3 December 1994: 25(L).

———. "Woman Upheld in Abuse Case Feels Vindicated." *New York Times* 30 March 1993: B1(L).

"North Carolina Appeals Court Voids 2 Child-Abuse Convictions." *New York Times* 3 May 1995: A21(L).

Northcott, Karen. Telephone interviews, 15 December 1998 and 13 January 1999.

O'Donnell, Patrick. *Latent Destinies: Cultural Paranoia and Contemporary U.S. Narrative.* Durhan, N.C.: Duke University Press, 2000.

Ofshe, Richard and Ethan Watters. *Making Monsters: False Memories, Psychotherapy and Sexual Hysteria.* New York: Scribner's, 1994.

Oldham, John and Stanley Bone, eds. *Paranoia: New Psychoanalytic Perspectives.* Madison, Conn.: International Universities Press, 1994.

Oldham, John and Andrew E. Skodol. "Do Patients with Paranoid Personality Disorder Seek Psychoanalysis?" In *Paranoia, New Psychoanalytic Perspectives*. Eds. John Oldham and Stanley Bone. Madison, Conn.: International Universities Press, 1994.

Olsmstead, Jane. "The Uses of Blood in Leslie Marmon Silko's *Almanac of the Dead*." *Contemporary Literature* 40:3 (Fall 1999). 464–90.

O'Neill, Kelly. Letter to *The Nation* 24/31 August 1998): 2, 23.

Orlando, William. "Dog Star Desperado." In *Doing Time: 25 Years of Prison Writing*, Ed. Bell Chevigny. New York: Arcade, 1999. 7–13.

Parenti, Christian. *Lockdown America: Police and Prisons in the Age of Crisis*. New York: Verso, 1999.

Payne, Cril. *Deep Cover: An FBI Agent Infiltrates the Radical Underground*. New York: Newsweek Books, 1979.

Pazder, Lawrence with Michelle Smith. *Michelle Remembers*. 1980. New York: Pocket Books, 1981.

Pearce, Richard, ed. *Critical Essays on Thomas Pynchon*. Boston: G.K. Hall, 1981.

Pipes, Daniel. *Conspiracy: How the Paranoid Style Flourishes and Where It Comes From*. New York: Free Press, 1997.

Pleynet, Marcelin. "The Readability of Sade." In *The Tel Quel Reader*. Ed. Patrick ffrench and Roland-Francois Lack. New York: Routledge, 1998.

Pollitt, Katha. "Justice, Not So Swift." *The Nation* 274:10 (March 18, 2002) 10.

Pynchon, Thomas. *Gravity's Rainbow*. New York: Penguin, 1973.

———. *Mason and Dixon*. New York: Henry Holt and Co., 1996.

———. *V.* New York: Harper and Row, 1961.

———. *Vineland*. Boston: Little, Brown, and Company, 1990.

Rabinowitz, Dorothy. "From the Mouths of Babes to a Jail Cell." *Harpers* May 1990: 54–63.

Rabinowitz, Dorothy. *No Crueler Tyrannies: Accusation, False Witness, and other Terrors of Our Times*. New York: Wall Street Journal Books, 2003.

Ricoeur, Paul. *Freud and Philosophy: An Essay on Interpretation*. Trans. Denis Savage. New Haven: Yale University Press, 1970.

Ridgeway, James. *Blood in the Face: The Ku Klux Klan, Aryan Nations, Nazi Skinheads, and the Rise of a New White Culture*. 1990. New York: Thunder's Mouth Press, 1995.

Reiman, Jeffrey. . . . *And the Poor Get Prison: Economic Bias in American Criminal Justice*. Boston: Allyn and Bacon, 1996.

Roach, Joseph. *Cities of the Dead: Circum-Atlantic Performance*. New York: Columbia University Press, 1996.

Robertson, Pat. *The New World Order*. Dallas: Word Pub., 1991.

Robins, Robert S. and Jerrold M. Post, M.D. *Political Paranoia: The Psychopolitics of Hatred*. New Haven: Yale University Press, 1997.

Rogin, Michael. *Fathers and Children: Andrew Jackson and the Subjugation of the American Indian*. 1975. New Brunswick, NJ: Transaction Publishers 1995.

———. *Ronald Reagan, The Movie and Other Episodes in Political Demonology*. Berkeley: University of California Press, 1987.

Rorty, Richard. *Achieving Our Country: Leftist Thought in Twentieth Century America*. Cambridge, Mass.: Harvard University Press, 1998.

Rosen, Barbara, ed. *Witchcraft in England, 1558–1618*. Amherst: University of Massachusetts Press, 1991.

Rosen, Kenneth, ed. *The Man to Send Rainclouds: Contemporary Stories by American Indians*. New York: Viking Press, 1974.

Rosenberg, Susan. "Lee's Time." In *Doing Time: 25 Years of Prison Writing*, Ed. Bell Chevigny. New York: Arcade, 1999. 206–16.

Russell, Diana E.H. *The Secret Trauma: Incest in the Lives of Girls and Women.* New York : Basic Books, 1986.

Ruoff, A. Lavonne. "Ritual and Renewal: Keres Traditions in Leslie Silko's 'Yellow Woman'." In *"Yellow Woman": Leslie Marmon Silko.* Ed. Melody Graulich. New Brunswick, NJ: Rutgers University Press, 1993. 69–81.

Sanders, Scott. "Pynchon's Paranoid History." In Levine and Leverents, *Mindful Pleasures,* 139–60. Reprinted from *Twentieth Century Literature* 21.2 (May 1975):177–92.

Savage, Dan. "Holiday in the Hole." *Village Voice* (December 9, 1997) 33–36.

Sayer, John William. *Ghost Dancing the Law: The Wounded Knee Trials.* Cambridge, Mass. and London, England: Harvard University Press, 1997.

Schatzman, Morton. *Soul Murder: Persecution in the Family.* New York: Signet, 1973.

Scheper-Hughes, Nancy and Loic Wacquant. *Commodifying Bodies.* London: Sage Publications, 2003.

Scheper-Hughes, Nancy. Critical Resistance colloquium unpublished transcript, University of California Humanities Research Institute. June 7, 2002.

Schrecker, Ellen. *Many Are the Crimes: McCarthyism in America.* Boston: Little, Brown, 1998.

Sedgwick, Eve Kosofsky. *Between Men: English Literature and Male Homosocial Desire.* New York: Columbia University Press, 1985.

———, ed. *Novel Gazing: Queer Readings in Fiction.* Durham, NC: Duke University Press, 1997.

Seltzer, Mark. *"The Princess Casamassima*: Realism and the Fantasy of Surveillance." In *Henry James and the Art of Power.* Ithaca: Cornell University Press, 1984.

Seltzer, Mark. *Serial Killers: Death and Life in America's Wound Culture.* New York: Routledge, 1998.

"Separatists Offer Aid to White Shut-Ins." *North County Times* (San Diego County, California) 14 March 1999: A-13.

Seyersted, Per. *Leslie Marmon Silko.* Boise State University Western Writers Series 43. Boise, Idaho: Boise State University, 1980.

Shakur, Sanyika. *Monster: The Autobiography of an L.A. Gang Member.* New York: Atlantic Monthly Press, 1993.

Shapiro, David. *Neurotic Styles.* New York: Basic Books, 1965.

———. "Paranoia from a Characterological Standpoint." *Paranoia: New Psychoanalytic Perspectives.* John Oldham and Stanley Bone, Eds. Madison, Conn.: International Universities Press, 1994.

Showalter, Elaine. *Hystories: Hysterical Epidemics and Modern Culture.* New York: Columbia University Press, 1997.

Siegel, Marc Richard. *Pynchon: Creative Paranoia in Gravity's Rainbow.* Port Washington, NY: Kennikat Press, 1978.

Silko, Leslie Marmon. *Almanac of the Dead.* New York: Penguin, 1991.

———. *Ceremony.* New York: Viking Penguin, 1977.

———. *Storyteller.* New York: Arcade, 1981.

———. *Yellow Woman and a Beauty of the Spirit: Essays on Native American Life Today.* New York: Simon and Schuster, 1996.

Silko, Leslie Marmon and James Wright. *The Delicacy and Strength of Lace.* Letters edited by Anne Wright. Saint Paul, MN: Graywolf Press, 1986.

Skow, John. Book review, *Almanac of the Dead. Time* 138.23 (9 December 1991): 86.

Slotkin, Richard. *The Fatal Environment: The Myth of the Frontier in the Age of Industrialization, 1800–1890.* Middletown, Conn.: Wesleyan University Press, 1986.

———. *Gunfighter Nation: The Myth of the Frontier in Twentieth-Century America.* New York : Atheneum, Maxwell Macmillan International, 1992.

————. *Regeneration through Violence: The Mythology of the American Frontier, 1600–1860*. Middletown, CT: Wesleyan University Press, 1973.

Smith-Rosenberg, Carroll. *Disorderly Conduct: Visions of Gender in Victorian America*. New York: Oxford University Press, 1985.

Southern Poverty Law Center. "The Rise of the National Alliance." http://www.splcenter.org/intelligenceproject/ip-index.html. Date of access April 28, 1999.

The Spirit of Crazy Horse. Parallax Productions and Access Productions in association with WGBH. Alexandria, VA: PBS Video, 1990.

St. Clair, Janet. "Cannibal Queers: The Problematics of Metaphor in *Almanac of the Dead*." In *Leslie Marmon Silko: A Collection of Critical Essays*. Eds. Louise K. Barnett and James L. Thorson. Albuquerque: University of New Mexico Press, 1999. 107–221.

St. Clair, Janet. "Death of Love/Love of Death: Leslie Marmon Silko's *Almanac of the Dead*." *MELUS* 21.2 (Summer 1996): 141–156.

Stanford, Ann Folwell. "'Human Debris': Border Politics, Body Parts, and the Reclamation of the Americas in Leslie Marmon Silko's *Almanac of the Dead*." *Literature and Medicine* 16:1 (1997): 23–42.

Steiner, Wendy. "Pynchon's Progress: Dopeheads Revisited," *Independent* (London) 3 February 1990: 30.

Stern, Kenneth Saul. *A Force upon the Plain: The American Militia Movement and the Politics of Hate*. New York: Simon and Schuster, 1996.

————. *Loud Hawk : The United States Versus the American Indian Movement*. Norman: University of Oklahoma Press, 1994.

Stevenson, Mark. "Lynching of Kidnapping Suspects Called Justified." *San Diego Union-Tribune* 28 March 1998: A12.

Stock, Catherine McNicol. *Rural Radicals: Righteous Rage in the American Grain*. Ithaca: Cornell University Press, 1996.

Summit, Roland. "Abuse of the Child Sexual Abuse Accommodation Syndrome," *Journal of Child Sexual Abuse* 1.4 (1992): 153–63.

————. "The Child Abuse Accommodation Syndrome," *Child Abuse & Neglect* 7 (1983).

"Survivor of Waco Blaze Detained." *North County Times* (San Diego County, California) 9 March 1999: B-3.

Sussman, Peter and Dannie Martin, *Committing Journalism: The Prison Writings of Red Hog*. New York: Norton, 1993.

Tanner, Tony. *City of Words: American Fiction 1950–1970*. New York: Harper, 1971. Also published as "Patterns and Paranoia or Caries and Cabals" in *Salmagundi* 15 (1971): 78–99, reprinted in Levine and Leverentz (*Mindful Pleasures*) and Mendelson, (*Pynchon: A Collection of Critical Essays*).

Tappan, Mel. *Survival Guns*. Rogue River, Oregon: Janus Press, 1976–77.

Theoharis, Athan G. and John Stuart Cox. *The Boss: J. Edgar Hoover and the Great American Inquisition*. Philadelphia: Temple University Press, 1988.

Thomas, Keith. *Religion and the Decline of Magic*. New York: Scribner's, 1971.

"A Time Line of the Wenatchee Case." *Seattle Times* 30 June 1998. http://.archives.seattletimes.com.

Trafzer, Clifford. Lectures in southwestern Indian history. University of California, Riverside, Fall 1994.

United States Senate Subcommittee to Investigate the Administration of the Internal Security Act and Other Internal Security Laws (Internal Security Subcommittee) of the Committee on the Judiciary. *Revolutionary Activities within the United States: The American Indian Movement*. Hearing, 6 April 1976. Ninety-fourth Congress. Washington, D.C.: Government Printing Office, 1976.

———— *Revolutionary Activities within the United States: The American Indian Movement.* Report, September 1976. Ninety-fourth Congress. Washington, D.C.: Government Printing Office, 1976.

United States vs. Mark Fleury, Reginald Dodge, Larry Johns, and Colin Wesaw, # CR74-L-14 (original conviction case # CR73–5160), and United States vs. Manuel Alvarado and Terry Williams, # CR 74-L-12. United States District Court, Omaha, Nebraska. May 31, 1975.

Victor, Jeffrey S. *Satanic Panic: The Creation of a Contemporary Legend.* Chicago: Open Court, 1993.

Waterman, Jill et al. *Behind the Playground Walls: Sexual Abuse in Preschools.* New York: Gilford Press, 1993.

Weisenburger, Steven. "The End of History? Thomas Pynchon and the Uses of the Past." In *Critical Essays on Thomas Pynchon*, Richard Pearce, ed. Boston: G.K. Hall, 1981. 140–156.

Weyler, Rex. *Blood of the Land: The Government and Corporate War Against the American Indian Movement.* New York: Vintage, 1984.

White, Edmund. "Flower Power-Broking," *Independent* (London) 4 February 1990.

Whittington, W. L. et al. "Incorrect Identification of Neisseria Gonorrhoeae from Infants and Children," *Pediatric Infectious Disease Journal* 7.1 (1988): 3–10.

Whitworth, John. "Not a Novel for Grown-Ups," *Spectator* 3 February 1990: 28.

Wilkins, John. "Innocent Family Awaits End to Child-Abuse Saga." *San Diego Union Tribune* 14 November 1993: B1.

Willis, Deborah. *Malevolent Nurture: Witch-Hunting and Maternal Power in Early Modern England.* Ithaca: Cornell University Press, 1995.

Wood, David. "Feathers on the Solar Wind." In *Doing Time: 25 Years of Prison Writing*, Ed. Bell Chevigny. New York: Arcade, 1999. 153–63.

Wood, James. "Seriously Unfunny, Truly Unreal America," *Times* (London) 3 February 1990: 38.

Wright, Lawrence. *Remembering Satan: A Case of Recovered Memory and the Shattering of an American Family.* New York: Knopf, 1994.

Young-Bruehl, Elisabeth. *The Anatomy of Prejudices.* Cambridge: Harvard University Press, 1996.

"Your Information Might Save Their Lives." *Akwesasne Notes* Early Spring 1976: 6–7.

Zand, Nicole Zand. "A la recherche du temps hippy," *Le Monde* 20 September 1991: 24 (review of French translation).

Index